THE ART OF *ageing*

THE ART OF *ageing*

S. K. Kulkarni

Indus Source Books

Indian Spirit, Universal Wisdom

Indus Source Books
PO Box 6194
Malabar Hill PO
Mumbai 400 006
INDIA
Email: info@indussource.com
www.indussource.com

The Art of Ageing

Published in India by Indus Source Books, Mumbai

ISBN: 978-81-88569-38-0

Cover design by Sanskruti Graphics, Mumbai

First published 2013
First reprint 2014
Second reprint 2015
Third reprint 2016

Printed in Mumbai

Dedicated to the memory of

my beloved wife Smt. Sumati

and also my two younger brothers Bhim and Madhu.

AASHIRVACHAN/BLESSINGS

Long life necessarily ends with old age. Old age is welcome to none. Nevertheless it awaits nobody's welcome or the invitation.

Every ailment may have a remedy but old age and its concomitants viz., infirmity and instability, fragility and certain deformity do not have any remedial course of action to check or halt them.

Since numerous and various are the problems faced by the elderly, it may be a bane for practical worldly ambitions and mundane aspirations but a boon for the pursuit of spirituality.

Lessons are best learnt in the school of life than the academic schools.

Happy old age is the guerdon of one's sober youth.

In old age it is advisable to learn to subdue one's passions and emotions, likes and dislikes if they are not detrimental to principles and philosophy of one's life.

Stern resolution is an adorable virtue of youth which enables a person to fulfil all his ambitions. But stubbornness and obdurateness are vices in old age for which man has to pay heavily and suffer a lot.

Adjustment is the golden mean for a peaceful and happy life.

It is advised in scriptures that old persons should learn to lessen their tendency of intervening in every matter of their younger generation and soften their bossing nature provided the matter is not of serious concern.

But it is exceedingly desirable on the part of the younger

generation to respect the old and learn good lessons they have derived from their whole life and imbibe great virtues they have inculcated.

Old age is a period when one should tune oneself up to derive more and more bliss of spirituality. This is the age one should turn towards the Maker of the Universe. Contemplate on the Ultimate Truth. Read spiritual books. Indulge not in the trivial. Involve more in others' betterment.

Youth is to earn. Age is to give. Youth is to learn. Age is to practice.

Understand the meaning of life. Try to see the Divine hand in everything and in each happening around you. It brings peace to you which has never been experienced.

Shri S. K. Kulkarni has penned down his thoughts and deliberations about old age in this book. He is a very good writer, deep thinker and erudite scholar. Unless he dives deep into the subject and researches he wouldn't express his views. He has already authored half a dozen books of great interest. Matured mind and unbiased intellect of this octogenarian bring out many facts to the surface.

Hope this book too will be helpful to understand the reality and see the path for the future. Pray God the Almighty to bless this thinker bountifully forever.

M.G. Vidyasimhacharya
Kulapati
Satyadhyana Vidyapeetha,
Mulund, Mumbai.
2 November 2013

CONTENTS

FOREWORD

One of the worst consequences of modernism—inevitable, one might argue—is the way the elderly are treated in Indian society today. Can one generalise on this subject? Yes and No. Society is multi-layered, multi-cultural and multi-religious and broadly-speaking, one can divide it into two parts: rural and urban, though with considerable hesitation. But increasingly, what has been painfully noticeable in recent years is the steady marginalisation of the elderly by the GenNext, with what can only be described as callous indifference. How did this come about?

In old world India where a joint family was the norm, the elderly were well taken care of as a matter of course. With gathering industrialisation, the compulsions on the young to migrate to the cities to make a living with constrictions on space had become so common place as to result in a new culture and today we are facing the consequences.

It is to this development that S. K. Kulkarni has devoted months and months of deep study and may it be said that he has done a remarkable job. The book discusses the demographic transition of population in India, replete with statistical support. With the aspiring young wishing to leave their homes for fresh fields and pastures new, the question arises: what has happened to the rural elders? In a different context one might also ask what is happening to the urban elders. To what extent are the old feeling emotionally bereft?

Three things confront the aged: Financial insecurity, health and allied affectations and lack of medical care and, worst of all, increasing feeling of being unwanted. Old persons, it now appears, are becoming soft targets for criminal elements. They are also becoming victims of fraudulent dealings and of physical and emotional abuse within the household.

The Government of India has, in its small way, sought to meet some of these problems. The finance minister, while presenting the budget for 2013-2014 said, "The National Programme for the Health Care of the Elders (NPHCE) is being implemented in 100 selected districts of 21 states. Eight regional geriatric centres are being funded for the development of dedicated geriatric departments. I propose to provide ₹150 crore for this programme." ₹150 crore is chicken feed.

As the author of this well-researched book rightly points out, "the National Policy is so wide and comprehensive that unless time based programmes are chalked out, and implemented with all vigour and sincerity, the policy, it is feared may prove to be only wishful thinking."

The fact is the burden of morbidity in old age is enormous. If a person, above sixty, happens to be a government servant, he can, at least, hope to be financially independent, thanks to the pension he receives. But, percentage-wise, the number of men and women entitled to pension is minute in the larger context of total retirees. What could be the fate of those not entitled to pension and will have to be totally dependent on their children for even their daily petty needs? They come in millions. Today it is not uncommon for both parents to be employed. Time was when the father—or husband—was the only bread-earner who had to see that his children—whether one, two or three, but seldom more than that—had to receive a decent education and were one of them a girl, arrange not only for her education but for a marriage as well, ending up with a big hole in his savings. At the time of his retirement he turns out largely to be poor.

But consider still another situation where one finds himself not only to be poor but additionally disabled, infirm, chronically sick and totally vulnerable, and a burden on the young. What family support can one expect to such? In India, unlike, say, the United States, there is no social security as such. One understands that a Welfare Fund for older persons is likely to be set up, hopefully with funding support from government, corporate sector, trusts, charities and individual donors.

According to the author, if one understands him right, "State policies will encourage children to co-reside with their parents by providing tax relief, allowing rebate for medical expenses etc." It sounds more like wishful thinking. Where there is unbroken love between parents and their children, no outside help is altogether necessary. Where that love is non-existent, no outside help can change the life style of the young which is almost self-indulgent.

The author draws our attention to the Maintenance and Welfare of Parents and Senior Citizens Act 2007, guaranteed under the Constitution and enacted by Parliament which received the assent of the President on 29 December 2007. One would like know how effective it has turned out to be. It is well to remember that as early as in 2001, India had 34.94 million elderly male population and 35.75 million elderly female population. This has since increased by 2011 to 48.41 million male and 50.33 million female elderly. The government, let it be said to its credit, has introduced Reverse Mortgage Scheme through the National Housing Bank, but again one might ask: how many of the elderly have, among their non-movable assets, homes to mortgage?

The author to his credit has discussed how every aspect of likely problems affecting the aged and suggested how each can be met by the government, by private bodies, by the children themselves and, just as importantly, by those elderly affected.

It is now a known fact that old age homes are now steadily on the increase and will continue to do so in the years to come.

But what is so outstanding about this work is the thoroughness with which the author has dealt with the subject of old age in all its multi-facets. This must be the first work of its kind and deserves the fullest attention of policy makers in government and may one add that it is also a matter for the young to ponder over their duties and responsibilities towards their parents with the hidden hint that Time is a greater Teacher and the young, too will also be old one day and would need the care they presently may be hesitant to give to their elders. Time and Fate may then seek to wield their own revenge.

M. V. Kamath
Manipal
May 2013

PREFACE

In 2011 at the book release function of my previous book titled *Women in Hindu Society*—a critical appraisal of their status in India from the Vedic period to modern times—I had mentioned that I was planning to study the present status of elderly in Indian society and reflect my views in the next book. I had also mentioned that not scholarship and intelligence but my sense of keen observation of the events taking place in the society with sensitivity forms the asset of my writing. The outcome of this churning of the thoughts is the present book. In this task my close family acquaintance, Dr. Arundhati Hoskeri, a scholar and author in her own right, agreed to write on alternate therapies and good health for all. Continuity and change in lifestyle is the essential feature of any individual or society. It cannot remain static for long. Joint family system in which the family members of two-three generations and lived together sharing joys and sorrows with emotional attachment was prevalent till the early twentieth century. Old age was not a problem. But in India the situation went on changing fast from the second or third decade of the twentieth century especially after independence in 1947. The whole social structure has undergone and is still undergoing many changes especially in respect of longevity, nuclear family, industrialisation, urbanisation, and globalisation, resulting in attitudinal changes particularly in the younger generation.

These issues are mutually dependent, greatly affecting the life of the aged, particularly those who are at present aged seventy-five and above who have spent their early life in the traditional joint family system. These challenges have made the government intervene to make the life of the elderly dignified. The elderly themselves have also to accept the challenges and change their life style. Financial problems have also to be tackled.

Due to increase in longevity the average life span which was roughly 30-35 in 1930s and 1940s has now increased to 65 and above. The average life span in the case of females is more than the males by more than 5 years resulting in more population of elderly females than males. Nuclear family system has also deprived the elderly of family ties and emotional attachment much needed in old age. Financial issues add to their problems.

Due to urbanisation and industrialisation young people in greater numbers have to move to the cities leaving the elderly behind in the rural areas because of which the elderly have to face many problems. This has also resulted in a way dividing the society into Rural and Urban with problems of their own.

Due to globalisation the young shift to foreign countries in search of jobs for better prospects leaving the elderly behind in India. This has its own problems both for the young as well the old. More and more elders are required to shift to old age homes for better personal and social life. Aged single males or females have yet again different problems to solve.

Taking into account all these issues social voluntary organisations and the state have stepped in with suitable legal provisions.

When a man or woman is born he or she is bound to become old in due course. With this awareness one has to plan old age to keep good health and ensure financial security. But much attention is not paid to this by majority of the people.

In order to get feedback on this and other issues by the present elderly a questionnaire was sent to about seventy five elders (both male and female) their responses are analysed in the book.

At my request another questionnaire was designed by Dr. G. B. Kolhatkar a social scientist of Pune. About sixty elderly responded which are analysed in the book.

In order to enable the readers to know the views of senior journalists and intellectuals on old age, I requested some such scholars to send articles expressing their views. The same are printed in the book.

Financial security is very important in leading a contended life in old age. For this, strict personal financial management solutions are absolutely necessary. On my request an article in this respect has been contributed by Mr. Kaushik Ramchandran and Shri Anand Kulkarni both of M/s Dyota Solution Pvt. Ltd. It is incorporated in the book. I thank them for their contribution. I would also like to thank Dr. Rajesh Jaria, MD, for his article on medical care for the elderly and Dr. Dhananjay Chavan, MD (Psychiatry) for his article on mental health of the elderly.

I have been working on this book for nearly last two years. As in the case of my previous books this venture would not have been succeeded but for the involvement of my present colleague Ms. Arati Desai and my former colleague Shri S. A. Harnahalli. Ms. Desai is Librarian and Documentation Officer at Nehru Centre. She was the first editor of the manuscript written in long hand. She also made available the relevant books and press clippings on the subject. In short, hers was a day to-day involvement in my writing.

Similarly Shri Harnahalli who is a critic and who has translated my earlier books into Kannada was also involved right from the beginning. He prepared the Glossary for the book. I have no words to express my gratitude to both of them.

Shri Satish Sahney (IPS Retd.) and presently Chief Executive of Nehru Centre who himself is a scholar and history student was of immense help to me. After the initial editing I used to send computer printed chapters for his study and guidance. True to his nature he meticulously went through the chapters and suggested certain modifications and additions. He specifically appreciated the sub-chapters (d) of Chapter IV which deals with Living Old Age. On my request he also obliged me with an article on his views on old age. I am extremely thankful to him for his interest and involvement.

Computer printing of the book involved typing of nearly four hundred pages. This tremendous task was at my request done by my colleague Shri Gopalakrishnan with his jet speed with full involvement. I am extremely thankful to him for his tremendous help.

Ms. Nina Vichare another colleague of mine helped in typing Sanskrit slokas. I am thankful to her.

I must express my gratitude and seek continued blessings from P.P. Vidyasimhacharyji, Kulapati Satydhyana Vidyapeeth, Mumbai who released my earlier book on Hinduism. He took keen interest in the progress of this book by saying that my writings of such books is in the interest of the society.

Shri M. V. Kamath, doyen of journalism, a guide and philosopher to me, was kind enough to write the Foreword to my earlier two books viz. *Challenges* and *Hinduism*. He is now 92 years old. Who else can be a better person to write the Foreword for this book? On my request he readily agreed to write it. I am extremely grateful to him for his excellent Foreword. On my request he has also contributed an article expressing his views on old age.

I also requested Dr. Usha Thakkar, Shri Satish Sahney (IPS Retd.), Prof. Vispi R. Balaporia, Indu Saraiya, a freelance writer and editor, and Prof. P. M. Kamath for articles on old age. They responded promptly. I am obliged to them for their excellent articles.

To my questionnaire I nearly sixty-five senior citizens, males and females, from different walks of life responded. I have already thanked them through letters. Analysis of the responses was a great education to me in many ways. I again thank them. I am also thankful to my former colleagues Shri V. N. Unde and D. D. Akolkar who took pains in getting the responses from the elders and also took keen interest in the progress of my writing.

Questionnaire II was prepared by Dr. Kolhatkar who also took pains in getting responses and analysing the response. I am extremely thankful to him.

My visit to "Niwara" an old age home in Pune and interacting with the inmates was possible when I accompanied Shri R. D. Pradhan, vice chairman, Nehru Centre. I am thankful to him for giving an opportunity to accompany him to Pune for this purpose.

Shri G. T. Rane, Smt. Smita Oghle and Shri J. J. Rane, my colleagues in the Library, readily made available the required books and Shri Arun Chavan made available the copies of the extracts of the books and periodicals. This made my tasks easy. I am thankful to them.

Fortunately I have a large number of friends and well wishers who always take keen interest and encourage me in my writings by providing materials/books relevant to the subject. It will be a long list to mention every name. To quote a few, I would like to mention Shri Aravind Bharucha, N. B. H. Kulkarni, Pardiwala, Satyapal Khanna, B. M. Patil, Jaya and Umesh Keskar, D. H. Kaulgud, S. G. Savadi (IRS), M. M. and R. B. Kulkarni, Prof. J. V. Naik, V. Balachandran (IPS Retd.), and S. S. Puri (IPS retd.).

Dr. Rekha Udani, Dr. Sandeep Sattur, Smt. Shubhada Kamathe, Smt. Shama Deshpande, Smt. Asha Nadgounda, Shri Rekha Bavdekar, Smt. Seetamma Kulkarni, Smt. Raju Altekar, Smt. Hema Joshi, Dr. (Mrs.) Vinita Joshi, Smt. Shailaja Hublikar also took keen interest in my writing.

I am thankful to all my colleagues in Nehru Centre for their support in my venture. To mention few Shri L. A. Kazi, Shri Arvind Paranjpye, Shri S. P. Verma, Shri M. B. Tawde, Shri C. M. Rane, Smt. Nina Rege, Shri Nageshkar, Shri Suhas Naik

Sattam, Shri N. S. Patil, Shri Imtiaz Kalu, Shri K. P. Nair, Shri Pramod Rane and Smt. Nirmala Carmen.

My family members—sons Sunil and Atul, daughters-in-law Varsha and Anjali, grandsons Aditya, Parth and Mihir, grand daughter-in-law Disha, nieces Vaishali and Sampada, sons-in-law Anand and Rahul, sisters-in-law Suman and Vijaya, brother Raghu and his family—always took keen interest in my work.

Shri A. P. Deshpande, chairman, Marathi Vijnan Parishad, Mumbai reviewed in Marathi my earlier book *Women in Hindu Society* and has since taken keen interest in the present book. I am thankful to him for his interest.

Nehru Centre is my greatest strength. I am extremely grateful to all especially Shri I. M. Kadri, Shri Deepak Parekh and Smt. Bakul Patel for their support and encouragement.

Dr. J. N. Banerjee, who is associated with Nehru Centre since its inception, has supported me in writing the present book. He spared books and other materials relevant to the subject. I am very much thankful to him for his interest and support.

Ms. Sonavi Desai, editor and publisher of Indus Source Books has published my two earlier books viz. *Hinduism* and *Women in Hindu Society*. I requested her to edit and publish this book also. She readily and gladly agreed. I am grateful to her. I must express my happiness and gratitude to her for taking keen personal interest and going out of the way in obtaining two articles on health from the eminent doctors mentioned by me earlier. She also obtained detailed material in making the chapter on finance more elaborate and useful.

I am thankful to SAP Print Solutions Pvt. Ltd. for their excellent work. I am also thankful to Sanskruti Graphics, Mumbai, for the attractive and meaningful cover design.

I shall feel my task accomplished if the readers, young and old, social and state agencies find the book useful.

S. K. Kulkarni
Mumbai
June 2013

Chapter I

FOUR STAGES OF LIFE

According to Hindu culture and tradition, whenever an elderly person gives his/her blessings, he or she says "शतायुषी भव सुखी भव" meaning "May you live a hundred years with happiness", which is naturally meant to be with sound health, equanimity and prosperity. This hundred-year span of life has to be of good quality and must be lived with a positive attitude and by discharging all the obligations that are expected during each span of life with a sense of both spiritual attachment and material detachment.

Our ancient scriptures and seers have divided the hundred years of one's span of life into four stages covering roughly twenty-five years each. All these stages of life are inevitably to be spent in succession and are also interdependent. This is because unless the first stage of life is productively utilised by an individual and a good foundation of life is laid down, one cannot lead a peaceful and contented existence in the second stage of life. In fact, the first two stages of life are most important as they determine the way of life an individual is going to follow in the third and fourth stages, which are commonly called the period of old age. This period roughly ranges from the age of sixty until death. Happiness in the third and fourth stages of life entirely depends on the quality of life and on the attitude adopted during the initial two stages of life.

Four Ashrams

The four stages of life that every human being goes through are known as *ashrams*. They can be briefly stated as under:

i) Brahmacharyashram: This roughly covers the first twenty years of one's life, and includes education and learning the basic ways of life.

ii) Grahasthashram: This is the second stage covering the next twenty-five years of one's life during which man starts earning his livelihood, acquires family and discharges all attendant responsibilities.

The first two are the most active stages of life in every aspect.

iii) Vanaprasthashram: This is the third stage of the next twenty-five years of one's life. This marks the phase of retirement from active life.

iv) Sanyasashram: This comprises the last twenty-five years of one's life during which the individual lives as a hermit in a secluded place and leads a completely detached life.

It may be stated that all the four stages of life put together make one's life. The success, happiness, and contentment in life depends on how best these four stages are rightly interwoven.

Mahatma Gandhi had appreciated the system of *ashramas* in our society and strongly advocated its adoption all over the world. (*Young India*, 23 April 1929)

It may be argued that everyone does not live a hundred years and that the division of life into four stages of twenty-five years each appears unrealistic. In this connection, it may be pointed out that what is important is not the exact or probable number of years of life of each stage but the inevitable four stages of life. If, unfortunately, a man dies at a very young age or in middle age, which is the age of *Grahasthashram*, he will not be required to face the last two stages of life. If a man's lifespan is about sixty-five years and more, which is normal in the present century, one has to live through all the four stages of life.

In order to make all these four chain links strong, our ancient seers and philosophers have prescribed certain "dos and don'ts" for each stage of life. It is therefore necessary to study and elaborate these regulations which are expected to be observed by each individual to make their life worth living.

I. Brahmacharyashram: Of the four, this is the first *Ashram,* which starts at childhood and lasts till the individual completes his education, starts earning his livelihood, gets married and starts living an independent life with his wife and other members in the family and the society. This normally takes 20-25 years of life. Our ancient writings (*Bharatiya Sanskrit Kosh* – Chapter VI) define this word as "ब्रम्हणे वेदार्थ चर्य आचरणीयम", that is the years devoted for the study of Vedas. During this period a person was expected to follow the four principles with attendant duties given below:

• To study the Vedas by staying in the teacher's house (गुरूकुल) and serving him with all sincerity (गुरूसेवा).

• To participate whole-heartedly in the teacher's assigned work and also serve the teacher's wife and son faithfully.

• To remember with gratitude and with full faith the teacher's teachings and blessings. This attitude moulds the positive character of the student during his entire life.

• After completion of education, to pay *gurudakshina* with humility according to his financial capacity.

In the ancient period all the students, irrespective of their social, family and financial status, had to stay in the same *gurukul,* and eat and study together. There was no sense of superiority or inferiority. Thus there was no scope for ego clashes. It may be recalled that Lord Krishna and his friend Sudama learnt lessons under one guru and were closest friends. This way of living automatically developed a sense of equality and a way of social life which is called समष्टी जीवन. This was how a sound and healthy foundation of social life was laid down.

The *Brahmacharya* stage of life is the foundation of the remaining three stages of life to follow viz. active period, old age, and very old age (renunciation). Success in life depends on the qualities acquired by the individual in the first stage. Hence, it is needless to emphasise that just as the durability and quality of any structure depends on the soundness of the foundation, so also the success or failure in our life. Our ancient scriptures like *Atharva Veda, Brahmanas, Upanishads,* and *Manusmṛiti* have therefore elaborately prescribed the duties to be performed and achievements to be aimed for during this stage of life. For instance, by acquiring the qualities of hard work, respect towards elders and guru, and abandoning one's ego and anger while studying in the guru's house, one lays the foundation for an exemplary and fruitful life during the later stages, says the *Atharva Veda* (11.8.1.6).

The great sage Manu in his *Manusmriti* (2.175-185) has elaborately prescribed a certain code of conduct for a *brahmachari* during his stay in the guru's house. It is meticulous and well thought out, and intended to groom the student to enable him to acquire the qualities essential to shape his later life.

The essence of Manu's teachings was the moulding of the life of a young man with the character and qualities required to face the problems of life with grace and equanimity. This is the basic feature of human life which was relevant in the past, is relevant in the present and will be relevant for the future too. The mode and contents are decided to suit the changing times. For instance, according to Manu, during one's childhood and young age one should whole-heartedly engage oneself in getting education suited to the times and acquiring certain qualities like respect for the teacher and elders – मातृ देवो भव़, पितृ देवो भव, आचार्य देवो भव. These qualities are required even in the twenty-first century. Unfortunately, over time we are slowly drifting away from the path to be followed. The result has been that the student's attitude towards life is fast changing. Money and physical pleasures are gaining predominance, which often results in crimes. This is mainly because of the lack of positive influences or *sanskaras.* Regrettably, both the teachers and parents are not, by their own behaviour, role models for the children. This situation is really a matter of concern. If the young do not possess the qualities of pure character and honesty in dealing with others, their subsequent three stages of life will result in misery and frustration. The best way to avoid such a situation is to acquire moral and physical strength by treading the path laid down by the parents, teachers and other elders in society.

The responsibility of moulding the character of a young boy mainly rests with the parents, teachers and leaders in the society. If these elders themselves lack the qualities of truth, honesty, hard work, and respect for others, how and with what moral authority can they advise the youth? Good *sanskaras* is the basic necessity in one's life especially in the young age.

Our philosophers and saints have specially emphasised this aspect. One philosopher-saint[1] from Maharashtra has said that it is much easier to imbibe good *sanskaras* at a tender age and that it has an impact on the culture of the man for the rest of his life. This he has illustrated by a simple example. He says that before *sanskara*, a man's body is like mud which has no value in the bazaar. The same mud becomes valuable and useful after being moulded into a beautiful earthen pot—with design, shape and size, including having been baked in the kiln. So also, the human body and mind after being moulded by good *sanskaras* becomes valuable and respectable.

Swami Vivekananda, a great philosopher-saint[2] also said that the sum total of all our impressions determines our character. The past determines the present and the present thoughts and actions shape our future.

II. *Grahasthashram*: This is the second stage of life and the most important one. While the first stage of life is basically meant to lay a solid foundation of life by acquiring sound body, sound mind, education, and pure character, the second stage of life which blossoms based on the seeds sown in the first stage, is the prime, mature, and responsible stage of life during which the individual is expected to discharge the numerous duties towards his wife, parents and children. This is also a stage of

---

[1]नित्य गुरवाणी (p.106)

[2]*Personality Development* (p.10)

life to act as a responsible member of the society. During this period he earns his livelihood and discharges his duties in an honest and faithful manner. These duties can be discharged fruitfully only if he does not fall prey to the temptation of earning money at any cost and by any means. He should not be tempted by vices like arrogance and sensuality. He should be spiritual in the true sense; a role model in his family, in his profession, and in the society.

In order to enable a man to acquire these qualities, our ancient scriptures and philosophers have prescribed certain norms for this stage of life which is normally from the age of twenty-five years to fifty-five or sixty years. *Dakshasmriti* (2.32) says that every man has a bounden duty to take care of his parents in their old age, take care of his guru and guests irrespective of whether he himself is rich or poor. If he is rich, his duty of help should cover his other needy relatives and also other members in the society.

This is a universal preaching which can be found in all religious scriptures. For instance Holy Quran says "Jannat ka Raasta maa-baap ka hai" meaning that the path to heaven is under the feet of your parents. One Maulana explains that "Allah has given the *paigam* (message) that if you wish to be happy in this world, serve your parents."

Every human being has the same stages of life and the duties and responsibilities of each stage are in essence applicable to everyone though their role may differ according to the prevailing conditions of the society. Manu has also elaborated the duties of man and woman (husband and wife) which are most relevant in the modern age also. The second stage of life is important for both of them as both have to face old age in due course of time. Mutual trust, mutual love, faithfulness if imbibed in the second i.e. prime age of life, is bound to make old age happy and constructive for both. It is important to shun ego, arrogance, selfishness, greed for money and power at any cost in their respective fields whether in running a house or in their professions. This in essence is a spiritual way of life. Contrary to what many people think, spirituality is not a religious term to take cognizance of only when one becomes old. Spirituality is a way of life which is essentially relevant from birth to death.

It may be briefly stated here that our ancient philosophy emphasises the sanctity and purity in one's life and also in human relations. That is why when a man is young he is advised to treat parents and guru as God and worship them.

"मातृ देवो भव पितृ देवो भव आचार्य देवो भव."

That is why a man in the second stage of life is bound by a moral duty to look after his parents whether he himself is rich or poor. He can also consider this as repayment of debt of bringing him up with great struggle and sacrifice.

During this span of life, a *grahastha* is advised to imbibe qualities which would enable him to lead a quality life. This by itself is a great asset which will come in handy during old age. The other qualities to be achieved are: a healthy and positive attitude, disciplined daily routine, and most of all job satisfaction i.e. enjoying one's own work. Developing satisfying hobbies is a good investment for old age. It is said that getting sound sleep is an indication of good health and contentment. To get good sleep one should follow the advice given in a Sanskrit sloka.

सुखं शेते सत्यवक्ता सुखं शेते मितव्ययी

हितभुक् मितभुक चैव तथैव विजितेन्द्रियः

This means that a human being who speaks the truth, who lives within his means, who eats wholesome or nourishing food in limited quantity and who has firm control over his senses gets sound sleep. In fact, these are the qualities which have to be acquired and are an asset in all stages of life. That is why our philosopher-saints have laid great stress on a positive and constructive approach to life.

It must be constantly remembered that happiness in old age, which is bound to follow the second stage, entirely depends on the quality of life lived in the active stage of life.

III. *Vanaprasthashram*: Of the four stages of life, this is the third stage lasting about 20 to 25 years of life after retirement from active life. In fact this is the exact stage of life on which the present book is based. Due to evolutionary and revolutionary changes in the family and social structure, and demographic changes in India during the last four to five decades, the issue of old age has become a matter of both concern and consideration. No longer is it purely a personal or family problem. In addition to family, NGOs and government have to play a role and assume responsibility in tackling the issue.

It may be stated that in ancient writings, scholars had stipulated that a man and woman, after fulfilling the obligations of *grahastha,* namely, getting married, bringing up children with proper education and inculcating in them the values of good health, moral character, taking care of the parents during their lifetime, and after discharging other personal and social obligations, should forsake close family ties and go to the forest (husband and wife together if the wife is willing; if not, she should stay in the care of the children). During the stay in the forest they were expected to lead a totally detached life and indulge in philosophical and spiritual pursuits. Going to the forest was also prescribed perhaps with a view that the children should have the liberty to lead life the way they like. It is also possible that this was made an ideological instrument to separate the young and middle aged from the elderly so that the elderly did not meddle in worldly affairs, which was considered the prerogative of the people in the young and middle age.

Bharatiya Sanskriti Kosh in the 8th chapter elaborates the norms for a *Vanasprasthi*. It states that an individual, after fulfilling his obligations as a *grahastha,* should go to forest and live on fruits and other products of nature and engage himself in prayers. Such an individual was called *vanaprasthi.* The great sage Yajnavalkya says that during the third stage of life a man should go to the forest. His routine should be to bathe thrice a day, and eat the little food which is obtained by begging. He should spend his time in studying the scriptures.

It seems that recourse to *Vanaprastha* was mainly taken by Brahmin sages and Kshatriya kings though others were free to do so. Vyasa, Valmiki, Vasishtha, and Atri were all Brahmin sages. Similarly, Yayati, Dhrutarashtra, and Raghu were all kings who were proud of this tradition.

IV. *Sanyasashram*: This is the fourth and last stage of human life. This is the stage of total renunciation from worldly life. During this span, one is expected to live life in total solitude. Our ancient scriptures and sages have stipulated certain regulations for this stage of life too.

Manu further says that after a man has spent the third stage of his life in the forest, then during the fourth span of his life he should abandon all attachments and wander as an ascetic.

वनेषु च विहृत्यैवं तृतीयं भागमायुषः ||

चतुर्थमायुषो भागं त्यक्त्वा सङ्गान्परिव्रजेत्

(Manu 6.33)

He further says that a man who has moved from one stage of life to another, conquered his sensory powers, exhausted himself by giving alms and propitiatory offerings, and then lived as a wandering ascetic—when he dies, he thrives. What it says is that by observing all the norms in all stages of life, he can be said to have lived and died with blissful existence.

आश्रमादाश्रमं गत्वा हुतहोमो जितेन्द्रियः ||

भिक्षाबलिपरिश्रान्तः प्रव्रजन् प्रेत्य वर्धते ||

(Manu 6.34)

Manu also elaborates how a sanyasi should conduct his daily routine during the last span of his life.

A sanyasi should get up early in the morning and offer prayers. He should not welcome death nor should he welcome life but wait for orders. He should endure hard words and never despise anyone nor become anyone's enemy. He should not respond with anger to someone who is angry. He should not speak untruthful words. These qualities and attitude towards life should be models that should be adopted during the earlier three stages of life also but for a sanyasi these are a must.

Further, he should go begging for alms once a day and not be eager to get a great quantity, because with an eagerness to get more quantity of food, there is a fear of getting attached to sensory objects. He should not be sad when he does not get alms nor delighted when he gets more but take only the required quantity for sustenance. Through yoga he should meditate on the subtleness of the Supreme. He should fulfil his own duty with equanimity to all living beings.

In the Bhagawad Gita also, Lord Krishna says, "The sages understand 'sanyasa' (सन्यास) to be the renunciation of work with desire. Totally giving up all activities prompted by desire is renunciation." (18.2).

It must be clarified that the four *ashramas* elaborated above only bring out the essential and eternal philosophy of man's life consisting of four stages of human life as practised in ancient times. The ways of their operation have continued to exist after changing periodically to suit the conditions of the relevant times. For instance, during *Brahmacharyashram* for education, the student was to stay in the house of his guru with regulations that were not relevant in the later times. But the essential feature of this *ashrama* i.e. devotion to education, respect for guru (teacher) still remain and will remain the same. Similarly, *Sanyasashrama* required totally abandoning family ties and wandering in the forest as an ascetic. This was not possible in the later period. In the modern context when a human being crosses the age of eighty, he/she is expected to live a totally detached life in the discharge of personal and social obligations though staying in the family.

Therefore, taking into account the demographic changes over the decades and centuries, in the modern context the four stages of life mentioned earlier may be broadly classified as under:

i) Young age (*Brahmacharyashram*) up to the age of 25-30 years (ब्रम्हचयाश्रम)

ii) Active age (*Grihasthashram*) up to the age of 30-60 years (गृहस्थाश्रम)

iii) Old age 60-80 years (*Vanaprasthashram*) (वानप्रस्थाश्रम)

iv) Old-old age beyond 80 years (*Sanyasashram*) (सन्यासाश्रम)

Chapter II

THE FIRST TWO STAGES OF LIFE IN THE MODERN CONTEXT

A)YOUNG AGE IN THE MODERN CONTEXT

Life is like a ladder with four landings, which have to be climbed one after the other in sequence. The concept of the four stages of life totalling hundred years was more theoretical than real. This was because hardly any individual lived that long. But with rapid progress in medical science, longevity has increased and a good percentage of people live beyond the age of eighty or ninety. The stages of life and their span have to be suitably modified as under:

I. Brahmacharya or young age comprises childhood and student age with roughly thirty years lifespan from birth. This, in fact, is the foundation or preparatory stage of one's life. During this stage one has to acquire education, a sound body and sound mind on the strength of which one enters the second stage of life.

II. Grihastha or the second age of life can be termed as "active age" and it roughly covers another thirty years. This is the most important stage of life not only for oneself but also for the society. During this period a person gets married, starts earning his or her livelihood and starts a family. During this period, one has tremendous duties and responsibilities towards the family, parents and towards society. One has also to plan and prepare for the next stage of life which is considered as the elderly or old age of life with which we are mainly concerned.

III. The third stage of life (*Vanaprastha*) can be considered to cover a span of twenty years from the age of sixty to eighty which is known as old age.

IV. The fourth and final stage of life (*Sanyasa*) can be considered to cover a span of twenty years from the age of eighty-one, that is till one attains the age of hundred and in very rare cases a little more. This is known as "very old age".

An attempt has been made in this chapter to critically analyse the duties and responsibilities of an individual during the first two stages of life viz. young age or student age and middle age or active age and the actual situation prevailing in the present day and the steps needed to improve the situation to make old age constructive and happy.

Young age - Student age:

The first stage of life covering a total span of about thirty years has two sub-spans viz. childhood until the age of eight to ten years and student age until the age of thirty years. During childhood, an individual is under the control and care of the parents and other elders. The child's mind is very open, sensitive, and receptive. Impressions formed in the mind of the child have a great impact on his thinking and behaviour. It is entirely the responsibility of the parents to shape the mind of the child by setting good ideals before him. The parents should bring up the child with great attention and proper nourishment. By the age of eight to ten, the child would have developed the ability to think and would be ready to go on with his education in school.

It may be pointed out that in view of the drastic changes in the family and social structure during the second half of the twentieth century and also due to globalisation, the youth of today should equip themselves to accept every challenge with the strength of a solid physical and mental foundation.

The main three ingredients of such a foundation are health, education and character, the perfect combination of which improves the quality of one's life. Health and character have to be acquired from childhood and maintained thereafter. Education, which has a wider dimension, has also to be acquired from one's youth. It is necessary to analyse each of these ingredients as stated in the ancient scriptures with their relevance to the twenty-first century.

Education

Education has a wide connotation. The purpose of education is training of the mind although it is commonly understood to mean acquiring certain academic qualifications mainly to earn one's livelihood. It should also be understood that only acquiring degrees is not education. As far as academic qualifications are concerned, the younger generations all over the world have exhibited tremendous intelligence in acquiring mastery over all subjects. India too has produced top class scholars in almost every subject. But educating oneself on the values of life has to be a constant effort for every human being.

In this connection it may be specifically pointed out that right from the ancient period to modern times our teachers, saints and philosophers have taught their students the values of life and also the means of adaptation to changing times. The right type of education and lifestyle relevant to the times should be mastered by the young. The choice is left to the student. However, there are certain teachings which have eternal values. For instance the teaching or advice such as the following has eternal value to everyone:

मातृ देवो भव |

पितृ देवो भव |

आचार्य देवो भव |

i.e. treat the mother, the father and the teacher as Gods and respect them.[3]

[3] *Light for Students* compiled from the writings of Sri Aurobindo and the Mother

Again, Indian culture always highlights the importance of spirituality for quality living. In his call to young India, Sri Aurobindo, the philosopher-saint said, "A spiritual ideal has always been the characteristic idea and aspiration of India. But with the progress of time and the need of humanity demands a new orientation and another form of that ideal. The old forms and the methods are no longer sufficient for the purpose of time spirit."

An intimate relationship between education and value based life from young age to old age has been beautifully spelt out in the following Sanskrit verse.

असतो मा सद्‌गमय
तमसो मा ज्योतिर्गमय
मृत्योर्मामृतं गमय

(Lead me from falsehood to truth
Lead me from darkness to light
Lead me from death to immortality.)

It is important that pride in these Indian values should be inculcated in children from a very young age. These are the inspiring objectives which go beyond the normal concept of education. According to Swami Vivekananda, education is not a negation of facts, but the cultivation of positive ideas. It is a development of faculty and not an accumulation of information and words. He said, "We want that education by which character is formed, strength of mind is increased, the intellect is expanded and by which one can stand on one's feet. Education is the manifestation of the perfection already in man." This can be acclaimed as a very comprehensive definition of education encompassing learning, earning and living a spiritual life.

Sri Aurobindo has stressed the importance of student age for betterment of future life which covers active age and old age. For better old age one should have had a better student age. He said, "One of the most important periods in the life of an individual is the time he spends as student. During this period, his personality develops and takes shape, determining to a great extent the course of his future. This is where one must utilise in maximum capacity, the absorption of the right educational values."

Mahatma Gandhi considered education to be the most important tool for the development of the individual as well as the society. He said, "By education, I mean an all-round drawing out of the best in the child and man, body, mind, and spirit."

It may be stated that the words "student age", "young age" and "youth" are synonymous. The period of about 20-25 years from the age of seven or so is called student age, young age and the period of youth. This is the most critical period when the youth, by virtue of his age, has developed the capacity to think and plan his/her present and future life. That is why importance has been given to youth by every right thinking person. Swami Vivekananda was of the firm view that youth is a reservoir of energy. Idealism finds ready response in them. Hopes, aspirations, ambitions and, above all, dreams have a free play in their mind.

Health

The next important ingredient in one's life is health, especially in young age. A majority of the present young generation do exercise regularly and lead a disciplined life, which they consider absolutely necessary to enjoy youth. This thinking is normal in a majority of cases. But realisation that for good quality life in old age it is absolutely necessary to have a sound healthy body in young age is not very common. Many elderly probably never thought of their becoming old as inevitable because longevity was earlier not so high. People did not live long after retirement. As demographic evolution clearly shows, now people do live beyond eighty years and it is therefore necessary to have good health many years after retirement. It is therefore absolutely essential that people should think of old age in their young age itself. It may also be emphasised that if one looks after himself when one is young and fit, his body will last longer, which in turn will lead to a better quality of life.

It has to be emphasised that physical education is meant to bring into the body, consciousness and control, discipline and mastery and all things necessary for a higher and better life.

It may be stated that young ones by and large during their young age or student age do some physical exercise in the form of sports, yogasanas or other physical activities. But their objective is to enjoy good health during their young age. The young do not think of getting old. Consequently, they do not realise the importance of ensuring good health in their youth with their old age in mind. This was a frank admission by many as revealed in a sample survey of the elderly above seventy years of age. This was alright when the lifespan three to four decades back was much less. Not many people lived more than 10-15 years after retirement. But the present young generation have to plan for about 25-30 years of life after retirement. That is why the social scientists emphasise proper planning of old age during their young age. Health consciousness becomes an important aspect right from childhood and young age.

Physical fitness, thus, is an important factor for the youth of today. This is especially important considering the effect of globalisation and unhealthy food habits and lifestyle.

Sport is one major activity for physical and mental fitness. During the last fifty years after independence, encouragement to students to participate in sports activities has been tremendous. As a result the country has produced many world class sportsmen in every discipline of sports. This is a matter of pride. But equally unfortunate is the situation in which a large number of students, almost fifty percent, are unfit for sports.

A recent nationwide survey found that one in every two children is unfit for sports. The study which involved nearly 50,000 students in 18 states between the age group of 7 to 17 years also found that one in every four children surveyed was obese. The survey concluded that children in the eight metros it covered were more prone to obesity compared to those living in 46 non-metros. In Maharashtra the survey covered the cities of Mumbai, Pune, Nagpur, Gondia, Amaravati, Akola and Malkapur. The survey used indicators like endurance, anaerobic capacity/explosive power, flexibility, body strength and BMI (Body Mass Index). Moreover, obesity was seen to be on the rise as children grew older.

The survey further points out that even though most children were able to walk and run non-stop for five minutes which displays the acceptable levels of endurance, almost 40 percent of them did not have anaerobic capacity—that is the fitness level to perform well in events like sprinting. Nearly one in every two children had poor flexibility levels and body strength making them unsuitable for sports. This can be made good by taking recourse to other type of activities like yoga which are elaborated in a later chapter.

This is a matter of great concern. To enjoy all stages of human life a healthy body and healthy mind are essential. This can be achieved by leading a strict and disciplined life right from one's youth with ideal food habits. With the increasing use of technology, physical activity is very limited. That is why it is all the more important to eat right and maintain a fitness regime throughout one's life.[4]

Character

The most important factor in the life of an individual is "character" which has to be acquired and developed right from childhood/young age and preserved till the last day of one's life. The essence of character is integrity and dependability. A man is known by the character he possesses through his life right from childhood to old age. Character is the strength and originality in a person's nature. A nice blend of all the virtues commonly understood makes a man with character. It has only a positive side and brings out a man's complete personality. Character formation must be taught to children in school and at home. These two places alone would build the character of a person for life.

[4] *Times of India* dated 24/11/2012

When we say that X is not a man of good character or that he is characterless, what do we mean by that? In simple words it means that he is violating the norms of behaviour acceptable or stipulated by the society of the time. Such a man indulges in vices like cheating, excessive drinking, drug addiction, promiscuous sex life etc. That is why our ancient scriptures, philosophers and social workers have prescribed certain dos and don'ts for man in all stages of life. The foundation of good character has to be laid during young age so that the entire life is built up on it.

From the previous paragraphs it is clear that good education, good health and good moral character make an ideal young man. Such a young man can plan and live a successful active age and also a happy and peaceful life in his old age. Judging by these standards where does the present youth stand? Or what are the positive and negative factors in the lives of modern young men in the background of technological advancement and globalisation.

As regards the first ingredient, namely education, it may be stated that the modern youth has tremendous avenues and scope for development educationally. With the available opportunities, they can excel in any branch of education available not only in India but also in other countries of the world. Many young Indians have excelled in their chosen field of education.

As regards the second ingredient, namely health, it may be stated that the modern youth has realised that keeping good health with regular exercise, leading a disciplined life and adopting other good habits from young age are absolutely necessary to have a sound body and mind especially in old age. Life is for living with quality and with least suffering till the end. The maxim that health is wealth should be remembered and followed in all the stages of life.

The third ingredient, namely character, is most important in the sense it makes or mars the personality of the individual. Due to globalisation, the world has shrunk and the modern youth is easily influenced by happenings in other countries. The Indian youth can easily see the lifestyle of youth in other countries. If a youngster gets influenced by the negative side of this lifestyle, his life will be ruined and this will have a far reaching effect on his future life, especially old age. The modern Indian youth have the advantage of studying the ancient teachings which can influence their lifestyle in a positive manner and help them to lead a sober and happy life. They need not be blindly carried away by the lifestyle of the youth of other countries. What is good should be adopted and what is bad should be rejected.

Another important development in the modern world is fast advancement during the last two-three decades in the field of technology. Technology has revolutionised the communication systems, both visual and print. One need not even move from one's house to know what is happening in other parts of the world. By using the internet and other communication technologies like mobile telephones and laptops, one can know visually, what is happening in the world, whether politically, socially or culturally. These facilities though have inherent dangers. In a way, they are double-edged weapons which can be used for good as well as for bad intentions; it all depends upon the users. Human nature being what it is and especially of the youth, they may be negatively influenced by technology.

In India, a section of the youth has been found to misuse such technology, thus ruining their present and future life. This is a cause for concern as they indulge in criminal acts and suffer from psychological stress when in fact they should be planning for a happy and contented future.

Swami Harshananda, in his analysis of "How the Modern Youth Can Confront their Problems", writes: "The youth problem is not a special curse of our times." More than 2300 years ago Plato wrote thus, "What is happening to our young people? They disrespect their elders. They disobey their parents. They ignore the laws. They riot in the streets, inflamed with wild notions. Their morals are decaying . . . The youth of yesterday have become the old people of today. The youth of today will be the aged of tomorrow. This is the inexorable law of life . . . The youth of any historical age is modern to that particular age . . . But there is a silver lining. In every age, such judgements have been passed. In spite of what Plato said, the fact remains that the Greeks in their time conquered the world and their ideas have survived till date."

Raising a question as to the characteristics of youth in general, and modern youth in particular, Plato states, "From the physical point of view, youth is the best period of life. It is the period of health, strength and brimming with energy . . . the young people are apt to feel courageous. Fired with the spirit of adventure, they can plunge themselves into acts of dare devilry. High ambitions come to them naturally. Guided by these, they can work hard and undergo any amount of suffering in the process." Indeed, this best period of one's life should give utmost scope for developing the qualities of a good person.

As pointed out earlier, these qualities have been very much imbibed by our present youth. Due to globalisation and technological developments in the last three-four decades, they have got ample opportunities to exhibit their skills and in fact they have seized upon these opportunities. While this is a positive development, on the other hand there is degeneration due to the same globalisation and technological advancement. There is a sharp rise in crime rates among youth who use the aid of technology to commit those crimes.

On this negative side, Swami Harshananda writes: "On the negative side their strength can degenerate into rashness and can be used to inflict cruelty and suffering. The power of the senses can get the better of the power of the mind, resulting in lack of poise and self control; courage can give way to impatience, ruthlessness, and anger. Ambition can force them into expecting quick results and giving up in despair if thwarted in their efforts. Pleasure seeking, which is a common instinct of all living beings can do them greater harm due to the strength of natural instincts at that age."

We find this undesirable situation in a lot in the youth of the twenty-first century in India. The young mind has a lot of ideas of living the luxurious life and does not stop at committing crimes like rape, theft and murder to achieve that. It may be pointed out that the general belief that only the illiterate and poor youth resort to crime is not correct. Many youth from middle class and affluent backgrounds also resort to crimes just to satisfy their greed and lust. According to the National Crime Records Bureau[5] out of the total number of arrests in 2005 for various offences, 43 percent were in the age group of 18 to 30. In Delhi it was 61 percent. This is not a good sign as it depicts the large number of youngsters who indulge in various crimes. However, one must not forget that there are very many young people who lead normal healthy lives.

According to the Maharashtra State Crime Record Bureau-2011 (i) child criminals have killed 145 persons (ii) attempt to murder cases are 135 (iii) rape cases are 125 and (iv) cases of other offenders like theft, house breaking etc are 2051. As compared to the position obtained in 2001, the crimes by youth below 18 years of age have increased by one and half times in 2011. In child crimes 94 percent are boys and 6 percent are girls.[6]

Illiteracy and poverty in the family are considered to be the main reason for the young to commit criminal acts. In addition domestic surroundings, lack of love and affection from the parents, influence of crime-based cinema etc are also attributed to the growing criminal acts by the youth. What would be the quality of life of these youths when they become adults? The social institutions should groom these future citizens of India to be responsible citizens not only in their own interest but also in the interest of the country and society.

In January 2006, six college students from Mumbai were arrested for stealing high-end mobile phones from a store

---

[5] *Times of India,* 11 November2006

[6] *Maharashtra Times,* 29 November 2012

as the parents were not willing to pay for their purchase. In another case, a seventeen year old boy of a wealthy family took a few lakhs of rupees from his parents' cupboard without informing them. Many times children do not feel guilty as their parents themselves are not role models and indulge in enjoyment at any cost. Nearly 3-4 years ago a young man of 26-27 years of age was driving back from a party and on the way back stopped the car to give a lift to a fifty-two year old woman[7] (old enough to be his mother). He allegedly gave her a sedative-laced drink and took her to a deserted place and raped her. A sixteen year old college student hatched a plot with his childhood friend to rob his own house to buy a fancy motorcycle.[8] Four youngsters aged between the age of twenty-one and twenty-four years were accused of gang rape of a minor who hanged herself at her house after the rape. The accused were sentenced to 10 year rigorous imprisonment by a court.[9] In October 2007, three teenagers in Ahmedabad allegedly killed their six year old neighbour. It seemed that the youngsters wanted to raise ₹25 lakh in ransom hoping to lead a life of luxury later on.[10] The same year a teenager was killed by a group of four youngsters who, it is alleged, demanded a ransom of ₹2 crore from his wealthy parents.

The cases mentioned above are of educated youngsters coming from well-to-do families. Greed, lack of morality and least or no respect for the parents, teachers and other elders are the main causes. "It is just not the street children, but those from middle and upper middle class families who have also been involved in criminal cases of late. Peer pressure and the thrill of being involved in crime could be important factors behind the offences," said former Mumbai police commissioner, Sanjeev Dayal.

The recent incident of gang rape and torture of a twenty-

---

[7] *Times of India,* 13 February 2008
[8] *Times of India,* 20 September 2011
[9] *Times of India,* 18 October 2011
[10] *Times of India,* 13 October 2007

three year old young girl in a bus in Delhi on the night of 16 December 2012 by six males including a juvenile is a national shame with no appropriate words to condemn it. Parents, teachers and leaders of all kinds need to put their heads down in shame for their indifference or failure in proper upbringing of such individuals.

These are only illustrative cases. Youth crimes are on the rise and now at least should make the society think seriously about remedial measures of refinement.

Cyber crime

As mentioned earlier, technological advancement can be used negatively also. The advent of the Internet has led to tech-savvy youth becoming involved in cyber crime. In April 2010 the Mumbai Cyber Crime Cell arrested a seventeen year old from Gurgaon near Delhi for posting abusive and lewd messages on a social networking site. Earlier in March 2008, the Mumbai police arrested a 16 year old class XII student from Ahmedabad for allegedly threatening to blow up the suburban Andheri railway station. During interrogation, the boy said that he sent the e-mail for the fun of seeing his prank flash as "Breaking News" on national television.

Such abuse of electronic media is common in other countries also. A survey of nearly 1000 teenagers aged between 14 and 19 years in Texas, found that "sexting" is common among this age group with nearly 28 percent of them admitting that they had sent nude pictures of themselves through electronic means.[11]

Researchers found that while 31 percent of the teens said they had asked for a nude picture to be sent to them, 57 percent said they were asked for such "sexts". The real worry is as to how these young will shape up in their future stages of their life. Unless the juvenile and young are properly disciplined by the parents, teachers, social workers, and political leaders by demonstrating themselves as role models and taking pains inculcating in them the ancient values of human life with

---

[11] *Free Press Journal,* 4 July 2012

spirituality and moral character their future life of middle age and old age is certainly doomed. This is against the essential feature of proper planning for a contented old age.

In conclusion, it is therefore absolutely necessary for the youth of today who have ample opportunities, to enrich their life by making positive use of the developments in keeping with the ancient teachings—in regard to duties and high level of character building. It is the responsibility first of parents, then teachers, then social activists and lastly political leaders to guide the younger generation not by sermons but by proving themselves as role models which alone carries conviction as well as moral authority. This surely will ensure happiness in all the stages of life including old age which should ideally be called a spiritual life. Dr. A. P. J. Abdul Kalam, former president of India, emphatically says, "What is needed is a grassroots initiative to create a new generation of Indians that learns the virtue of integrity at a young age. Our biggest hope and our greatest resource is our children and youth. We need to ignite and inspire their minds. We need to activate their ingrained spirit of 'What can I give to the nation, society, and environment?'"

B) ACTIVE AGE IN THE MODERN CONTEXT

"The householder is the basis, the prop of the whole society. He is the principal earner. The poor, the weak, the children, and the women who do not work—all live upon the householder; so there must be certain duties that he has to perform and these duties make him feel strong." ~ Swami Vivekananda.

"Just as all living creatures depend on air in order to live, so do members of the other stages of life subsist by depending on householders." (Manu 3.77)

"Since people in other three stages are supported every day by the knowledge and the food of the householder therefore the householder stage is the best." (Manu 3.78)

Active age

It should be clear from the above that our ancient scriptures and philosophical writings have attached the greatest importance to the life of an individual in the second stage which is that of a *grahastha* and which is also known as the "active age". In fact, at this stage he/she is the central figure in the family and the society. During active age which is about 30-35 years one has tremendous duties to perform and responsibilities to discharge. In this connection Swami Ranganathananda of Ramakrishna Math has said, "Because the Grahastha by his productive labour sustains constantly all other three (non productive) ashramas with education and food, therefore the Grahasthashrama is the preeminent ashrama."

In the modern period the first thirty years of one's life are spent in acquiring good education. After this, one starts earning in one's chosen profession like business, agriculture etc. One then gets married and starts a family life. During this stage of life, he/she has to discharge the responsibilities of looking after the family. He/she plays the dual roles of spouse and parent and that of the provider of financial comfort.[12] During one's active age, one also has to discharge the duties of being an honourable member of the society. For living a successful life, one has to live and follow certain social norms.

Our traditional teachings stress the fact that active age is the most important of the four stages of life. It is a stage not meant for enjoyment but for fulfilling one's duties and responsibilities.

This is a balancing stage of life when one enjoys worldly pleasures and yet at the same time leads a responsible life. As in the other three stages of life, so also in the active stage of life, one has to abide by four *purusharthas* in an absolutely balanced way to make life peaceful. The four *purusharthas* are: dharma (duty), *artha* (wealth), *kama* (physical enjoyment) and moksha (salvation). It is necessary to elaborate the contents and meanings of these.

---

[12]*Guruwani* (Marathi), p. 107-08

a) Dharma (Duty)

Dharma is one's own duty and should not be mixed up with religion as understood in the normal sense of the term i.e. belief in God, read religious scriptures etc. Dharma is a way of life and involves performing one's own duties and discharging the responsibilities expected from one within the accepted and expected norms of one's framework of living. In discharging of duties towards the family and others in society, one should be sincere, honest, and spiritual without pride and prejudice. One should shun ego which is the stumbling block to one's progress.

Essential features of Dharma

Swami Ranganathanda says, "Dharma has two dimensions. One is law with its rules and regulations by the state. That is compulsion imposed upon you from the outside. The second is moral and ethical awareness. That is the subject of the science of values, something coming from within yourself spontaneously. One is legal and the other is moral or spiritual. The legal dimension of Dharma cannot become effective unless there is the moral dimension."[13]

Shri Shri Anandamurti elaborates ten characteristics of Dharma:

- *i) Dhriti* or patience
- *ii) Kshama* or forgiveness
- *iii) Damah* or control
- *iv) Asteya* or not to steal anything physically or mentally
- *v) Shaocha* or cleanliness
- *vi) Indriyanigraha* or self-control
- *vii) Dhi* or benevolent intellect
- *viii) Vidya* or assimilation
- *ix) Satyam* or truth
- *x) Akrodha* or without anger

These may be briefly elaborated as under:

---

[13]*Practical Vedanta and the Science of Values*, p. 64

The first one is *dhriti* or patience. One cannot expect immediate result after starting the work. He has to be patient and wait for the results.

The second character is *kshama* or forgiveness. A man's basic nature is tit for tat. If one beats somebody for no provocation the man receiving the beating does not keep quiet. This effort will be a revenge which is not a good quality. A man should be firm but forgive the man who beats first.

The third character of dharma is *damah* or control. *Damah* is the state of achieving control over internal enemies.

The fourth is *asteya* which literally means not to steal anything physically or mentally. This is an attitude or way of life. Be content with what you have.

The fifth is *shaocha* or cleanliness both internal and external. While the external cleanliness refers to body, the internal cleanliness refers to that of mind.

The sixth feature of dharma is *indriya nigraha* which means controlling. The *indriyas* (the organs of sense and action) are to be kept in check with mental and spiritual power.

The seventh characteristic of dharma is *dhi*, which means benevolent intellect. If human intellect is not used well it becomes destructive, it corrupts and exploits society. It may even become a destructive force. *Dhi* means intellect that helps to regulate the society which can benefit not only human beings but all beings.

The eighth characteristic of dharma is *vidya* meaning internal assimilation of external objectives. It is of two types. *Vidya* and *avidya*. *Avidya* is mainly concerned with external life, whereas, *vidya* is concurred with internal life.

The ninth characteristic of dharma is *satyam* or truth and it is to be observed in one's individual and collective lives.

The tenth and final characteristic is *akrodha* or absence of anger, a very subtle propensity. One should not get upset or swayed by *krodha* or anger at the slightest provocation. This sort of anger has adverse effect on nerve cells which is dangerous for general health. One should develop a balanced and controlled approach to every problem.

***b)Artha* (Wealth)**

The second of the four *Purusharthas* is *artha* (wealth) which one should necessarily have in one's life to fulfil one's obligations towards one's family and also to contribute to society. Wealth has a wider connotation which includes not only money but also land, dwelling place, gold, cattle and other moveable and immoveable assets. Though the possession of wealth is absolutely necessary for oneself and one's family members to lead a comfortable life, the manner in which it should be earned has been stipulated in our ancient scriptures, the following of which alone will ensure peace of mind. Kautilya in his *Arthashastra* has emphasised that money or any other acquisition of property should be earned with honest means without harming anybody's interest. Then only will one have the mental satisfaction of having adequate money to meet the needs. Our philosophers-saints have also warned that if a man has too much wealth, especially when it is not earned by honest means, he tends to become arrogant to the extent that he forgets his duties towards his family and society.

Unfortunately, during the last three to four decades, earning money by any means whatsoever has become the way of life of majority of the people. Corruption also has become an accepted way of life. It is bewildering how such persons can enjoy the active age and also old age without any sense of moral values and remorse. In the context of planning and living old age, the young generation should themselves imbibe a sense of duty and moral values and avoid greed in every aspect. In this connection, the following guidelines for an emphasis on spirituality should always be kept in mind both while earning money and also for proper utilisation of money.

Swami Chinmanayanda said, "Wealth is not a taboo for the seeker, but the constant craving for wealth or property is not prohibited, but one is enjoined to use it in the service of society."

In the Bhagawad Gita (IV.28) the spending of part of the money and property acquired for the benefit of the poor in the society is highlighted as sacrifice. Sacrifice of wealth is to be understood in its largest connotation. Charity and distribution of wealth honestly acquired in a spirit of devotion to and in the service of the community or the individual who is the recipient of the benevolence is called *dravya* (द्रव्य) – *yajna* (यज्ञ). The term *dravya* includes everything that one possesses. To pursue a life of charity, serving the world as best as one can, with all that we possess, physically, mentally and intellectually is the noble sacrifice called "Wealth Sacrifice" (दान यज्ञ).

What is to be depreciated is the earning of money or acquisition of property much in excess of that sufficient for the removable needs of the house holders. "One should not develop attachment to or weakness for money," said Swami Lokeshwarananda.

To fulfil his obligations as the householder, a man has necessarily to earn money. Swami Vivekananda therefore said, "A house holder who struggles to get wealth is immoral if he is lazy and content to lead an idle life. He is immoral, because upon him depend hundreds. If he gets riches, hundreds of others will be thereby supported."

Going after wealth in such a case is not bad because that wealth is for distribution. The householder is the centre of life and society. It is a worship for him to acquire and spend wealth nobly, for the householder who struggles to become rich by good means and for good purposes is doing practically the same thing for the attainment of salvation. Swami Tejomayananda, head of the Chinmaya Mission says, "Wherever there is less water, the fish start suffering as unintelligent householders suffer without money. The householder should understand the importance and value of money, earn and cherish it. They should not resort to unacceptable and deceptive methods to earn and amass wealth. A householder should be smart, efficient and practical in handling worldly affairs. They should know how to manage their finances."

It is therefore necessary that people in the Grihastha stage of life understand the value of earning and spending money nobly to enjoy mental peace in this stage of their life and to enjoy blissful life in their old age.

c)Kama (काम)

The third Purushartha is kama. It covers both ordinary desire and carnal desire relating to physical urges. Another common quality of a human being related to kama (desire) is raga i.e. attachment. We find their elaboration in the Bhagawad Gita (VII.11). [14] Shankara explains the distinction between the two. He says kama is desire for what is absent in the scheme of our life and raga is affection for what one already has. These are the two emotions by which individuals generally express their might and strength.

Carnal desire relating to sex also plays an important role in determining the character of a man. Indian philosophers recognised and emphasised that for a man's proper and balanced living, it is necessary to satisfy the carnal desires also, which if properly enjoyed give pleasure and satisfaction to the mind and body. This makes a man an ideal human being. However there are strict dos and don'ts in fulfilling carnal desires. If one does not observe these restrictions, it becomes similar to animal behaviour. Swami Chinmayananda states that uncontrolled and excessive indulgence in sexual enjoyment causes dissipation of one's personality and leads to sorrow and misery. Such a man cannot enjoy old age. So for enabling a satisfactory old age, a man in his active age should keep equanimity in his behaviour. This is possible only when a man keeps his head above the storms of the heart. Only then can he live a successful life in active age and later in old age.

d) Moksha (Salvation)

This is the last of the four Purusharthas. This concept is wrongly identified with one's religion at birth. It is generally believed that the one who believes in the God of his religion

[14] *The Holy Geeta* by Swami Chinmayanda

and devotes his life in prayers etc to please God will, after his death, reach heaven, which should be the ultimate aim of one's life.

In practical terms of life, moksha is nothing but the ultimate bliss or results of his life lived with truthfulness and with virtues as elaborated earlier. Such a human being dies enjoying the sweet fruits of the attached and detached life in all the four stages of life.

Duties and Responsibilities

Before analysing the duties and responsibilities of people who are in active age, it is interesting to read what Swami Vivekananda has said about the householder. He writes:

> Excessive attachment to food, clothes, and the tending of the body should be avoided. The householder must be pure in heart and clean in body, always active and always ready for work.
>
> To his enemies the householder must be a hero. Them he must resist. That is the duty of the householder. He must not sit down in a corner and weep, and talk nonsense about non-resistance. If he does not show himself a hero to his enemies he has not done his duty. And to his friends and relatives he must be as gentle as a lamb.
>
> It is the duty of the householder not to show reverence to the wicked; because, if he reverences the wicked people of the world, he patronizes wickedness; and it will be a great mistake if he discards those who are worthy of respect, the good people. He must not be gushing in his friendship; he must not go out of the way making friends everywhere; he must watch the actions of the men he wants to make friends with and their dealings with other men, reason upon them and then make friends.
>
> These three things he must not talk of. He must not talk in public of his own fame; he must not preach his own name or his own powers; he must not talk of his wealth, or of anything that has been told to him privately.

> A man must not say he is poor, or that he is wealthy—he must not brag of his wealth. Let him keep his own counsel; this is his religious duty. This is not mere worldly wisdom; if a man does not do so, he may be held to be immoral. If he has done something weak or has made some mistake, he must not say so in public; and if he is engaged in some enterprise and knows he is sure to fail in it, he must not speak of it. Such self-exposure is not only uncalled for, but also unnerves the man and makes him unfit for the performance of his legitimate duties in life.

Every householder should read these guidelines and strive to emulate them.

The duties and responsibilities are many and varied. Firstly, one has duty towards oneself, then to one's family and lastly to the society and the nation.

Duties towards self

The first and foremost duty of an individual is to oneself. One has to be both physically and mentally fit to discharge the obligations to the best of one's ability. Physical and mental fitness are not attained automatically. One has to strive to achieve them by leading a self-disciplined life. This is absolutely necessary to enjoy an active life to the fullest extent and build a good foundation for a happy old age.

In this connection, it may be stated that there are three categories in the age of an individual. The first one is chronological age i.e. the age by calendar, the second one is biological age i.e. how old your body is in terms of critical life signs and the third one is psychological age i.e. how old you feel you are.

In terms of counting the age by years, months and days, the first age i.e. chronological age, is fixed, but it is most unreliable judging from other standards. Two persons born on the same day, month and year are of the same age, say forty. One's body may look like that of a thirty-year old man and the other's body may look like a fifty-year old man. This is the biological age; the psychological age is based on one's thinking and attitude. A sixty-year old man, as a result of good physical fitness and positive attitude towards life may feel that he is just fifty years old. On the other hand, another of the same age may feel that he is seventy years old because he is physically unfit and has a negative approach to life. Leroy Satchel Paige, a philosopher, rightly said, "How old would you be if you did not know how old you are?"[15]

An individual in the active age should thus lead life in such a way that he/she looks and feels younger than the actual age. But how should one do so? One should follow strictly the following three norms viz. (a) Health (b) Discipline and (c) Contentment.

Health

It is said that "health is wealth". Another proverb says, "If money is lost nothing is lost, if health is lost everything is lost." But still a man greedy of wealth neglects his health. A man who neglects his health neither enjoys his own life nor allows others dependent on him to enjoy their lives. If for any reason one does not pay much attention to build a healthy body in young age, then one should make extra efforts to make good this omission during middle and old age. In fact, in all the four stages of life one should realise that a healthy body and healthy mind are the *sine qua non* for a contented life. But this is most necessary in the stage of active life. Regular physical exercise is a must for everyone. The exercises that are suitable for every stage of one's life have been elaborated in a separate chapter of this book. In brief, it may be stated here that long silent walking in the early morning for about three to five km is the best exercise. It is ideal if this is preceded by morning prayers, yoga *sadhana* etc. which help in developing a positive mental attitude to face the ups and downs of one's life. If during young age one has played some outdoor sports

[15]*Chicken Soup for the Golden Soul*, p. 9

like tennis, badminton, swimming, football, and others, then he should continue the same to the extent age permits without feeling the strain of it.

Dr. Shigeaki Hinohara, Japan's ninety-seven year old physician says, "To stay healthy, always take the stairs and carry your own stuff," which is worth emulating. On the human tendency to be greedy and to amass wealth and other materials, he says, "Don't be crazy about amassing material things. Remember: You do not know when your number is up, and you cannot take it with you to the next place."

Discipline

This is the most important aspect of one's life as it enables one to lead a quality life. Ideally, discipline should be imbibed in one's nature and should be a way of life in every activity. Discipline loses its value if one gets a feeling that it is thrust by parents, teachers or bosses. Regularity and punctuality should be a part of one's life. A daily routine should be fixed depending on the activities related to one's job or profession. It should include the following:

i) Getting up early in the morning at fixed hours after a good sleep of six to eight hours

ii) Morning exercises as detailed earlier

iii) Moderate breakfast, lunch and dinner

iv) Punctuality and regularity in attending place of work

v) Avoidance of habits like alcoholism, smoking and chewing tobacco

A disciplined life should be a role model for others, especially for the members of the family.

Contentment

Of all the qualities, contentment is the most cherished quality in a human being. It is a state of mind, it is an attitude towards life. After working hard with dedication, one should develop an attitude of being satisfied with what one gets in return. One should never grumble, never be envious of others and always be content. Of course, there is no fixed formula for living a contented life. The following are some of the factors which contribute to one's contentment towards life.

i) Happy marriage or long term relationship:

This involves another person sharing the same likes. Mutual love and affection, mutual respect and an attitude of adjustments are the essential qualities that one should possess in a relationship. If one has a happy married life or relationship then one will be content, thus making way for a happy old age.

ii) Job satisfaction:

This is also another important factor responsible for a contented life. One should fully get involved in discharging the duties expected from him/her. One should take pleasure and get a sense of satisfaction in the job. If one does not do so, then his active span of thirty years will be full of hurdles and will affect future life. One either gets what one deserves or what is destined. One should learn the art of being content to make one's life and that of one's near and dear ones worth living.

Negative factors like lack of regular routine, job dissatisfaction and a pessimistic attitude accelerate the aging process in addition to physical ailments during active age.

In every longevity study[16], job satisfaction emerges as the most reliable indicator that shows a person to be at low risk for heart ailments. Another study[17] has pointed out that about 15-20 years ago, hardly 2 percent of people below forty years of age suffered from heart ailments. Now the percentage has risen to 40. This is largely due to increased stress levels brought about by discontent in one's life.

ii) In addition to married life and working for one's bread and butter, one should develop some interesting hobbies like music, reading or writing and also get involved in some social work. These will enable one to lead a satisfactory active age. More than that, these will prove as long term assets which will

---

[16]*Ageless Body, Timeless Mind* by Deepak Chopra, p.21

[17]*DNA*, 29/9/2011

enable one to lead a satisfactory old age after retirement.

It may be stated here that in India the old age problem and planning for it is only a recent phenomenon. In foreign countries however, old age problems are being scientifically and socially analysed since several decades. In 1973, at a major gerontology conference at Duke University, three papers were delivered describing the type of person who can expect to live to a healthy old age—between 85 and 100 years old. Such people amount to less than 5 percent of the current population. In her psychology research at the University of Chicago, Dr. Bernice Neugarten concentrated on "life satisfaction" that entails five factors. The person

i) takes pleasure from daily activities,
ii) regards his life as meaningful,
iii) feels he has achieved his major goals,
iv) holds a positive self-image and regards himself as worthwhile, and
v) is optimistic

Another benefit of a balanced lifestyle emerged in 1965 when a Southern California research team headed by Nadia Belloc and Lester Breslow decided to follow the ageing pattern of more than seven thousand aged persons and discovered that the most important distinguishing feature of those who lived a long life was not their income, physical condition or genetic inheritance but a handful of extremely simple lifestyle habits. These are to be followed not after one becomes old but during young age and more so in active age.

Duties and responsibilities towards family members, spouse, children, dependents and parents

i) Towards spouse:

Our ancient scriptures and scholars like Manu have sanctified the rules for the husband and wife. While the basic tenets have remained the same, the ingredients have naturally evolved to suit the changing times. In the modern period and in the context of living a happy old age, the relationship of husband and wife needs elaboration.

Husband and wife are compared to the two wheels of a chariot. Both the wheels have to play an equal role in driving the chariot i.e. running a family smoothly and enjoying good family life. In order to live a happy active age and old age there should be mutual affection, love and respect. Loyalty and mutual trust are most important in making one's life happy and enjoyable.

ii) Towards children:

It is the joint responsibility of the parents to give their children an ideal upbringing. They have to maintain both their sons and daughters till they grow old enough to earn their own living. The children should be given a proper education and should be given a free hand in selecting their line of education. Moral upbringing is another important duty. Parents must shower all love and affection but never pamper them. The children should be taught to obey and respect their elders and teachers. For this, schools and homes should be ideal places and the parents and teachers should prove themselves to be role models. The old concept of children blindly following the dictates of parents and teachers does not hold good in the present times. Children today are watchful and vocal. If a father is corrupt and accepts bribes, and if the son sees this, then the father loses his moral right to guide the son.

What should the son do in such a situation? If by nature he is upright he resists and desists his father, or otherwise he ignores his father's misdeeds and decides to lead a luxurious life with all bad habits. If this happens (and unfortunately it is happening on a large scale in the society) then the entire society gets corrupt. The future life of both son and father will become blotted and unhappy.

It is, therefore, the essential duty of the person in the active age to desist from the temptations of hoarding ill-earned money and make his old age a satisfying one. Then the son will be disciplined both in the school and outside it.

In this connection, it is appropriate to know the reaction of David Cameron, the prime minister of England, after the recent students' riots under the caption "Families and Parenting". Some excerpts:

> Let me start with families:
>
> The question people asked over and over again last week was "Where are the parents? Why are not they keeping the rioting kids indoors?" Well, join the dots and you have a clear idea about why some of those young people were behaving so terribly. Either there was no one at home, they did not much care or they had lost control.
>
> So if we want to have any hope of mending our broken society, family and parenting is where we have got to start.

Schools

The next part of the social fight-back is what happens in schools. We need an education system which reinforces the message that if you do the wrong thing you will be disciplined, but if you work hard and play by the rules, you will succeed. This is not a distant dream.

Towards dependants:

Sometimes, a man in the active age is required to fulfil his obligations towards his brothers or sisters cast upon him due to premature demise of his father. He should give them a proper education and take care of them till they start their own independent life. This is a satisfying duty which he can relish in his old age.

Towards parents:

This is the most important aspect in one's life. Whatever one is, it is because of the efforts of one's parents. They have given him education to the best of their ability. They have also brought him up with love and affection. By the time he completes his education, starts earning and gets married, his parents would have retired from active life. Now it is his turn to take care of them with a sense of duty and affection, irrespective of his financial position. If it is a joint family, there is more than one person to take care of the parents. But as the joint family system is fast disappearing, it has become the sole responsibility of the sons to look after their parents. Whether the son is rich or poor, it is his moral responsibility to take care of the parents.

Planning for old age

Due to the increase in lifespan and the growing break-up of the joint family system, one has to meticulously plan for one's old age. This has necessarily to be done during the span of active age when one has the capacity to do so both physically, mentally, and financially. For this, one has to live a very disciplined life. As mentioned earlier one must take utmost care of maintaining good health by regular exercise and balanced diet so that one does not suffer from any serious illness in later years of one's life.

Planning for old age has main three constituents. They are: (a) Financial planning (b) Psychological or attitudinal planning (c) Social and occupation planning. If a man successfully plans these three constituents in his active age, then his old age will be happy and worth living.

a) Financial planning

In order to have a contented life which is the key for a happy present and secure future, financial planning is most important. Financial planning is not just a way of saving but also of spending in a prudent way. Most Indians from middle class families try to establish themselves in life by hard work and dedication. Economic conditions vary from person to person. It is, therefore, necessary to have a clear idea of oneself, one's capability of earning and one's duties and responsibilities towards one's family. There are some who complete their education by borrowing money and their first duty is to repay the loans after they start earning. There are others from higher middle class families who have a satisfactory financial background. Their planning should be to build and expand their financial position. There are few born with a silver spoon. In their case, a different type of financial planning is necessary to take care that they do not become victims of lust and arrogance which may dwindle their wealth and character.

It should be remembered that whether a man comes from a poor and lower middle class family or from a higher middle class family or from an affluent family, in the matter of earning money, one should remember what David Niven, author of *100 Simple Secrets of Happy People* said, "Although people believe that as you get wealthier, you get happier, studies show that if you have enough money to feed and clothe yourself, more money does not increase happiness. It should therefore be clear that one should earn money to the best possible extent with the ultimate objective of contentment and happiness. Such persons are likely to live long and their old age will naturally be happy. This caution is necessary because of the allurements which are abundant in the present social life."

Savings for the present and future needs

Saving for the present needs mainly constitute the finances required to meet the expenses on education of the children and in due course, for their marriage. Depending on the earnings, a part should be set aside to meet these expenses. Whether one is in public service or in private sector, there is a provision for pension, provident fund, and gratuity after retirement. One can bank upon these returns. It is, however, prudent to discharge the responsibilities without banking on these items and utilising the savings from one's salary income and other income like return on investments, agricultural income, rent from the property etc. so that the returns on these items can be used after retirement i.e. in old age for financial security.

Investment of savings in life insurance policies is a safe investment with guaranteed return when needed. This is a guaranteed return even if the earning member unfortunately expires before the maturity period of the policy. In short, investments should be meticulously planned to ensure a good standard of living both during the active service and after retirement. No rigid rules can be laid down as circumstances vary from person to person. But the ultimate aim should be to have a good standard of living both during the active age and after retirement i.e. during old age. Modes of investments go on changing from time to time. One should, therefore, consult some financial planning experts and invest so that return on investment is fairly assured.

Housing

This is an equally important aspect to ensure a contented life during active age and during old age. When one is in active service, one should give priority to have one's own house. Often when one is provided with housing by one's employer during service, one tends to ignore the necessity to have one's own house. A house should be acquired during one's active service period during which a person will have the psychological strength to establish this asset. There is an increasing trend of young working couples buying their ownership properties with housing loans. This helps them to save on tax and also creates a lifelong asset.

b) Psychological or attitudinal planning

As every human being born has to die one day, so also every human being has to retire from active service at a certain age depending on the prevailing practice based on certain rules and regulations. This applies to everyone, whether in service, business or profession. Should one get worried on this account? Certainly not, provided one has the satisfaction of fulfilling all obligations and achieving major goals including providing satisfactory financial security for the years after retirement.

In many cases, it happens that a man, by nature, has cultivated other hobbies like reading, writing, painting, social service etc., but could not develop them during active service because of the pressures of work and family responsibilities. Such persons should be eagerly waiting for the date of retirement so that they can keep themselves busy in pursuing those hobbies.

A positive attitude has to be developed—that will be the key factor after retirement.

c) Occupational planning

This is another key factor in making post retirement years healthy and enjoyable. A man during active service, whether as professional or in business, devotes more than 8-10 hours in a day to give the best of himself to his work. After retirement, he suddenly becomes idle and does not know what to do and also how to utilise these 8-10 hours. Unless an alternative plan to spend these hours fruitfully is ready much before retirement, he becomes nervous and depressed. This naturally affects his health adversely and he loses interest in living. In order to avoid such a situation, one must necessarily develop some plans to keep busy after retirement. Day to day and hour to hour plans, if executed properly will keep the person busy and active. One should remember that an idle mind is a devil's workshop. Never keep your mind idle. There should be a chain of activities planned and also executed. This gives immense pleasure to the mind and helps the man to be proud of his achievements.

Women in active age

When we analyse the duties and responsibilities of a person in the active age, we have the man (head of the family) in mind, as he has the main role to play in the family. Traditionally, in the house, the wife is assumed to play a secondary or supportive role. But one cannot forget that she has her own independent life and she is also an active partner in the family. It may be stated that the four stages of life briefly analysed in the first chapter are applicable in their essential features to all human beings both male and female.

When we say that during the first stage of life, i.e. during young age, boys should acquire sound mind and sound body by regular exercise, it applies to young girls in equal measure. They should lead a disciplined life with regular exercise and with sound body and sound mind, from a young age. This is more so because women's lifespan is more than that of men by at least 5 to 6 years.

The traditional role of a woman to look after the home and children does not fully meet the expectations of today's modern women. Fortunately, today's women have realised their additional duties and responsibilities and have accepted the present challenges and excelled in every aspect of life like sports, education, service, business and management. Their role has become wider and equally important. The number of working women is increasing, especially in urban areas. During their active age, they have to shoulder major responsibilities like bringing up the children, teaching them proper values and extending financial support to the family with their earning. Their role goes much beyond the old concept of *ardhangini* (one half of a whole, in this case the wife).

Their dual role as housewife and also as earning member entails moulding the lives of children with proper *sanskara*s. Character building is the most important. This has become more relevant as today's children are growing up in a globalised and industrialised world. The present younger generation of women is more intelligent and has more opportunities for progress in career due to availability of advanced technology. Young women are in equal danger of going astray as young men, as we see happening in society. Today, women are taking on roles outside the house and parents have the onerous responsibility of bringing up their girl-children in an ideal manner by inculcating in them a sense of responsibility, high ideals and good moral character. For this, the parents have to be role models. They should set an example for their children by working with integrity and displaying high morality in every field of life.

Chapter III

AGEING

A. INTRODUCTION

This chapter proposes to highlight the various aspects of the third and fourth stages of life to help one to live a quality life with happiness and commitment.

The issue for analysis therefore is how to live old age so that old age becomes worth living. Here it may be pointed out that till the first half of the twentieth century old age was not at all a matter of concern for either the society or the government. This issue had however received the attention of developed countries much earlier and they prepared blue prints to tackle the situation. But in India, old age was not an issue till the middle of the twentieth century, mainly because of the strong joint family system, emotional attachments and a sense of duty towards the aged that prevailed then as also because of a shorter life-expectancy. A person hardly lived for 5-10 years after retirement and during the period commanded love and respect of the younger family members. This was the general position. But it cannot be vouched that this span of 5-10 years was really enjoyable for everyone. Old persons had to live in the family system whether it was enjoyable or not. Living in old age homes was rarely considered as a solution to the old age problems. If unlucky they had to put up with the situation in the family. There was no way out.

Since the problem of old age was considered a problem of the concerned individual and his/her family, the social organisations or the government rarely got involved with the family in finding out the problems of old age. They acted more as observers and not as interveners in settling the matters affecting the elderly in the family. The Directive Principles of State Policy enjoined in the Constitution as to the state's obligation in respect of old persons remained only in the statute book for many years after independence. However, during the last three to four decades the situation in the family and social structure changed continuously mainly due to demographic evolution with its attendant consequences on the problems of old age.

Certain statistical data and its effect on the issue of old age has to be briefly understood in order to understand and appreciate the issues of "living old age" especially pertaining to the growth in the elderly population in comparison with the growth in general population, decline in the growth of young population and its effect on caring of the elderly population, ratio of elderly population of women and men in rural and urban area and their standard of living and other relevant factors which needs to be studied and analysed to suggest measures to make the retired life of elderly satisfactory.

Growth in the elderly population—a global phenomenon

Growth in the elderly population and its impact on the life of elderly people themselves, on family and social structure, has been an issue in all the countries in the world though in different degrees. Internationally, ageing has been on the United Nations agenda, since the International Plan of Action was adopted by the United Nations member states in Vienna in 1982.

Following this, the Government of India adopted the National Policy on Elder Persons in 1999 which was declared as the International Year of Older Persons. The National Policy, constitutional and legal provisions relating to it, has been separately elaborated.

It may be clarified that ageing is a global phenomena; the solutions thereto however are not and cannot be uniform. Solutions to ageing problems in a developed country like USA cannot be adopted as a matter of course by India, as India has its own peculiar features, in regard to density of population in rural and urban areas, source of income, literary status, family and social structure. Various aspects have to be considered before formulation of any policy and legal provisions. In order to understand the magnitude of the problems and their possible solutions, to enable the elderly to lead a happy and contented life, the demographic evolution in regard to elderly population needs a little elaboration.

Growth in the elderly population in India

Persons in the age group of 60+ are considered elderly. It may be stated that together with the growth in the general population, there has been an increase in the growth of elderly population also. In 1951, the elderly population was roughly 20 million; it increased to 44 million in 1981, which means the population doubled in thirty years. In 2001 the total elderly population was 71 million and in 2011 it was 99 million. Another important feature is that growth in the female elderly population is higher than the growth in male elderly population.

A person is generally considered old when he completes the age of sixty. But while analysing elderly problems and remedial measures, all cannot be clubbed in one group, as their problems especially relating to health and finance change roughly every five years. It is necessary therefore to further break up this span of old age as below:

Age group	Proportion among elderly	Proportion to the total population
60-64 – Young Old	35.9	2.7
65-69 – Old	25.8	1.9

70-74 – Old	19.2	1.4
75-79 – Old	8.6	0.6
80 Plus – Old Old	10.05	0.8
All elderly	100	7.4

According to a projection by United Nations, the present 7.4 percent of the elderly population will increase to 12.7 percent by 2025, and to 21.3 percent by 2050. A country is said to be "ageing" when at least 7 percent of the population is elderly. India is therefore an ageing country.

It can also be seen from the above that 61.7 percent of the elderly are in the age group of 60-69; 27.8 percent are in the age group of 70-79 and 10.5 percent in the age group of 80 and above.

Special features of social structure in the ageing society of India

India is one of the major ageing countries of the world and it has its own peculiar features. The division of the population into "rural" and "urban" sections is one of its special features. More than 70 percent of the Indian population lives in rural India. Growing urbanisation and industrialisation has a direct impact on the migration of rural population to urban areas and also partial re-migration to rural areas after retirement. Such shifting affects the lives of elderly both in the rural areas and urban areas in many ways. In order to understand the problems of the elderly it would be helpful to know the distribution of the aged population by age in urban and rural areas, which is as under:

Age groups (Years)	Total (million)	Rural (million)	Urban (Million)
60-64	27.5	20.6	6.9
65-69	19.8	14.08	5.0
70-74	14.7	11.1	3.6
75-79	6.5	4.8	1.7
80+	8.0	6.0	2.0
Total	76.5	57.8	19.2

(Source: Census of India 2001)

The above statistics reveal that the distribution of elderly persons between urban and rural areas is 1:3. So whenever the state or any social organisation intends to address the issues pertaining to elderly, they have to take into account not only the number of elderly living in rural and urban areas, but also their peculiar and varying problems in respect to their financial status, health status, working conditions, living conditions etc. which have certain advantages and disadvantages for both. The common disadvantage is, however, due to break up in the traditional joint family system, adoption of nuclear family system, change in the attitude of younger generation, years of dependency etc.

With all of these problems, one with a cynical approach may wonder whether increase in the lifespan from 60-70 years to 90-100 years during the last three to four decades is proving to be a curse or a boon. One need not be pessimistic. It is emphasised that by benefitting from the results of progress, one can surely turn the increased lifespan of about 20-25 years into a boon by availing of all opportunities and by maintaining the traditional value system of life and with a positive attitude of adapting to the inevitable but natural changes in one's lifestyle. That is the essence of fruitful and happy "old age life".

Magnitude of the elderly problem in rural areas

As pointed out earlier, 57.3 million elderly live in rural areas. Out of this, 20.06 million people are in the age group of 60-64 and 14.8 million are in the age group of 65-69. Most of them work in agricultural areas which either they own or as tillers on somebody else's land. For them, there is no retirement age as such. They can work as long as their health permits and earn money to support the family. Savings for the future are little or nil. The problem arises when they become completely incapable of doing any physical work. They have to entirely depend on their children for their living. The sons, because of their sense of duty towards parents, may look after them. But if the sons also have limited resources, the parents become a burden after a particular period. The lives of the parents then become miserable and many times they pray to be relieved from living in humiliating circumstances. Of course this happens if the son fails in his duty and becomes too selfish to have a sense of attachment for his parents. He forgets that he will also become old one day and may have to face a similar situation. The son may not have behaved in this manner if the old parents were financially self supporting. Hence, there is the necessity of saving for old age.

In such a situation it is up to the government to provide security through financial aid in the form of monthly pension with suitable provision for contribution by the person during his earning years. This aspect has been dealt with elsewhere.

Magnitude of the elderly problem in urban areas

It has been pointed out earlier that out of the total 76.5 million aged people, only 19.2 million aged live in urban areas, which means that 75 percent of the elderly live in rural areas and only 25 percent of the aged live in urban areas. The majority of the urban elderly during their active life would have worked in organised sectors where the retirement benefits like provident fund, pension etc. are available for their maintenance. After that, there are reasonably good opportunities, though not guaranteed, for getting re-employment which would give financial security for a longer period. But the rural elderly mostly working in unorganised sectors like agriculture, daily wages etc. can work for longer years i.e. till they are physically fit. Then they have to depend on others. According to the census, dependency ratio as percentage of all India working population is 9.8 in the case of rural elderly and 3.28 in the case of urban elderly. Family members of the elderly, and the state, have to take the responsibility of taking care of such dependent elderly.

Status of elderly by gender

From the point of view of "living old age" both males and females have their peculiar problems to face and solve to make their old age a happy one. A new approach to the customary practices at family and social level is absolutely necessary to avoid any conflict.

It has been pointed out earlier that the total male population in different age groups is 53,21,56,772 and that of females is 49,64,53,356 with sex ratio of 933 females for 1000 males. But in contrast, in the case of elderly population (60+) the females outnumber the males (7.8 to 7.0 percent and in terms of number 1029 to 1000). Therefore when we think of various measures to ease the problems of the elderly, peculiar problems of male elderly and female elderly have to be considered separately as the extent of dependency varies rather substantially.

Marital status of elderly

The quality of life of elderly males or females with spouse is definitely better than those without spouse. Togetherness has its own benefits in leading a contented life in one's old age, but statistics show that women are less fortunate than men in this respect.

Marital status of elderly in rural areas

Among the rural males in the age group of 60-69 years, 86.18 percent are married and living with spouse whereas 11.58 percent are widowers. In the case of rural females however only 56.98 percent are married and living with their spouse but 45.57 percent are widowed.

In the age group of 70-79 years, 78 percent of males are married and living with their spouse and 19 percent are widowers. In the case of females, however only 37 percent are married and living with spouse and as high as 62 percent are widowed.

In the age group of 80 and above, 65 percent of males are married and living with their spouse and 29 percent are widowers. In the case of females, the position is more worrying. Only 26 percent are married and living with their spouse and as high as 71 percent are widowed.

Marital status of elderly in urban areas

The position of male and female elderly in the urban area is more or less the same. In the age group of 60-69 years 89 percent of males are married and living with their spouse and 9 percent are widowers. In the same age group, 54 percent of females are married and living with their spouse and 44 percent are widowed.

We find that in the age group of 70-79 years, 79 percent of males are married and living with their spouse and 17 percent are widowers. In the same age group 33 percent females are married and living with their spouse and as high as 64 percent are widowed.

In the age group of 80 and above, 65 percent males are married and have their spouses and 28 percent are widowers. In the case of females only 24 percent are married and have spouses whereas 72 percent are widowed.

All-India marital status of elderly

The general position in the whole of India can be briefly stated as under:

81.64 percent rural males live with spouse and 18.36 percent live without spouse. In the case of urban males 83.66 percent live with spouse and 16.34 percent without spouse.

From this it may be concluded that nearly 80 percent of the elderly males have life partners and only about 20 percent are widowers.

In the case of females, however, the position is rather gloomy. 48.18 percent rural females live with spouse and 51.82 percent life without spouse. That is, nearly 52 percent of the rural females are widows.

In the case of urban females 44.84 percent live with spouse and 55.16 percent live without spouse. That is more than 55 percent. It may be easily concluded that while only about 20 percent of the elderly males are widowers, in the case of females however nearly 55 percent of the elderly females are widows. This has a great impact on the life of the widows in old age and also on the social and religious customs and practices. This needs elucidation.

Firstly, the age of marriage prevalent in the society during the ancient period and in the present century is largely responsible for the large difference in the total number of widowers and widows. Till the Sharda Act was passed in 1829 by the British there was no minimum age for the marriage of girls. The minimum age of fourteen was fixed by law, which has now been increased to eighteen. There is no provision regarding the age difference between the bride and bridegroom at the time of marriage. It is largely governed by the family and social customs and practices. Until the mid-twentieth century, a difference of five to eight or even more years was considered as normal. Due to increase in the literacy and also employment opportunities for girls, the age difference of two to four years is now considered as normal which is a welcome change in the attitude. But still there are a number of cases where the age difference is more than ten years which extends even up to fifteen years which has adverse effects in the later stages of a person's life.

It has been pointed out earlier that the longevity of women is at least five-six years more than men. That means, by and large women live at least five years or more as widows. Due to a general increase in the longevity for both men and women, the number of elderly widows has been increasing.

Another major reason for this situation is that many men, after the demise of their wife, remarry girls who are normally younger by more than twenty years. Such girls, when they become widows, have to live many years as elderly widows, which adds to the number of widows with related problems. This was a common feature about six to seven decades ago. One expected that because of the unpleasant situation it created, the practice of marrying a young girl with wide difference in age would stop. To the contrary, there are many instances even in the twenty-first century where marriages of elderly widowers with young girls take place. As this is a great social problem the widowers on their own should stop such an evil practice for getting a companion in the advanced age.

This situation can be eased at least to some extent if the widowers, instead of remarrying young unmarried girls, marry suitable widows. That is why widow remarriage should be preferred and encouraged. This has more than one advantage. First, many such widows would have crossed the age of reproduction. This avoids the problem of bringing up children at a very late stage of life. Secondly and more importantly, both get companionship which is absolutely essential to build a happy old age.

Of course this is easier said than done as it has many hurdles. Firstly, thinking on these lines by both widower and widow itself is difficult in view of the existing social and religious customs and practices. Even if one finds a suitable companion, it is difficult to get the consent of other family members, especially of children. Legal hurdles in property matters add to the problem.

But taking into consideration the fast changes in the family and social structure during the last three to four decades the scope of remarriage by the widows and widowers is a possible solution in the modern period for a happy old age.

The concept of "live-in relationship" with widows and widowers as major players is being discussed and debated during the last few years. Just as the concept of widow remarriage has so many ifs and buts, this too has many ifs and buts. In the concept of widow remarriage, at least marriage is contemplated, but in a live-in relationship even marriage is not contemplated. Men and women who are mostly elderly widows, widowers and divorcees, decide to stay together as companions and share their feelings, love and affection so that the remaining years of their lives become enjoyable.

A questionnaire was sent to about seventy senior citizens who are aged seventy and above to express their views on various aspects of planning and living old age. One of the questions was to ascertain their views on live-in relationships. Almost one third of the respondents did not favour the idea, as it is against the traditional system of living. Nearly an equal number, though not against the concept, expressed their view that it has many difficulties in its implementation and the best way is remarriage. Of course, a few were in favour of the concept.

It may be stated here that the concepts of widow marriage or live-in relationship are mooted with a view to encourage good companionship at the advanced age of life. Widow remarriage was a mission for social reformers and instances of widow remarriage have more or less proved successful. The concept of live-in relationship is very recent. It may be pointed out that though both the concepts appear to be good, they have many hurdles which are briefly explained below.

Widow/widower remarriage

The widowers and widows who intend to remarry may be comparatively young with many years of life to live. In such cases remarriage gives the required solace. But if either or both have children from their first marriage, great understanding and adjustment is required on the part of everyone involved i.e. widow, widower, children and their relatives to make the remarriage happy.

Live-in relationship

The concept of live-in relationship has added problems. It still hasn't been accepted by many. Moreover, the age is an important factor. In a unique match making meet organised last year by a social organisation at Ahmedabad,[18] it is reported that three hundred men and some seventy women participated and that seven pairs of elderly men and women agreed to enter into a live-in relationship. It is also reported that the ages of the participants, mainly consisting of divorcees, widows and widowers, ranged from fifty to eighty-three years. It is not known whether they had any children from their earlier marriage.

The following points arise for consideration:

---

[18]*FPJ*, 21 November 2011

1. If the participants are above seventy-five years of age, very few years of life are left to get to know the nature of the aspirant partner unless for any reason they have known each other for a long time. It is a fact that even in marriages at an early age it takes a long time to understand each other. It is more difficult at an advanced age.

2. Live-in relationship is not an experiment to be carried out without any attachment or commitment. Marriage even at this stage may bring a sense of commitment and sanctity to the relationship.

3. If there are children for either or both, the consent of the children would help to really enjoy old age or else life may become miserable.

These are the various ifs and buts in a live-in relationship; of course, the problems and considerations vary from individual to individual and can be solved with proper understanding by all concerned.

It may, however, be stated that in remarriage and live-in relationship both, the attitude and mind set of the widows is crucial. The examples of widow remarriage and live-in relationship are negligible. They are just drops in the ocean. Since ancient times, strict dos and don'ts had been stipulated for widows. Whether widowhood came as a child or at a late age, she was supposed to adhere to a strict code of conduct denying her rights as a human being. Widows also accepted the situation taking it as either destiny though with a rigid mind set. They suppressed their feelings. This is why at least some of them now think of remarriage irrespective of their age.

Continuity and change is the essential feature of any civilisation. So, Indian civilisation is not an exception. During the last one or two centuries human social values have been changing rapidly. That is how the issue of widow remarriage and concept of live-in relationship are at least discussed and debated with a favourable approach to the issues of widow remarriage and their legitimate rights to live as human beings.

Continuity and change are an ongoing and inevitable process and one has to accept them whether for the good or the bad; which time alone will prove.

Living conditions—continuity and change in the family and social structure

As we have seen earlier, there are peculiar features in the living conditions of Indian people irrespective of their age and gender. More than 70 percent of the Indian people live in rural areas and only about 30 percent live in urban areas. The peculiar family structure of the Indian society is that an adult male lives in a dwelling place along with his wife, children and elderly parents. This is a family unit. In rural areas agriculture is the main occupation and also a source of income. Love and affection for each other in the family, emotional attachment and respect for the aged was more or less the set pattern of family life. A section of the village or town population was engaged in other supporting occupations like teaching or trade etc.

It may be stated that about a century prior, agriculture was the main occupation of India on which the civilisation was built. This pattern of family and social structure could not be static as the years and decades passed. Continuity and change as mentioned earlier are the basic philosophy of any society. The population as expected grew and new avenues had to be found for the progress of the society by adapting to the changing circumstances. People thus moved out of the villages for better prospects in education, profession etc. That is how urbanisation started.

After independence in 1947, ambitious plans for the growth of industries, better facilities for higher education, and employment opportunities for both males and females were available. India has made tremendous progress in all fields of human activity—arts, science, medicine etc. Due to growth in technology all over the world, people are closely connected to each other. The number of students going abroad for studies and better prospects has increased, which was very rare a few decades ago. Many students permanently settle abroad but their parents have to stay in India as they cannot join their children for various reasons.

About 50-60 years previously it was common for almost every couple to have five or six children. In the joint family system, looking after the children was also not a problem. The housewife had time and support in looking after the children. Due to non-availability of medical facilities infant mortality was also common.

The joint family system was a strong binding force under which a good number of children, middle aged earning members and old parents could live under one roof with good understanding and caring for each other. Looking after the aged was no problem as everyone in the family considered it to be their moral responsibility and duty. Old age was not an issue, whether the family was rich or poor. The riches and poverty were shared by all. The aged parents who lived for about five to ten years after their active life were looked after with a sense of duty and respect. That is, there was an inbuilt system for the welfare of the aged.

Caring for the aged by the children and grandchildren was a noble practice passed down the ages. In ancient India an aged person had a vital role to play in the family and society. They also enjoyed social security and had the privilege of being cared for by the younger generations. They were accorded a high status as the decision makers in the joint family system. However, this system could not continue as a permanent feature due to changes taking place in the socio-economic and demographic dimensions such as drop in the number of children in a family, increase in longevity, greater involvement of younger women in economic activities and other social activities depriving the aged of their natural caretakers. Adults and children had to migrate from rural to urban areas often leaving the aged behind.

This resulted in moving away from the traditional, well

established joint family system depriving the aged of the most essential emotional support from family members. Because of the longevity, aged people have to face the adverse situation for a longer period as their dependency on the children for financial and health security increases. From what has been elaborated in the previous paragraphs it should be absolutely clear that the problem of the elderly is not confined to the individual himself or herself, or to the family of the aged individual. After all, the aged are also citizens of free India and hence the society and the state both have legal and moral responsibility to adequately address their problems and solve them. It has to be a coordinated effort by all the four players viz. individual, family, society, and the state.

Caring for the aged—a joint responsibility

It has been pointed out in the previous paragraphs that out of the total 76.5 million elderly people (60+), 57.3 million elderly live in rural areas and 19.2 million elderly live in urban areas, that is, in terms of proportion it is 3 to 1. Gender wise for every thousand males the general female population is 933. But when we come to the elderly population the female population is more than the males with the ratio of 7.8 to 7.0. It has also been pointed out with statistics that both in rural and urban areas, the number of widows by far exceed the number of widowers. As most of the widows entirely depend on their children for their livelihood, their care needs to be attended to by everyone involved i.e. self, family, and state. In view of the break up in the joint family system, and change in the attitude of children in the family, the state has to necessarily step into provide at least financial and health security as enjoined in the Constitution of India.

Constitutional and legal provisions

Article 41 of the Constitution—Directive Principle of State Policy has directed that the state shall within the limits of its economic capacity and development make effective provision for securing the right to work, to education and to public assistance in cases of unemployment, old age, sickness and disablement.

It may be stated that if these provisions, though termed as directives, were implemented sincerely it would make the life of every citizen dignified and happy from young age to old age. Education is one of the primary needs in the young age and is necessary to enable a citizen to get good employment which in turn gives him financial security in old age. Unfortunately, the state has failed in its duty during the last sixty-five years of independence. Sincere and determined efforts have not been made by the state to treat the directive principles as mandatory. As a result a number of problems have to be faced at the family and social level in regards to education, employment, and old age as all of these problems are interdependent. Unless and until education and employment are guaranteed, giving the citizen economic stability, old age cannot be happy.

It was only in the 80s i.e. after more than thirty years after independence that a decision was taken to frame a policy for older persons, following the World Assembly on Ageing held in Vienna in 1982. After six years i.e. in 1987-88 an Inter Ministerial Committee was constituted by the Government of India for the purpose. In 1999 a National Policy was formulated.

Constitutional and legal provisions of National Policy

This policy was formulated by the Social Justice and Empowerment Ministry which was adopted by the Union Cabinet on 13 February 1999. The policy highlights a few basic features of the issues of older persons. Some of the important features are briefly stated as under.

Demographic trends

People are living longer; this is a global phenomenon. Expectation of life at birth in India for males has shown a steady rise from 42 years in 1951-60 to 58 years in 1986-90, and it is projected to be 67 years in 2011-16, an increase of about 9 years in a 25 year period. In the case of females the increase in expectation of life has been higher by about 11 years during the same period.

Increased life expectancy has contributed to an increase in the number of persons in the 60+ category in India from only 12 million persons in 1901 to more than 24 million in 1951 and 57 million in 1991. In its projections further than 2016, United Nations (1996) has indicated that India will have 198 million persons who are 60+ by 2020 and 326 million by 2050.

The percentage of widowhood is much higher among females who are 60+ than among males of the same age group because it is customary to get married to men older than them by several years, they do not remarry and they have a longer lifespan. There were in 1991, 18 million widowed females who were 60+ as compared to the 4.5 million widowers. In other words there were four times as many widowed females as widowers.

National Policy statement

The National Policy seeks to assure the elderly that their concerns are national concerns and that they will not live unprotected, ignored, or marginalised.

The goal of the National Policy is the wellbeing of older persons. It aims to strengthen their legitimate place in society and help them to live the last phase of their lives with purpose, dignity, and peace. The policy visualises that the state will extend support for financial security, health care, shelter, welfare, and other needs of older persons, and provide protection against abuse and exploitation.

The policy views the life cycle as a contiguous one of which post 60 phase of life is an integral part. It does not view the age of 60 as the cut off point for beginning a life of dependency. It considers 60+ years of age as a phase when the individual should have the chances and opportunities to lead an active, creative, productive, and satisfying life. An important driving force is consequently an active and productive involvement of the elderly and not just their care.

The policy recognises that older persons too are a resource. They render useful services in the family and outside. They are not just consumers of goods and services, but also their producers.

The policy recognises that larger budgetary allocations from the state will be needed and the rural and urban poor will be given special attention.

Financial security

A great anxiety in old age relates to financial insecurity. When the issue is seen in the context of the fact that one-third of the population (1993-94) is below the poverty line and about another one-third belongs to the lower income group, the financial situation of two-thirds of the population of the elderly can be said to be fragile.

For the elderly below the poverty line, old age pensions provide some succour coverage under the old age pension scheme for poor persons and will be significantly expanded with ultimate objective of covering all the older persons below the poverty line.

Pension is a much sought after income security. The base of pension coverage needs to be considerably expanded to facilitate the establishment of pension scheme both in private and in public sector for self employed and salaried persons in non-government employment with provision for employees also to contribute.

Health care of the elderly—operational guidelines

The National Sample Surveys (NSS) of 1986-87, 1995-1996 and 2004 have shown that:

- The burden of morbidity in old age is enormous.
- Non-communicable diseases (lifestyle related and degenerative) are extremely common in older people irrespective of socio-economic status.
- Disabilities are very frequent which affect the functionality in old age compromising the ability to pursue the activities of daily living.

The National Sample Survey (NSS) of 2004 provides a comprehensive status report on older persons. According to it, the prevalence and incidence of diseases as well as hospitalisation rates are much higher in older people than the total population.

However, very little effort has been made to develop a model of health and social care in tune with the changing need and time. The developed world has evolved many models for elderly care e.g. nursing home care, health insurance etc. As no such model for older people exists in India, it may be an opportunity for innovation in health system development, though it is a major challenge. At present, elderly are provided health care by the general health care delivery system in the country. At the primary care level, the infrastructure is grossly deficient. And otherwise the health system machinery is geared up to deal with maternal care, child health, and communicable diseases. The elderly suffer from multiple and chronic diseases. They need long term and constant care. Their health problems also need specialist care from various disciplines e.g. Ophthalmology, Orthopaedics, Psychiatry, Cardio-vascular, Dentistry, Urology etc. to name a few. Thus, a model of care providing comprehensive health services to the elderly at all levels of health care delivery is imperative to meet the growing health needs of the elderly. Moreover, the immobile and disabled elderly need health services that are close to their homes.

As per the National Policy on Older persons, the Ministry of Health and Family Welfare was entrusted with the following agenda to attend to the health care needs of the elderly:

- Establishing geriatric ward for elderly patients at all the district level hospitals.
- Expansion of treatment facilities for chronic, terminal and degenerative diseases.
- Providing improved medical facilities to those not able to be present at medical centres.
- Inclusion of geriatric care in the syllabus of medical courses

including courses for nurses.

- Reservation of beds for elderly in public hospitals.
- Training for geriatric caregivers.
- Setting up research institutes for chronic elderly diseases such as dementia and Alzheimer's.

The vision objectives and expected outcome

The National Programme for the Health Care of the Elderly (NPHCE) is an articulation of the international and national commitments of the government as envisaged under the United Nations Convention on the Rights of Persons with Disabilities. As mentioned earlier National Policy on Older Persons was adopted by the Government of India in 1999.

The vision of the National Programme for the Health Care for the Elderly is:

- To provide accessible, affordable, high-quality, and long-term comprehensive and dedicated care services to the ageing population.
- Creating a new "architecture" for ageing.
- To build a framework to create an enabling environment for "a society for all ages".
- To promote the concept of active and healthy ageing.

Specific objectives

- To provide an easy access to promotional, preventive, curative, and rehabilitative services to the elderly through community based primary health care approach.
- To identify health problems in the elderly and provide appropriate health interventions in the community with a strong referral backup support.
- To build up the capacity of the medical and paramedical professionals as well as the care-takers within the family for providing health care to the elderly.
- To provide referral services to the elderly patients through district hospitals, and regional medical institutions.

Core strategies to achieve the objectives of the programme are

- Dedicated service at the health centres including provision of machinery, equipment, training, and additional human resources.
- Dedicated facilities at district hospitals with 10 bedded wards, additional human resources, machinery and equipment, consumables and drugs etc.
- Strengthening of 8 regional medical institutes for the elderly, introducing post-graduate courses in geriatric medicine and in-service training for health personnel at all levels.
- Education and communication using mass media and other communication channels to reach out to the target community.
- Continuous monitoring and independent evaluation of the programme and research in geriatrics.

The United Nations General Assembly in the sixty-sixth session (March 2002) also called upon member states to address the well-being and adequate health care needs of older persons as well as any cases of neglect, abuse and violence against older persons by designing and implementing more effective prevention strategies and stronger laws and policies to address these problems and their underlying factors.

The United Nations General Assembly direction and Government of India's policy adopted in 1999 are ideal and comprehensive. It is unfortunate that though more than twelve years have passed, the effective implementation of the policy is not yet visible. The finance minister while presenting the budget for 2013-2014 said, "The National Programme for the Health Care of Elderly is being implemented in 100 selected districts of 21 states. Eight regional geriatric centres are being funded for the development of dedicated geriatric departments. I propose to provide ₹150 crore for this programme."

This is a welcome measure, though provision of ₹150 crore appears to be too small. But the National Policy is so wide and comprehensive that unless time based programmes are chalked out and implemented with all vigour and sincerity, the policy it is feared may be considered by many as only "wishful thinking".

Shelter

Shelter is a basic human need. The number of houses for different income segments will be within housing schemes for urban and rural income segments. 10 percent of the houses or house sites will be earmarked for allotment to older persons.

Welfare

The main challenge of welfare will be to identify the more vulnerable among older persons such as the poor, the disabled, the infirm, the chronically sick and those without family support and to provide welfare services to them on priority basis.

Voluntary organisations will be encouraged and assisted to organise services such as day cares, multi social citizens' centres, reach out services etc. for the elderly.

A welfare fund for the elderly will be set up. It will obtain funding support from the government, corporate sector, trusts, charities, and individual donors.

Protection of life and property

Old persons become soft targets for criminal elements. They tend to become victims of fraudulent dealings and might also face physical and emotional abuse at the hands of family members who are trying to force them to part with their ownership rights. Widows' right of inheritance, occupancy and disposal which are usurped by their own children and relatives should be returned and protected. It is important that security is made available to older persons.

Voluntary organisations and associations for older persons should be assisted to provide protective services and help senior citizens through support services, and legal and other measures.

Family

Family is the most cherished institution in India and the most vital non-formal social security for the old. The elderly mostly stay with one or more of their children particularly when independent living is no longer feasible. It is the most preferred living arrangement and also the most emotionally satisfying. It is important that the family support system continues to be functional and the ability of the family to discharge its caring responsibilities is strengthened through support services.

State policies such as providing tax relief and allowing rebate for medical expenses will encourage children to co-reside with their parents.

Implementation

The National Policy on Older Persons will be very widely disseminated for which an action plan will be prepared so that its features remain in constant public focus.

The policy will make a change in the lives of the senior citizens only if it is successfully implemented. While the government and the principal organisations have some basic responsibilities in the matter, other institutions as well as individuals will need to consider how they can play their respective roles for the well being of the elderly.

Collaborative action will go a long way in achieving a more humane society, which gives older persons their legitimate place.

The Ministry of Social Justice and Empowerment will be the nodal ministry to coordinate all matters relating to the implementation of the policy.

The policy statement as briefly stated above sounds and reads well. But the ground reality is that the state has to go a long way with all sincerity and vigour which unfortunately is absent as very little has been done so far.

Some of the legal provisions made by the state in fulfilment of its objective are briefly stated as follows:

The Maintenance and Welfare of Parents and Senior Citizens Act, 2007

The elderly, who after retirement from active service do not have financial security and dwelling place of their own, have to depend on their children for survival. In the joint family system where the parents are taken care of as a sense of duty, the elderly had no problem in living their old age. But the declining joint family system has resulted in reduced attachment to the family and consequently emotional attachment among the family members has also lessened.

Due to change in attitude on the part of children, there has been a growing tendency to refuse to look after the aged parents, making their old age miserable. In order to protect the interests of such ignored parents, government had to interfere to make legal provisions to bind the children to provide the parents financial security to enable them to live an independent life of their own.

An Act to provide for effective provisions for the maintenance and welfare of parents and senior citizens guaranteed under the Constitution was enacted by Parliament which received the assent of the president on 29 December 2007. Some of the important provisions of the Act are:

Maintenance of Parents and Senior Citizens

A senior citizen including a parent who is unable to maintain himself from his own earning or property owned by him shall be entitled to make an application under Section 5 in case of

i) Parent or grandparent, against one or more of his/her children not being a minor

ii) A childless senior citizen against such of his/her relative referred to in clause (g) of Section 2.

(According to the above mentioned Section, a relative means any legal heir of the childless senior citizen who is not a minor and is in possession of or would inherit his/her property after his/her death).

An application for maintenance under Section 4, may be

made

a) by a senior citizen or a parent, as the case may be or

b) if he/she is incapable, by any other person or organization authorised by him; or

c) the Tribunal may take cognizance *suo motu.*

The Tribunal may, during the pendency of the proceeding regarding monthly allowance for the maintenance under this section, order such children or relative to make a monthly allowance for the interim maintenance of such senior citizen including parent and to pay the same to such senior citizen or parent as the Tribunal may from time to time direct.

An application for maintenance may be filed against one or more persons.

(Provided that such children or relative may implead the other person liable to maintain parent in the application for maintenance.)

Order for Maintenance

If children or relatives, as the case may be, neglect or refuse to maintain a senior citizen being unable to maintain himself, the Tribunal may on being aware of such neglect or refusal, order such children or relatives to make monthly allowance of such monthly rate for the maintenance of such senior citizen, as the Tribunal may from time to time direct.

The maximum maintenance allowance which may be ordered by such Tribunal shall be such as may be prescribed by the State Government which shall not exceed ten thousand rupees per month.

Deposit of Maintenance Amount

When an order is made (by the Tribunal), the children or relative who is required to pay any amount in terms of such order shall within thirty days of the date of announcing the order by the Tribunal deposit the entire amount ordered in such manner as the Tribunal may direct.

The provision by itself is very good. But many elderly may

not avail of these provisions as in practice it amounts to filing a case against their own sons and daughters which they may not like to do. Thus, other alternative method needs to be found out for the needy elderly needs to be explored.

Medical Support for Senior Citizens

The State Government shall ensure that:

i) The Government hospitals or hospitals funded fully or partially by the Government shall provide beds for all senior citizens as far as possible

ii) Research activities for chronic elderly disease and ageing is expanded

Protection of life and property of senior citizens

The Central Government and State Government Officers including the police officers and the members of the judicial service are given periodic sensitization and awareness training on the issues relating to this Act.

The State Government shall provide a comprehensive action plan for providing protection of life and property for senior citizens.

This needs to be implemented honestly and sincerely and be treated as a satisfying service for the needy elderly.

The policies and programmes described above sound very well in theory. But the main issue is whether any of these benefits have been actually given to the elderly who need them the most.

Even a general survey indicates that hardly any of the schemes have actually benefitted the elderly who are in dire need of financial security in the form of monthly pension or return on property planned insurance schemes. The present situation indicates that the state and other institutions have much more to accomplish to ensure financial security to every elderly.

B. LIVING OLD AGE

After retirement, old age is the final but most important stage of life. Even if one has reasonable financial security and health security, happiness and commitment depends on several factors mainly on the individual's nature and attitude and also on the determination to be happy and make others happy.

Living old age is both an art and a science. It is an art in making the best use of one's qualities for enjoyment of self and also of others. It is a science because one has to carry out his day-to-day activities by adhering and working to certain well established norms in a systematic way. For this, one has to follow certain regulations. "Old age can be creative or self destructive; it is your choice to decide. Old age need not be painful and death may not be frightening, it is possible to learn in the days of retirement."[19]

What Swami Chinmayananda has said is that if the aged looks to the surroundings and changes with negative approach his old age will not be a happy one. First he should consider himself lucky to survive with fairly good financial position and health at the age of sixty-five or more and should intend to live some more happy years with his children and grandchildren. He should accept the inevitable changes in the family and social structure both in regard to the living arrangements and the change in the attitude of the youngsters in the family. Children and grandchildren have to go out of the house, out of the city and even out of the country to avail of brighter career prospects. He should desist from the temptation of even comparing his behaviour with the parents and other elders during his younger days and should not express unhappiness even remotely over the change in the attitude of his children. In fact, there is absolutely no reason to be unhappy. As Swamiji has said, "One has to have a creative attitude to enjoy old age."

A man or woman requires certain additional qualities and sense of values which he has to acquire for graceful ageing.

---

[19]*Active Ageing in the New Millennium*, ed. Aabha Choudhary, p. 31

Once the people are able to secure these core values in their old age, they are said to be "ageing gracefully"[20]. Graceful ageing is a process of optimising opportunities for physical, social and psychological well-being to ensure a healthy, independent quality life in old age.

Graceful ageing allows older people to optimise their potential for independence, good health and productivity while providing them with adequate protection and care from the family, the society and the state. In this task, apart from the aged themselves, there are three additional players: family, community and state. All of them have specific responsibilities towards the aged. The state has to intervene and coordinate. As pointed out earlier, the aged are also required to behave in a manner that is conducive to a healthy life.

Intergenerational relationship:

It is true that due to urbanisation and industrialisation, the joint family system has almost disappeared to make way for nuclear family system. But even then, the present younger generation considers taking care of their aged parents as their moral responsibility. That is how even today more than 70 percent of the aged parents live with one of their children.

When one retires from active service and starts getting older, the quality of future aged life mainly depends on the intergenerational relationship which again is dependent on several factors. The main one is the living arrangement. For instance a middle class man in active service living with his wife, son, daughter-in-law and infant grandson is the head of the family and manages all household affairs himself. He retires at the age of sixty-five, with a modest monthly income by way of monthly pension or return on investment. At the same time if his daughter-in-law takes up a job, the old parents have to look after the house and in addition take care of the grandson which adds to their physical strain in the house in old age. What should be the attitude of the aged in such

[20]*The Greying of India*, p. 306-307

a situation? If the grandmother starts grumbling that after toiling for most of her life in managing the household and in bringing up the children, she has to continue to work hard in the house, friction starts in the family and old age becomes a burden.

On the other hand, if the aged parents, especially the grandmother, keep a positive attitude and accept this as a golden opportunity to keep themselves physically fit, help the son and daughter-in-law in earning more money and take pleasure in taking care of the grandson then without any arguments, not only does their old age become enjoyable but they also maintain the happiness of the entire family. The parents should engage themselves in home chores like cooking, cleaning, child care, marketing etc. without much strain and this will help to keep them physically fit. Sense of belonging as a part of the family gives them dignity in the house. The son and daughter-in-law can go to work without being concerned about the children at home and concentrate on bettering their career prospects.

The relationship between grandchildren and grandparents is the most sublime experience, which is manifest in interacting with them, in giving them their meals with affection and love, in telling them bed time stories etc. In return the grandchildren, as they get love, affection, and care from the grandparents, develop respect and strong bonds of attachment with grandparents. There cannot be any better pleasure for the aged.

Even in their relations with their son and daughter-in-law, in addition to natural affection, they should develop an attached yet detached attitude. Do not interfere with their daily working and do not advise unless asked.[21] By this the aged get peace of mind, and the son and daughter-in-law develop affection and respect towards the aged and voluntarily seek advice, because the aged have vast experience behind them. This is also in keeping with the Indian cultural tradition. These

[21]Swami Sukhbodhananda

are typical examples of the persons belonging to middle and higher middle class families who form the largest section of the Indian Society. They are the symbols of the problems of the aged in India.

There is another class of aged parents whose children are abroad—in countries like USA and England—and their chances of returning to India are almost nil. In such a situation, which is very normal in the present days, what are the options for the aged? Either they also could go to the foreign country and live with the children or continue to stay alone in India. Both have psychological and practical problems. Separation from the sons and daughters and their families in old age, when they need their company, is painful. If they opt to go and stay with the children in a foreign country, they lose the benefit of social contacts or family contacts nourished for decades in India. In addition, because of the peculiar lifestyle in foreign countries they have to stay alone in the house from morning till evening until the son, daughter-in-law, grandchildren return from office and school. The day becomes boring. This dullness becomes unbearable if the parent is a widow or widower.

The best way would be to continue to stay in India with spouse and enjoy. Wife and husband are the best natural companions and together they can spend life enjoying past memorable memories and planning for the remaining years of life. Love your spouse even more than you loved him/her during young age. Age is no bar for love and respect. What is important is to accept the changed situation wholeheartedly and capitalise on the changes for a happy aged life. If health starts failing they can even join a good old age home which provides better medical facilities and also social contacts with other inmates of the same age.

In the previous paragraphs an attempt has been made to explain the various living arrangements available for the aged and the necessity of adjusting to the changed circumstances willingly and completely. This is only one side of "living old age". The second side is equally important: the aged have to maintain certain rigidity for ensuring good health and to develop a positive attitude of making best use of the available opportunities. It may, however, be pointed out that four factors viz. financial security, living arrangements, health and attitude are inter-dependent. Balancing of these four factors is both an art and a science. The key words are "keep yourself busy" both physically and mentally. Be active and optimistic at any cost. Life is for living with quality and minimal suffering."

Health or physical aspect

The health of an individual in old age is basically determined by the genetic inheritance received from the parents and by the way one has lived in the young and middle age. There is not much one can do regarding the former but a lot can be done regarding the latter. In this connection a gist of the views expressed by the renowned writer and journalist, Khushwant Singh, who is now ninety-eight years old, are worth mentioning.

He writes: "Earlier I had written that longevity is in one's genes; children of long living parents are likely to live longer than those born to short lived parents. This did not happen in my own family. Nevertheless I still believe gene is the most important factor in determining one's lifespan.[22]

"More important than analysing longevity is to cope with old age and make terms with it. As we grow older, we are less able to exercise our limbs. We have to devise ways to keep them active.

"Equally important is the need to cut down drastically on one's intake of food and drink.

"Never allow yourself to be constipated. The stomach is a store house of all kinds of ailments. Our sedentary life tends to make us constipated. Keep your bowels clean however you can.

"Impose strict discipline on your daily routine.

"Try to develop peace of mind. For this you must have a healthy bank account. Shortage of money can be very

---

[22]*Afternoon*, 17 January 2012

demoralising. Savings should be enough for your future needs and provide for the possibility of falling ill.

"Never lose your temper, it takes a heavy toll and jangles one's nerves.

"Never tell a lie. Always keep your national motto in mind. *Satyameva Jayate*—truth alone triumphs.

"Give generously. Remember you cannot take anything material with you after your death. You may give away things to your children, servants or charity. There is joy in giving. Drive out envy of those who have done better than you in life.

"A practice which I have found very effective is to fix my gaze on the flame of a candle, empty mind of everything, but in my mind repeat 'Aum Shanti, Aum Shanti, Aum Shanti.' It does work. I am at peace with the world."

The lifestyle and attitude of Khushwant Singh should act as a role model for all, especially for the elderly. The discipline, regularity and spirituality that have moulded his approach to life are worth emulating. He has actually put into practice the philosophy contained in our ancient scriptures. What he has said about speaking the truth, frugal living and food habits are contained in the following Sanskrit sloka:

धृतिः क्षमा दमोस्तेयं शौचमिन्द्रिय निग्रहः

धीविद्या सत्यमक्रोहाः दशकं धर्म लक्षणा

Meaning:

Steadfastness, forgiveness, self control, non-exploitation, purity of mind, control over senses, intellect, knowledge, truthfulness, and tranquillity (not giving vent to anger) are the ten attributes of a truly religious person.

There is yet another example in Dr. Shigeaki Minohava of Japan who at the age of ninety-eight is one of the longest serving physicians. He says that "energy comes from feeling good".

On the concept of generosity, emphasised by both Khushwant Singh and Dr. Shigeakit for a long and healthy life, it may be stated that a recent study conducted by an institution in

America confirms this premise that if one wants good health and longevity then one must make a habit of giving. The five year study was conducted by three universities.

One's physical health at the time of retirement mainly depends on the type of life lived during young age and active age. Even if one does not have very good health at the time of retirement it can be improved with will and determination. Age is no consideration for starting afresh. Sardar Fauja Singh became the first hundred year old to compete in a marathon in Toronto. He commenced running only at the age of sixty-three.

How to maintain good health in old age

The keywords to maintain good health in old age are discipline and activity.

The aged person should as far as possible exercise in the morning as one is fresh then and it is the right time of the day. The selected exercise should be good enough to stretch all the muscles and joints and increase pulse and respiration rates. This may be anything from gardening, brisk walking, games like badminton and tennis, swimming or even cycling. Golf is a favourite pastime of many senior citizens. The most preferred exercise is regular walking in the morning though the distance covered depends on one's health.

Advantages

Participation in regular, moderate physical activity can delay functional decline and reduce the risk of chronic diseases in both healthy and chronically ill older people. Regular moderate physical activity reduces the risk of cardiac death by 20-25 percent among people with confirmed heart disease. It can substantially reduce the severity of disabilities associated with heart disease and other chronic illnesses. When an old man is in a position to exercise regularly it has other advantages. The first is that he feels healthy which itself is morale boosting. It improves his mental health and promotes social interaction which was a normal feature in active age. The feeling of loneliness, a sense of inferiority and dejection, vanishes and the man becomes confident and bold in his dealings with others in the society. He feels that he is as good as he was in his active age and will remain so till the end by maintaining a disciplined life with good exercise.

It is not your age but how you behave that defines you as old. In particular, people who still do their own shopping, travel alone or do their own house chores are less likely to be perceived as old. According to a study by Michelle Barnhart of Oregon State University, which is based on interviews with octogenarians, their families and caregivers, she concludes that when people in their 80s or 90s are active, safe or independent they are treated as younger themselves allowing them to "age without getting old".[23]

A study of more than 10,000 people in Britain and the United States found that although physical life goes down after middle age, the mental satisfaction increases.

The researchers found that people reported better mental quality of life as they aged, despite decrease in their physical abilities.

The study also found that those who slept between six and eight hours per day tended to have better physical and mental health scores than those who slept on an average fewer than six or more than eight hours.

Role of Yoga exercises for physical fitness

Since many centuries, our ancestors believed in and practised yoga exercises for good health and mental peace. In course of time other methods of exercises and sport also gained popularity as in addition to physical fitness they could also inculcate a sense of fellowship and team spirit. During the last five or six decades the role of yoga as a means of maintaining physical and mental health, along with sport has been gaining popularity and many yoga institutions have been established. Some that focus on yoga for seniors are becoming increasingly

[23]*Harmony - Celebrate Age*, January 2013

popular. The various aspects of yoga are dealt with in a separate chapter.

Habits and health

It is needless to emphasise that good habits keep a man healthy in all the stages of life while bad habits create health problems. The impact of these habits is felt more in old age. In respect of food habits the terms used are undernutrition, overnutrition, malnutrition and balanced diet.

Under nutrition implies eating too little. With advancing age most people tend to eat less with the apprehension that eating more has an adverse effect on health, forgetting that eating less itself will have an adverse effect. Each one should decide the quantity of intake in consultation with their doctors. Similarly, over eating will also have a negative effect on health.

The best way is to balance one's diet, both in quantity and quality, with due regard to one's health. Normally a balanced diet should contain adequate amounts of: (a) Protein (b) Carbohydrate (c) Fat (d) Vitamins (e) Minerals and (f) Fibre. Of course the actual proportion varies from person to person.

Problems of the aged

Nutrition

Malnutrition in older adults includes both undernutrition in poorer households and excess calorie consumption in richer households. Malnutrition is caused by a number of factors like limited access to food because of poverty conditions, tooth loss, lack of nutritional knowledge and information, and lack of physical activity. With advancing age certain nutrients are not easily absorbed in the body and thus it loses its energy requirements. Therefore it is important for older people to eat a variety of nutrient-rich foods that are culturally acceptable and regionally available at affordable prices. Excess calorie consumption greatly increases an older person's risk for chronic diseases and disabilities. Obesity and a high fat diet are directly related to diabetes, high blood pressure, arthritis and some cancers. Insufficient calcium and vitamin D intake can result in loss of bone density in older age and increase in painful, costly and debilitating bone fractures especially in older women.

It is essential for persons with a medical condition to be disciplined with their diet. For example, persons suffering from diabetes, especially the old, are tempted to eat sweets, which is strictly prohibited. The aged should desist from such temptations in the interest of their own health.

Smoking

This is one of the major common habits which, if not restricted, does more harm than providing enjoyment. Habits die hard, it is said. Temptation, lifestyle, and wrong notions of enjoyment have a bearing on one's life.

It is again our common experience that middle-aged people and the aged, who smoke, are more likely to suffer from serious disabilities and die prematurely of smoking related diseases. Smoking may also decrease the effect of the essential medication. Constant exposure to passive smoking can have a negative effect on health generally and more so on older people's health, especially if they suffer from asthma or other respiratory problems. The aged should stop smoking altogether even if they were smokers during their active age.

Alcohol

Like smoking, this is another common habit which does more harm than good unless it is strictly kept within limits.

While older people tend to consume less alcohol than younger people, the metabolism changes that accompany ageing increase their susceptibility to alcohol related diseases, including malnutrition, liver disease and peptic ulcers. Older people also have greater chances of experiencing alcohol related falls and injuries as well as dementia and other potential hazards that result from mixing alcohol and medication.

According to a recent WHO report, there is evidence that

alcohol consumption at very low levels (up to one drink only) may offer some degree of protection against coronary heart disease and stroke for people aged forty-five and over. However, in terms of over excess mortality, the adverse effects of drinking outweigh any protection against coronary heart disease, even in high risk populations.

From the previous paragraphs it is clear that in order to maintain good health in old age, regular exercise and stopping of or at least restricting certain habits like smoking and alcohol consumption would help in living old age with good health and tranquillity.

Keeping occupied in old age—A key to graceful ageing

As stated earlier, financial security, health security and attitude are the three important factors for ageing gracefully. The first two aspects have also been examined. After retirement one knows where he stands in respect of finance and health. It may or may not be satisfactory. Income gets reduced and so also health. This change is inevitable. But one has to plan to improve this situation wherever possible. One should also plan as to how to utilise the years of life available after retirement. Otherwise as a saying goes, "an empty mind is a devil's workshop" and it will be harmful if one sits idle after retirement. Therefore, one should plan to be active or occupied and be positive in his working and thinking.

A study of almost 4000 people in the age group of 52-79 done by the University College London has proved this point. Following are the well recognised simple guidelines for happiness:

i) Free your heart from hate
ii) Free your mind from worry
iv) Live a simple life
v) Give more and expect less

One should develop the attitude or mindset of being content with what one has. This attitude brings happiness. This is our ancient philosophy stressed by the great saints and thinkers.

"Who realises all the happiness he desires? Everything is in the hands of God. Therefore one should learn contentment," said Chanakya.

Sri Sri Ravi Shankar, the renowned spiritual guru, says, "Want or desire arises when you are not happy. Have you seen this, when you are very happy then there is contentment. 'Contentment' means no want."

Another saint Swami Sivananda observes: "There is no end to craving. Hence, contentment alone is the best way to happiness."

Lao Tzu advises: "Be content with what you have; rejoice in the way things are. When you realise there is nothing lacking, the whole world belongs to you. When you are content to be simply yourself and do not compare or compete, everybody is with you."

This is the essence of spirituality, which is nothing but a way of life. Dr. S. Radhakrishnan, the great philosopher-thinker says, "My belief in spirituality is based on this faith: 'Do your duty without expecting anything in return. Spirituality is a way of life based on the doctrine of *Karma-Phala-Tyaga* or doing your duty without being attached to it.'"

Lokmanya Tilak too stated that to work with a stable mind without expecting anything in return is spirituality.

As stated earlier one should keep oneself fully occupied after retirement so that no vacuum is created. If the financial position at the time of retirement is not very good, then one should try to get a full time or part time job to keep oneself busy.

If one has a natural talent for painting, music or writing but could not devote time to pursue these hobbies during active service, then one should treat retirement as a blessing and devote more time in pursuing and enjoying these hobbies. Reading and writing is an enjoyable hobby if one has a good command over the language and an analytical mind. The results are fantastic as one gets joy, satisfaction and recognition in the society. He can continue this hobby as long as he is physically fit and mentally agile. Age is no bar. We see around us great authors and journalists of repute who have crossed eighty or ninety years of age and are still devoted to their profession.

Captain C. P. Krishnan Nair, who retired as chairman of the Leela Group of Hotels in early 2013, belongs to this category. When he was young he was told by his guru that his path is that of a karma yogi[24]. He has since lived like a karma yogi. Even after retirement at the age of ninety-two, he says that he still has unfinished tasks such as opening of six new hotels and managing them. Not age but inner strength is important to remain fully occupied.

A classic living example of this is of Dr. Sushila Rani Patel, who is highly educated and a greatly respected musician. She is ninety-four years old. The key to the success of her life lies in hard work, mental attitude and full devotion to her occupation. When asked the secret behind her graceful ageing she said, "I have led such an active life right from my school days, through college days, through married days and as a widow. As my husband, late Baburao Patel, was a popular journalist, I took to journalism and music which has been with me since childhood."

She further said, "If the mind and body are in perfect control, a lot can be achieved. Even today at ninety-four, my day is full from morning till midnight. I am still working furiously. I have established a charitable trust. This keeps me busy. I sing, I teach music, I write, I attend big functions. Old age is inevitable. People unknown to me often give a helping hand when required. I begin my day with pooja and prayer and end the day with a short thanksgiving to God Almighty for all the boons he has showered on me. My old age is beautiful and meaningful because I have dedicated my artistic life for the welfare of the nation. People are shocked when they hear my age. My old age is a gift from God. I look after my health as best as I can. I eat frugally and follow scrupulously the medical instructions and the advice of our family doctor."

---

[24]*Economic Times*, 26 February 2013

Another veteran thinker, Henry Van Dyke, says, "Be glad of life, because it gives you the choice to live and to work and to play and to look up at the stars."

A ninety-six year old lady faithfully attended a women's club of Bible studies. She came prepared with her lessons and knew all the answers. One day a tactless member asked her, "Why do you work so hard on these lessons when you are so old?"

The old lady looked up and replied confidently, "I am cramming for my finals." This is the spirit to emulate.

When a young one after completing his education takes up a job he feels happy and on the first day itself, plans for future life. Likewise one should look at retirement as the first day of the rest of one's life rather than the beginning of the end. In the present days of longevity, the end cannot be immediate and the period may stretch to 25-30 years which cannot and should not be allowed to take its own course. The course has to be decided by you to make the period fruitful. One would take it as an opportunity to make the best use of it to fulfil one's unfulfilled ambitions in various fields of interest.

For this, one should be happy for happiness makes one live longer and be healthier and more determined to achieve what one wants.

Family and social life for the aged

It is said that man is a social animal. This holds more relevance in old age. In addition to taking care of finance, health, hobbies etc., man requires family life and social life to make ageing graceful.

After fulfilling one's duties and obligations towards one's wife and children, the relationship during old age takes altogether a different aspect. During old age a man or woman require good and trusted friends to share one's thoughts, joys and sorrows. One can find friends both in the family and outside. When the children are settled in life, the relation between the aged parents and well settled children should be more as friends with a free exchange of ideas. The relations between aged grandparents and grandchildren should be more free and enjoyable too.

For the aged couple, the spouse is most often the best friend with no family responsibilities of active age. Having lived together for more than forty-fifty years they know each other's nature and needs. They can start a fresh life of love and affection without any shyness or reservation. That is how both can spend their old age gracefully and with great happiness.

The aged couple should consider themselves fortunate if they live with their children and grandchildren in the same house. They can help the children in many ways and also guide the grandchildren. It is a common experience that grandchildren are more frank and friendly with grandparents.

If for any reason they have to live independently, they should consider this as an opportunity to stay together with more love and affection and remembering their long and happy married life. This has its own charm. But they should stay connected emotionally with the children and grandchildren with reciprocation.

It must be understood that no one is more important than our family. In times of crisis they are the only ones whom you can count on entirely. So value and cherish them.[25]

Unfortunately if the aged is a widow or widower the problems are different and a lot of understanding and adjustments are necessary if one is required to live alone. The best way is to stay with children and shower your love and affection on them. Do household work to the extent that your health permits. This will change the normal attitude that the aged are a burden. If this is also not possible for any reason other than the psychological conflicts, one can stay even in old age homes where one gets to interact with other elderly, make new friends, and also get access to medical facilities. To avoid despair stay connected emotionally with children.

What is important for the aged is to understand and accept the inevitable changes in the family system over the decades in both rural and urban areas. It may be stated that in India

[25] *Mumbai Mirror*, 23 May 2011

about 94 percent of the aged have at least one living child, but only 32 percent live with their children. About 62 percent live with their spouse or alone.[26]

Social life for the aged

Various aspects of living arrangements and various avenues of keeping oneself occupied after retirement have been briefly analysed in the previous paragraphs. But just these two aspects are not sufficient for a man or woman to make their life complete. Social life, in addition to self and family life, is necessary to make old age more meaningful and enjoyable.

Friends circle

A man or woman should have one's own circle of friends with whom he can interact and from whom one can expect a friend, guide, and a philosopher. It has been pointed out earlier that husband and wife are mutually best friends and also companions. Beyond family relations there should be good friends with whom they can mutually, confidently and also confidentially seek help and guidance for various problems bothering them. It is our common experience that in addition to one's spouse, a good friend plays a most important role in one's life. He is always available when needed. To broaden the scope one should also have a wider friends circle who can meet often for social interaction.

Senior citizens' associations

Friends circle is more of a personal nature but on a somewhat larger scale, in comparison to spouse, children and grandchildren who are also friends. A senior citizen has to go beyond this on a societal level to participate in the activities which give him an opportunity to contribute to the society and also benefit from others. Needs and aspirations and vigour to lead an active old age are to be planned and achieved by coordinated efforts of many who are similarly placed.

To achieve this, senior citizens associations have been formed all over India with the objective of bringing together

[26]*Hindustan Times*, 15 May 2006

the senior citizens and carrying out activities which help in creating a greater sense of brotherhood, caring for each other and enjoying life together so that ageing becomes graceful.[27]

In the case of most of the senior citizens' associations, activities like birthday parties, get-togethers, festivals and religious discourses, picnics, educational lectures and voluntary work are carried out on a regular basis. At times, activities such as yoga, eye and blood camps, and counselling services are carried out, helping the participants to keep healthy and to know their health conditions. By active participation in these activities an aged person becomes more agile, forgetting other problems normally related to old age.

Associations for retired persons

As the name itself indicates, retired persons form the associations to deliberate the problems regarding their pension and other related problems. Mostly they are also members of the senior citizens associations. These associations address specific problems like settling their pension related issues, legal aid, lectures on pre- and post-retirement and felicitations for their members which are more specific for the retirees.

Day care centres

Day care centres are of great service to the elderly especially in metropolitan cities. Day care centres provide a service for the elderly during the day time so that they can pass some time outside the house and interact with other persons of their age group. At the same time, their children or caregivers get some time free, especially in cases where the elderly require constant attention.

As one ages, one turns sensitive and emotional in approach and expects the people around to respect him/her for the accumulated experience. Humiliation and suffering encountered by seniors make them depressed and frustrated about their very existence towards the end of their life. Even

---

[27]Ref. Networking of Organizations working for care of older persons – Edited by S. Siva Raju (BR Publishing Corporation)

an elderly neighbour living on his own needs love, respect and affection. A courtesy call once in a while, visits and spending some time in the company of the elderly makes them feel elated with the idea that the society has not rejected them.

It is the duty and also moral responsibility of the family members, friends whether young or old, and social organisations taking care of the elderly to understand the psychology of the aged persons and relieve them of their anxiety.

C. ACTIVITY AND EXERCISE

Loneliness and depression can affect the physical and mental health of the elderly. Senior citizens often live alone or with younger family members who are busy with their own lives. This makes them feel neglected and isolated. It is therefore important that they are involved in social and other activities that keep them occupied, help them interact with others and ensure that they feel accepted in society. There are several ways in which the elderly can keep occupied and interact socially with people:

- Senior citizens clubs and groups are a good way to socialise. Interaction with other people of the same age helps them to share problems, exchange news and feel accepted.
- Senior citizens can also enjoy board games, playing cards and video/computer games. These help to keep them mentally active and to spend time with other people.
- Pursuing an old hobby or taking up a new one is an enjoyable way of keeping mentally active. This could be gardening, sewing, learning a language, music, painting or anything else that the individual enjoys.
- Senior citizens often have vast professional experience which they can share with others. Teaching youngsters

or members from underprivileged sections of society is a satisfying occupation for several individuals after retirement.

It is important for the well-being of the elderly to find an activity in which they can involve themselves. It will ensure that they remain cheerful and alert, which will help them to stay mentally and physically fit.

Physical activity

As you get older, it is very essential to remain physically active so that you are in good health and maintain your independence. Physical activity, exercise and doing your regular activities can help you remain healthy and energetic. As people get older, the level of physical activity begins to reduce. Sometimes the elderly develop health problems that hamper physical activity. However, if you don't stay active, your health deteriorates and over a period of time you may be unable to do all the things that you enjoy. In all probability, your body may begin to experience aches and pains that you never had before. Your energy levels may dip. And worst of all, you may be more vulnerable to falling which could lead to fractures or broken bones.

As you age, your lifestyle often becomes more sedentary. This could result in obesity, falls, heart disease, diabetes, stroke, and even dementia and depression. It is therefore extremely important to be physically active and to keep moving. Listed below are a few tips about physical mobility:

- Avoid sitting down for long periods either before the TV or computer or to read.
- Include walking or moderate exercise or a sport in your daily routine.
- Doctors advise about two and a half hours of moderate-intensity aerobic activity per week. This could be done as routine half hours sessions over the week.
- Moderate-intensity activity is exercise that increases the heart rate like brisk walking, riding a bicycle or playing a sport. This exercise would be in addition to normal physical activity

around the house.

- Muscles and bones become weak with age. Weight training twice a week is recommended to strengthen them.
- Take up any exercise that you enjoy doing whether it is yoga, dance, pilates, swimming or walking.

D. CARING FOR THE ELDERLY: RURAL AND URBAN

From ancient times caring for the elderly parents/grand-parents has been accepted as a duty that is to be performed with love and affection. Elders were respected and played an advisory counselling role in family affairs. Caring for the elderly posed no problem either to the youngsters or to the elderly themselves. This was mainly due to the then prevailing joint family system in which the duty of caring for the elders was shared by the members in the family. Also, due to the shorter span of life then prevalent, the period of caring was on average ten years. This was the position till the middle of the twentieth century.

After the mid-twentieth century the demographic position underwent revolutionary changes due to the increase in the lifespan from 60-65 years to 90-95 years. The years of caring for the elderly increased from about ten years to twenty-five years or more. Due to the break-up in the joint family system, the issue of caring for the elderly could not be confined to the family. The society and the state had to step in, in large measure.

Due to the adoption of the nuclear family system for economic and other reasons, a question is being raised as to whether there will be sufficient number of young people available to care for the elderly given the fast growth in the elderly population. Such a situation has arisen in the developed countries, where there is already a large proportion of aged persons. In such a structure there will be fewer younger people to take care of a large number of aged persons. This brings more pressure on the younger generation. In a developing country like India, this will take some more decades. Nevertheless the situation calls for an elaborate scrutiny and proper planning.

In regard to the question of examining the issue of caring for the aged, two important factors need to be taken into account. One is the status of the elderly in rural areas and another in the urban areas as the social structure and living conditions of elderly in the rural areas are quite different from those in the urban areas. The aged persons need to adjust to a new kind of family and social situation. This adjustment means making room for others, that is, youngsters. This results in a series of mental, physical, and emotional adjustments, for which most of the aged are often not prepared. This is because of the loss of the respect and authority which they enjoyed earlier under the joint family system.

More than 70 percent of the population of India lives in rural areas. Due to lack of employment opportunities in rural areas most of the rural people in their young age shift to towns and mostly work in unorganised sectors where no future economic plans exist. After working in the unorganised sectors till the age of sixty or sixty-five there is reverse migration to their rural native place; they return mostly empty-handed and totally dependent on their local family members for the rest of their lives of about 15-20 years. This also results in the growth of elderly population in rural areas.

In order to understand the magnitude of the issue of caring for the aged, it would be useful to know the distribution of the aged population by age in urban and rural areas as the caring problems are different from one age group to another.

Age Group	Total population(Million)	Rural (Million)	Urban (Million)
60-64	27.5	20.6	6.9
65-69	19.8	14.8	5.0

70-74	14.7	4.1	3.6
75-79	6.5	4.8	1.7
80+	8.0	6.0	2.0
Total	76.5	57.3	19.2

(Source: Census of India 2001)

The above mentioned statistics bring out the following facts:

i) The proportion of population of elderly urban and rural areas is one to three.

ii) There being no stipulated date of retirement it can be presumed that a majority of the elderly in the age group 60-69 (35.4 million) do some odd jobs for their living. Still, an elderly population of 21.9 million needs special analysis.

Joint family system

From the various writings on the problems of elderly it may be said that the main reason attributed to this situation of elderly suffering is due to

(a) break-up of the ancient joint family system in which elders enjoyed respect and good care from the youngsters and

(b) change in the attitude of youngsters: loss of respect towards elders and an increasingly materialistic selfish attitude, forgetting their moral responsibility.

It may be clarified that both the reasons are true to a great extent but can be remedied with a proper approach. It is true that under the old joint family system, family members of two, three and even four generations used to live under one roof. This living arrangement in the family could not and cannot be continued indefinitely, not because of internal problems in the family but due to the necessity of migrating to towns and cities and also abroad for higher education and employment. It is true that in a joint family the aged in the family could be easily taken care of so that their old age was happy and contented. The main reasons for this were companionship, love, affection, respect, a sense of duty, and emotional attachment. Now it is an essential requirement to imbibe these qualities even when the aged and youngsters are living in different places. Many times the aged have to live separately with their spouse or alone due to unavoidable circumstances. Both young and old have to adjust their lifestyle to suit the changed family and social structure. This is all the more necessary so that the aged in the family can live with contentment. The watchword for this is to maintain family ties and emotional attachment irrespective of the place of their stay.

There is no use in brooding over the past which only makes elders unhappy. Enjoy the best of the opportunities now available and be happy. It is gratifying that even today 80 percent elderly in India stay with their family as against only 18 percent in USA and several other developed countries.

Elder care

When the issue of caring for the aged is to be examined, it should be borne in mind that India's elderly population is of two kinds—rural elderly and urban elderly. Their living conditions differ substantially in terms of number and also other relevant factors. It was pointed out earlier that out of the total elderly population of 76.5 million, 57.5 million live in rural areas. Again the position of rural elderly both in respect of literacy and economic dependency is far from satisfactory. The statistics indicate that at the all India level 54.51 percent of the elderly are illiterate. In some states the percentage is still higher. In UP, Bihar and AP it is more than 61 percent and in Punjab and Rajasthan it is more than 66 percent.

In the case of rural females, the position is still more unsatisfactory. On an all-India basis the illiteracy is 86.99 percent and in some states like Rajasthan, UP and Bihar it is more than 90 percent.

This is a sad reflection on the education policy and its implementation and a total disregard for the Directive Principles of the State Policy enjoined in Article 45 of the Constitution which casts a responsibility on the state to provide all children compulsory education within a period of ten years from the commencement of the Constitution. In the case of illiterate persons who are elderly in the twentieth century, efforts should have been made to educate them well in time. Education and employment go together and the first step of the progressive state should have been to provide them with education and employment which would have made the life of every citizen of all ages dignified and self supporting. If the provision in the Constitution had been implemented to the letter, perhaps there would not have been a problem of the existing magnitude.

Marital status of the elderly is also an important factor which makes or mars the process of a happy old age as dependency increases with age. At the all-India level 18.36 percent of the rural male elderly are widowers and in the case of females number of widows is as high as 51.42 percent. Most of them have to depend entirely on family members, primarily sons and daughters.

Issues of the elderly

It has been pointed out earlier that the active life—earning life—normally ends on attaining the age of sixty in urban areas and after attaining the age of sixty-five in rural areas. It is natural that every man and woman wants to lead a happy and contended life of about 20-25 years after active age which may be called elderly or aged life. But what are the essential requirements to enable them to lead such a life?

The first one is financial security including a dwelling place. The second is health security and the third is emotional support. These are the common essential requirements both for rural elderly or urban elderly.

Financial security

Financial security comes from the assured monthly income from whatever source—pension, insurance returns, interest on savings etc. This income has to be sufficient enough to take care of food, clothing and day-to-day medical expenses. For this income to be suitable enough, earlier planning during active age is necessary.

Health security

Naturally everyone desires to maintain good health till the end. This in reality depends on several factors. It is important that he/she is conscious of the importance of good health right from youth and makes efforts to ensure it with regular exercise and moderate habits of eating and drinking. Even then, to meet the medical expenses if required on account of sickness in old age, one has to make provisions for health insurance schemes etc.

Emotional support

This is a very wide concept involving human relations. The emotional satisfaction has to come from one's spouse, sons, daughters, and others. In this the elderly themselves are major players. Love begets love it is said; love and affection can come from near and dear ones, if he in his earlier age had set an example for this.

Economic dependency of the elderly

Financial security of the aged being the basic feature on the quality of the life of elderly, the issue has been examined by various agencies during the last 15-20 years even before the formulation of the National Policy by the government in 1999.

The data collected by the National Sample Survey (52nd Round, 1995-96) brings out the fact that as many as 70 percent of the aged had to depend on others for their livelihood. The situation was particularly worse for elderly females. Over 85 percent were found out to be dependent partially or fully on others. The elderly position of men was a little better with 49 to 52 percent of them not dependent on others. The situation, however, was slightly better in the urban areas than the national average. Among the elderly rural males, 48.5 percent were not dependent on others, 18 percent stated that they were partially dependent on others and 31.3 percent stated that they were fully dependent on others. In the case of elderly rural females, 70.6 percent were fully dependent on others, 14.6 percent were partially dependent on others and only 12.1 percent were not dependent on others.

In the urban areas, 51.5 percent of elderly males stated that they were not dependent on others 29.7 percent stated that they were dependent on others and 16.9 percent stated that they were partially dependent on others.[28] In the case of urban females, 75.7 percent were fully dependent on others, 11 percent were partially dependent on others and 11.5 percent were not dependent on others. The question that thus arises is about giving economic support to the elderly. The NSS data provides details about those people who support the economically dependent elderly—children, grand children, spouse and others. The data indicates that children support 71.1 percent of the rural elderly and 70.8 percent of the urban elderly[29]. The grand children support 5 percent of the rural elderly and 5.4 percent of the urban elderly. The share of the spouse is 53.8 percent in rural and 15.2 percent in urban areas. Surprisingly, among others, which includes the government, the share is only 5.9 percent in urban and 6.9 percent in rural areas. The information collected by the NSS 52nd Survey, 1995-96, gives information on the retirement benefits received by the rural elderly which is indicated in the following table. [30]

Percentage Distribution of Aged Persons (engaged in wage/salaried jobs or as casual labour) by Category of Retirement Benefits.[31]

	Rural				Urban			
	Pension only	Pension with other benefits	No pension but with other benefits	No benefits	Pension only	Pension with other benefits	No pension but with other benefits	No benefits
Male	9.9	15.7	6.9	67.5	17.1	37.2	18.9	26.8
Female	2.6	1.8	2.8	92.8	0.5	15.3	9.8	67.4
Total	6.7	9.3	5.0	79.0	15.1	32.8	17.1	35.0

[28] *The Graying of India: Population Ageing* by Rajagopal Dhar, p. 271

[29] Ibid., p.274

[30] Ibid., p.280

[31] Source: National Sample Survey Organization (NSSO), The Aged in India; A socio-economic Profile, NSS 52nd Round, July 1995-June 1996, NSSO, Department of Statistics, Ministry of Planning and Programme Implementation, Government of India, Calcutta, 1998

It may be seen from the above that 67.5 percent of the rural male elderly retire with no retirement benefits. In the case of women it is 92.8 percent. That means they have no regular source of income to maintain themselves after retirement unless they have substantial savings while earning. Generally and for a majority there is no scope for that as with the increased cost of living they hardly make both ends meet. In such cases some post-retirement income is possible only if right from a young age they had meticulously planned to save some part of their meagre earning for old age and government and non-government agencies induced them to do so with very attractive plans.

Experience shows that neither the individual nor government nor any social agencies have taken any particular interest in the matter though the National Policy by the government recognises the necessity of such an action. In whatever manner one looks at the issue, the retired elderly come under the category of poor, totally depending on the family members for their future life.

The poor aged are more vulnerable if their main source of support, namely their children, also happen to be earning a very meagre income and can offer only limited support to the aged parents out of a sense of duty during their long years of ageing. The younger ones who support the parents have also to take care of their own children in the matter of education etc. as a result of which they feel that the aged parents are a burden.

This cannot be considered an inevitable situation in a democratic country where every citizen has a right to life and to live with dignity. The policy statements announced by government realise this but the actual implementation with meticulous planning and extending its benefits need to be done with determination.

As pointed out earlier, there are more than 57 million rural elderly in the second decade of the twenty-first century whose financial status has to be studied in detail and regular financial assistance in the form of monthly pension has to be given to the needy elderly to enable them to live with dignity.

This has two advantages. One is financial security, which itself makes the aged confident of living with the necessary security and dignity. Secondly, with their regular monthly income they can help the family in running the house, instead of becoming a burden on them.

If the aged do not become a burden on their sons, they get respect. The teaching of sense of duty and affection for the parents which is intended to be a part of our culture has become meaningless in the present materialistic world.

RURAL ELDERLY

Financial status of the rural elderly (males)

On the subject of earning for longer years the position of rural elderly is much better than their counterparts in urban areas. Being engaged mostly in agricultural work, there is no age of retirement and they can work as long as their health permits. This may sometimes extend up to the age of seventy or even more. It is only after that, when they are physically incapacitated, that they have to depend partially or fully on others.

Statistical reports[32] point out that in the age group of 60-69, 76.04 percent are workers and 23.96 percent are non-workers. In the age group of 70-79, 54.12 percent are workers and 45.88 percent are non-workers. In the age group of 80+ only 36.76 percent are workers and 63.24 percent are non-workers.

It is clear from this that as age advances, the physical capacity decreases, making them unfit to earn a living.

Status of the rural elderly (females)

It may be stated that in regard to women in the age group of 60-69, 31.36 percent are workers and 68.64 percent are non-

[32] Census 2001

workers. In the age group of 70-79 only 15.77 percent are workers and 84.23 percent are non-workers. In the age group of 80+ only 9.97 percent are workers and 90.03 percent are non-workers.

In this connection it may be clarified that female workers or non-workers cannot be compared with the male workers or non-workers. In Indian society, the role of women is mainly to look after the household. The percentage of women who work to earn money is therefore less. Their role and utility in the house is very important and valuable even though they do not actually earn money by service. Unlike males, their contribution and utility in managing the household affairs is in bringing up the children and grand children, which is equally important. This also stops only when they become physically incapacitated to do any work. Due to the Indian family set-up a majority of women have to depend on others in the family—husband and son—for their living. Total dependency comes if they become totally physically incapable of doing any work in the family.

Health security of the rural elderly

The World Health Organisation (WHO) defines health as "a state of complete physical, mental and social well being and not merely the absence of disease or infirmity."

Health security or good health in all the stages of life requires proper planning with conscious efforts. Good health in old age is the fruit of earlier efforts. If one enjoys an easygoing and luxurious lifestyle during the early three stages, it is likely to create health problems in old age. In the case of rural elderly, the health is comparatively better than the urban elderly because they were required to work hard physically through most of their life. Even then, the prevalence of chronic diseases is very common. In rural area there are few or no medical facilities to detect and treat the illness.

According to National Sample Survey Organisation (NSSO)[33]

[33]Ibid., p.286

joint problems are the most common ailment. Nearly 36.3 percent of the rural elderly (males) and 40.4 percent of the rural female elderly have this problem. Another common ailment[34] is cough. Nearly 25 percent of the rural elderly males and 19.5 percent of the rural females suffer from this ailment. Yet another common ailment reported is high or low BP; more than 10.5 percent of the rural male and female suffer from this problem. Of course they are more fortunate than their urban counterparts who tend to encounter high stress levels.

In addition, the elderly suffer from other physical disabilities such as lack of vision and hearing. Nearly 2 percent of the rural male and 30 percent of the rural females suffer from this disability. Nearly 14 percent of the rural elderly males and 16 percent of the rural elderly females suffer from this disability.

Health facilities

The rural elderly lag behind on two counts: one is lack of awareness and the second one is absence of medical facilities. One depends on the other. The necessity of routine regular medical check-ups to detect and treat ailments in time is not realised by most. In rural areas, there are very few government run hospitals for people to avail of the facilities.

Now what is urgently required is to provide medical check-up facilities at a walking distance from their residence so that the elderly make it a habit to have regular medical check-ups to prevent/treat the ailments in time.

Psychological aspect

The psychological aspect of the elderly, whether rural or urban, towards self and towards family is very important in making the elderly happy or otherwise. Adjustments in their life, expected due to changes in the family and social structure, are absolutely necessary to make their own life worth living. This aspect is elaborated in a separate section of this chapter under the caption "Living Old Age".

---

[34]Source: NSSO 52nd Round

URBAN ELDERLY

Status of the urban elderly

The statistics elaborated earlier show that 19.2 million elderly live in the urban areas. Out of the total 19.2 million in urban areas, 6.9 million are in the age group of 60-64, 5 million are in the age group of 65-69; 3.06 million are in the age group of 70-74; 1.7 million are in the age group of 75-79; and 2 million are in the age group of 80+.

It may be stated that the male members living in urban areas during their active life work in organised sectors like government institutions, companies etc and non-organised sectors like personal business, construction activities etc. Persons working in organised and non-organised sectors work till the age of retirement at the age of sixty or sixty-five years. Casual workers in the non-organised sector like construction activities re-migrate to rural areas. Most of the persons working in organised sectors retire at the age of sixty or so with retirement benefits. Some of them seek and get service in private institutions even after retirement. There are people in personal business and other occupations who continue to work beyond the age of sixty. In the case of females, those who work in organised sectors also retire at the age of sixty or so. The rest of the women are homemakers.

After attaining the age of sixty, there is a category of workers and non-workers both for males and females in different age groups.

Urban males

In the age group of 60-69 the percentage of workers is 51.13 and of non-workers is 48.87. In the age group of 70-79 it is 34.37 percent and 65.63 percent respectively. In the age group of 80+, it is 27.83 percent and 72.17 percent respectively.

Urban females

In the age group of 60-69, the percentage of workers is 10.98 and non-workers 89.03. In the age group of 70.79, 6.17 percent are workers and 93.83 percent are non-workers. In the age group of 80+ the figures are 4.68 percent and 95.32 percent respectively.

After enjoying an active life both in terms of earning and fulfilling obligations towards family and society, one has to plan the future life of 25-30 years or even more which one naturally expects to be satisfactory and contented on the strength of one's earnings and savings for the future, good health earned, and also on the basis of a will to lead a satisfying life with the right attitude.

For this the following three requirements are absolutely necessary: financial security, health security, and psychological security. Though these are essential requirements for all elderly, whether rural or urban, their ways of achieving them differ qualitatively as the working conditions during active age differ in substance.

Health care

It is obvious that most of the aged cannot afford to take medical treatment in private hospitals. Government hospitals and also private hospitals run by the business houses should provide free medical treatment in separate reserved wards for the aged poor.

During active service, people working in the organised sector get the benefits of medical facilities provided by the employer. Whether one should plan for additional coverage like health insurance depends on the extent of medical facilities provided by the employer. If it is restricted or if one does not have any medical facilities from the employer or if one is in a profession or business it is absolutely necessary to go in for health insurance of a reasonably good amount. After retirement it is all the more necessary to continue such a health insurance. In addition, one should set apart a certain amount of cash to meet the emergency situation of health. As financial security and health security for self and spouse are absolutely necessary during the old age, one should study health insurance schemes during one's youth and invest in them, and should always remember that the earlier one invests in health insurance, the less premium one has to pay. **The premium on health insurance will increase with increase in age.** Thus, investing early in health saves undue worry about illnesses in old age and provides financial security too.

Financial security

A man in active service with the help of the money that he earns as salary or from the amount he receives as professional charges or from business profits normally discharges his duty as father by giving proper education to the children and getting them married at the appropriate time. After this he has to provide for regular income for himself and his spouse so that they can lead a good life with the same or reasonable standard of living during their post-retirement lifespan of 25-30 years. Needless to emphasise that this requires meticulous planning during active age depending on the conditions under which he works. If he retires from service from organised sector where there is provision for pension, more or less financial security is guaranteed. But the number of persons eligible for such benefits is very limited.

The information collected by the National Sample Survey Organisation (NSSO) regarding the retirement benefits received by urban elderly is as follows:

	Pension only	Pension with other benefits	No pension but with other benefits	No benefits
Male	17.1	37.2	18.9	26.8
Female	0.5	15.03	9.8	67.4

It may be seen from the above table that the various retirement benefits which females get is less than half of the benefit the males get. 26.08 percent of the males retire with no benefits and in the case of females it is as high as 67.4 percent. Unless they have made other savings/investment for a steady income after retirement, this large number of males and females has to depend on the goodwill of sons and daughters for years. Persons who retire after modest earning and not enough savings to last for the rest of their life, will outlive their savings.

Fortunately, in spite of the breaking up of joint family system and attitudinal changes on the part of the youngsters, due to the deep impact of traditional culture more than 70.75 percent of the dependent elderly are looked after by their children and grandchildren. But a situation where the elderly after retirement from their active age do not have any savings of their own and have to look to children even for petty expenses on medicine, pocket money etc. cannot be described as a healthy situation. Such elderly cannot live their old age happily. This creates innumerable problems for the children if they themselves have limited resources and for the elderly too.

Persons living in urban cities, both males and females, whether working in organised institutions or unorganised institutions or pursuing some profession or business can be classified into four categories (i) Poor (ii) Lower middle class (iii) Upper middle class and (iv) Rich. It is necessary to do a realistic analysis of the financial and health status of the elderly persons of the twenty-first century who belong to these categories.

Financial status of the poor

These are persons who did not acquire higher educational qualifications and worked in the lower and middle category of jobs like clerks, peons, carpenters, technicians, drivers etc. on a modest salary. The spouses are mostly homemakers and in few cases do some odd jobs to add to the family income.

Among the poor, there was generally no concept or awareness of nuclear family or family planning till late in the last century. On an average every couple had three to four children, if not more, adding to their financial and health burdens. In the absence of an awareness for the need of savings, as also due to limited earning they would have spent all their earnings on children's education, marriage and medical expenses of the family members. So inevitably the aged parents had to entirely depend on the children for their sustenance during old age. If the children had comparatively better education, better jobs with fair earning, taking care of the parents with due regard for their duty and obligation towards them was not a serious problem. But this cannot be considered as an ideal situation. There is considerable strain both on the children and the aged parents. The aged parents are almost destitute. The other alternative is to go to old age homes run or aided by the government and other philanthropic institutions where the destitute are admitted free of cost. With no other better alternative, parents go to live in an old age house with a psychological setback. Old age homes as a facility for old age has been analysed in detail in another section.

Here comes the intervention of the state, society, and other philanthropists to help the destitute aged with reasonable financial security so that they can spend the evening of their life with some satisfaction. As pointed out earlier the state has announced a policy for the aged but what is required is meticulous planning and implementation to help the present aged destitute with financial support.

The state and other institutions should work out a policy and plan for making young employed persons aware of the necessity of savings to the extent possible for their future life of old age and participate in saving plans. Because for the old, however poor they may be, it is a blow to their pride and self respect to receive money from the state as "dole".

Financial security of the lower middle class, middle, and higher middle class aged persons

Aged persons belonging to any of the three categories, now living, were well educated on account of which they could get good jobs with good salary. Because of good education, good salary, awareness of the necessity of planned savings for old age, and receiving pension, balance amount of provident fund amount accumulated and also gratuity admissible under the rules, their old age does not present a problem. But people with such benefits are only about 6-7 percent of the total work force. Also working in formal sectors only has the advantage of getting financial benefits whereas in business, the professionals have to make their own financial planning when they cease to be active workers and retire. Here the government agencies and other institutions managing the investment amount should take active interest and come out with various plans of investment with good returns after some years coinciding with retirement.

The children of such retired aged persons would have settled with their own family whether living with parents or living separately. During their active age they would have acquired a dwelling place big or small depending on the size of the family and also financial capacity to acquire a house.

After retirement from active life the aged live with their spouse either along with children or independently. Whatever option they exercise, they need not normally expect any financial help from the children. Owning a house with reasonable financial security would enable them to live independently while giving freedom to the children to lead their own life. It may be emphatically reiterated here that in whatever manner the aged and the children decide to live as an agreed arrangement, the family binding and emotional attachment should be kept intact.

If an aged person decides to stay with his wife in his own house he should prepare a budget of his monthly income and expenditure including the possible expenditure on medicine etc. if required. It is observed that after retirement from active service at the age of sixty or sixty five, at least 60-70 percent of the elderly are physically fit. If opportunities are available they should take up part time or full time jobs which add to their monthly income in addition to the chances of continuing to be physically fit on account of both physical and mental activity.

The elderly after retirement and after receiving lump sum

amount from provident fund balances, insurance maturity amount and other returns should meticulously plan for its investment to ensure monthly return on investment which can be used for living expenses. The amount received can be classified into three parts for the purpose of investment. The first is investment in annuity, the profit received by way of dividend can be utilised for unavoidable expenditure. The second investment should be in the schemes which give higher rate of interest in the form of profit. The amount so received on such investments should be reserved for unforeseen expenditure. The return on investment in lower risk schemes like mutual funds may be set apart to meet the expenditure on unexpected medical treatment etc. In what proportion the amount should be invested in the three schemes should be decided based on personal needs.

If one needs much more income for living with the same standard of lifestyle and if the aged owns a house there is one more scheme of recent origin called "Reverse Mortgage Scheme". The salient features of the scheme have been elaborated later in this book in the chapter on finance.

E. ABUSE OF THE ELDERLY

In common parlance, the word "abuse" indicates derogatory language or the improper use of something. Therefore, on the face of it there is contradiction in the use of the words "elderly abuse", because the elderly are traditionally respected and not abused. However, the words "abuse of the elderly" have a deeper meaning. During the last three to four decades, a selfish materialistic approach is gaining predominance and young persons are becoming more self-centred. Even if the financial position is good, the children find it inconvenient to take care of their parents who cannot look after themselves due to ill-health, old age, and other problems. They think of their parents a burden, not realising that someday they too will become old and need someone to care for them. The following folk tales illustrate this very well.

In a Bangladeshi folk story,[35] a disabled grandfather is carried by his son in a basket to be abandoned in the forest so that he will meet his death in due course. On seeing this, the grandson calls out, "Father, please be sure to bring back the basket. I will need it when you grow old like my grandfather."

A similar story appeared in a monthly magazine. There was a hard working farmer who worked on his small land holding. He had a son who grew up and married at the proper age. Father and son both worked in the farm and maintained the family. In course of time, the wife of the senior farmer (father) died. In spite of this personal tragedy the old farmer helped his son in his work on the farm. Growing old is an inevitable thing. Soon the father became too old to help his son in farming. He just lay down in the hut. The son had to work hard alone. He served his father for some months out of a sense of duty. In course of time, the father became too old and invalid. This then became both a physical and financial burden on the son.

One day, he questioned himself, "How long should I serve this invalid old man? Why not get rid of him so that I can pay full attention to my farm and I live comfortably with my wife and son." After a few days of dilly-dallying he made up his mind to get rid of the old man. He put his father in a container and took it to the top of the hill to push him down the hill.

When he was about to push the container downhill, he heard a feeble voice from the container. The son said to himself, "Let me see what this old man's last wish is." He opened the container and the old man said in a very low voice, "Son, anyway I am going to die. Just push me down and take back the container for use by your son when you also become old and helpless like me."

These two stories speak for themselves.

---

[35]*Hindustan Times*, 3 May 2012

Some realities

We see around us how old parents are treated badly by their children. The following are some real examples:

a) A lower middle class couple had three sons who, after completion of education, got employment with a moderate salary and were married. The parents who became old shifted from the village to the city to stay first with their elder son. After two to three years, the old man died leaving the old lady who also developed some infirmity and required constant attendance. After some time, the daughter-in-law started having arguments with her husband as to why only they should look after the old lady since there were two other sons in the same city and questioned why they should not share the burden. After heated arguments, the sons ultimately argued that the old mother should be looked after by all three sons for four months in rotation which they rigidly and mechanically followed till her death without caring for her physical and mental condition. The emotional attachment was completely missing in this family.

b) A couple in a fairly good financial position had two sons who were also well placed. When the parents became old, the sons adopted a strange way of sharing the burden of the aged parents. The mother was staying with one son and the father with another son. When companionship is considered necessary in old age, both husband and wife had to stay separately in different towns. Is it not a failure of one's duty?

c) This is a typical case of a well-to-do couple staying in a flat in a posh locality. The couple has two sons. The first son is a brilliant doctor with a lucrative practice. His wife is also a doctor with roaring practice. They own a spacious apartment in a posh locality with servants etc. Even then the daughter-in-law does not want the old in-laws to come and stay with them even for a single day.

The second son and his wife are highly educated and settled in U.S.A. drawing huge salaries. This daughter-in-law also says that they will never return to India and stay with the parents.

They are prepared to help the old couple financially but do not want to stay with them in India.

d) An old wealthy lady has yet another reason to feel frustrated. She complains that her daughter-in-law talks with her in such harsh language that the old lady feels that she (daughter-in-law) is virtually piercing a needle or knife in her body.

In all these cases, where is the love and affection, where is the emotional bond and the sense of duty? The highly self-centred children who are intoxicated with riches never think that they will also grow old which is an inevitable truth and their children may treat them in the same way.

According to the definition accepted by the World Health Organisation (WHO), "elder abuse" (also called "elder mistreatment", "senior abuse", "abuse in later life", "abuse of older adults", "abuse of older women and abuse of older men") is a single or repeated act, or lack of appropriate action within any relationship where there is an expectation of trust, which causes harm or distress to an older person.

The core element to the harm of elder abuse is the "expectation of trust" of the older person towards their abuser. Thus it includes harm by people the older person knows or with whom they have a relationship such as spouse, partner or family member, a friend or neighbour, or people that the older person relies on for services. Many forms of elder abuse are recognised as types of domestic violence or family violence.

There are several types of abuse of older people that are generally recognised as being elder abuse including

a) Physical e.g. hitting, punching, slapping, burning, pushing, kicking, restraining, excessive or improper medicine.

b) Psychological/Emotional e.g. humiliating a person. It may take verbal forms such as name calling, ridiculing constantly criticising, accusations, blaming etc.

Common abusers

An abuser can be a spouse, partner, relative, friend or neighbour, a volunteer worker and paid worker, practitioner, solicitor or any other individual with the intent to deprive a vulnerable person of their resources.

Health Consequences:

The health consequences of elder abuse are very serious. Elder abuse can destroy an elderly person's quality of life in the form of:

- Declining functional abilities
- Increased dependency
- Increased sense of helplessness
- Increased stress
- Worsening psychological decline
- Premature mortality and morbidity
- Depression and dementia.

Prevention: Doctors, nurses, and other medical personnel can play a vital role in assisting elder abuse victims. Studies have shown that elderly individuals on an average make 13.9 visits per year to a physician. Although there has been increase in awareness of elderly abuse over the years, physicians tend to only report 2 percent of elder abuse cases mainly due to lack of knowledge concerning state laws, pressure of work and non-cooperation from the elderly and their family members.

Educating and training those in the criminal justice system, such as police, prosecutors and the judiciary about elder abuse, as well as increased legislation to protect elders will also help to minimise elder abuse and provide improved assistance to victims of elder abuse.

Role of individuals

Instead of meekly surrendering to the abusive acts from close relatives and others, an individual should face the situation boldly. He should keep himself financially and legally protected.

Distinguish between the deceptive, cunning, selfish relatives, and genuine ones, and stay connected with genuine loved ones. Instead of becoming victims of abuse and suffering silently, giving an impression that you are vulnerable, challenge such persons with the help of genuine relatives and friends by taking recourse to legal action if necessary.

In the Indian family system the abuse of elderly in whatever context and form was very rare and also was strictly within the family. It was considered as a domestic problem. But during the last four to five decades, the abuse of elderly has become a social issue at the national and international level. The problem is getting more and more complex. Hence, in December 2011, United Nations (UN) recognised elder abuse as a global social issue which affects the health and human rights of millions of older persons around the world.

The United Nations (UN) Committee on Economic, Social and Cultural Rights (CESCR) has maintained that "side by side with older persons who are in good health and whose financial situation is acceptable, there are many who do not have adequate means of support, even in developed countries and who feature prominently among most vulnerable, marginal ,and unprotected groups". Older people and all those who support fulfilment of their needs believe that the crux of elder abuse and neglect in society is violation of right of seniors. The rapidly increasing numbers of older people, especially in Asia, where China and India take the lead in growing ageing population, are at considerable risk of abuse, neglect and marginalisation. In developing countries like India, older people do not always fully enjoy fundamental human freedom and rights.

It is common knowledge that for older people the right to accessibility—including physical and economic accessibility, access to education and information, and non-discrimination—as a key component of the normative content of the rights, is not followed. There are numerous examples of older people not having access to a reasonable standard of living (adequate food, water, and housing), health, and education. There is a high percentage of illiterate older people, especially women, and yet there is limited emphasis on this age group in adult education programmes or in financial literacy campaigns in spite of the growing numbers of older people becoming victims of financial frauds and abuse.

The vulnerability of older people to the risk of various forms of abuse is not only on the increase but there are not adequate mechanisms to address them and provide relief to victims of abuse and neglect both from the family and the community. World Health Organisation (WHO), in its publication *Abuse of the Elderly*, estimates that 4–6 percent of older persons at home and in community settings have suffered some form of abuse including physical, psychological, emotional, sexual or financial abuse or neglect.

There is no doubt that concerns relating to older persons are increasingly being addressed from human rights perspective by the government[36], civil society, growing number of NGOs and other stakeholders. But until an adoption of a new, comprehensive, international instrument to protect the rights of the ageing population is not in place, responses will remain fragmented, non-specific, and inconsistent to address elder abuse concerns, a malice which must be combated urgently in fast demographically changing societies.

Elderly abuse in India—causes and effects

It is an established fact now that elderly abuse is a matter of concern for both developed and developing countries like India. From what has been analysed in the previous chapters it should be absolutely clear that basically lack of education and lack of employment are the major reasons for suffering of individuals at all ages and especially in old age when dependency both in financial and health matter increases. Abuse of elderly is one such major form of suffering receiving attention at all levels: individual, societal and government.

The following headlines which have appeared in some of the leading newspapers during the last few years should be enough to understand the gravity of the issue of elderly abuse in India.

i) 47.3 percent elders abused by own children – study reveals.

[36] http://www.asianage.com (*Asian Age*, 15 June 2012)

Only one in six cases gets reported. [37]

Some excerpts:

• There are 70 million 60-plus elderly in India and the number is expected to touch 177 million by 2025.

• Elder abuse is a closeted and complex phenomenon.

• According to HelpAge India, most elders are ill-treated by their own children, who have emerged as the largest group of perpetrators at 47.3 percent. Spouses follow next at 19.3 percent. Other relatives and grandchildren follow at 8.8 percent and 8.6 percent respectively. However, only one in six cases gets reported.

• The United Nations International Plan of Action adopted by all countries during the Madrid Signatory in April 2002, clearly recognises the importance of addressing and preventing abuse and neglect of older adults and puts it within the framework of the Universal Human Rights.

ii) "It is shocking that the largest perpetrators of elder abuse are their own children. . ."[38]

Some excerpts:

• A study on abuse of senior citizens across nine cities including Mumbai has found that a high proportion of elderly people are subjected to abuse and ill treatment by their daughters-in-law and sons.

• The report was released on the eve of World Elder Abuse Awareness Day by HelpAge India.

• In the lower economic strata, the daughter-in-law was seen as the major abuser in 63.4 percent cases.

• In the higher economic bracket, in 53.6 percent of the cases, the son was responsible for ill treating his parents.

• The survey also revealed that abuse is highest among women above 70 years as they are more dependent on their sons than their male counterparts.

• The report also stated that more than one fifth of the elderly in India face violence, neglect or maltreatment with Bangalore

---

[37] *DNA*, 15 June 2007

[38] *Hindustan Times*, 15 June 2011

topping the list at 44 percent.

• 98 percent of the elderly do not report abuse, even while the option for legal action exists.

• 66 percent of the elderly were financially dependent on someone with 85 percent particularly dependent for their medical expenditure.

iii) Can retirement homes help to prevent abuse of elderly?[39]

Some excerpts:

• A universal concern is how to have provisions which enable older people to live safely and secularly. How can we generate thinking and action that would work towards ensuring that older men and women enjoy a life free of violence, mistreatment and neglect?

• Increasingly, older people are recognised as a significant group having rights requiring special care, services and programmes for living a life of dignity and respect. But on the other hand there is growing incidence of their exploitation, abandonment, neglect, becoming victims of crime and abuse at home, in community and society. While narrations of exploitation, abuse and neglect by family members, including spouse, children and siblings are now being voiced out, friends, acquaintances and strangers being perpetrators and victimising older people by cheating, robbing, fraud of money, transfer and property grabbing has been publicly more visible...

iv) 1 of 3 senior citizens faces abuse—Survey[40]

Some excerpts:

• Nearly one in every three senior citizens in Mumbai faces some form of abuse reveals a survey undertaken by HelpAge India which interviewed 5600 people across India. The report highlights that much of the abuse takes place within the home. Nearly 62 percent of the elderly victims in Mumbai had borne abuse at the hands of their sons followed by their daughters-in-law (21 percent).

• The survey found that 83 percent of senior citizens silently

---

[39] *The Age*, 15 June 2011

[40] *Times of India*, 14 June 2012

faced the abuse mainly due to "family honour" and the 17 percent who spoke out mainly told family members in 44 percent of cases, relatives 37 percent or friends 19 percent.

The above mentioned few examples clearly bring out the gravity of the situation. Elderly abuse has become a part of social life, and also a common feature especially in poor families where the elders have to depend wholly on the good sense of the sons and daughters.

Before analysing the causes and remedies of elderly abuse it would be interesting to understand the situation highlighted by some of the social groups and institutions. HelpAge India is one such institution wholly dedicated to the cause of the elderly. Results of research studies conducted by HelpAge India on Elder Abuse are narrated in "A HelpAge India Report 2012". The salient features are briefly analysed below.

There are an estimated 100 million older people in India and by 2050 their number is expected to rise to 326 million (non projections).

The older persons considered disrespect, neglect, and verbal abuse as elderly abuse. The all India average of elderly abuse is 31.13 percent. In some states it is very high. For example in Madhya Pradesh it is 77.12 percent, Assam 60.55 percent, Uttar Pradesh 52 percent, Andhra Pradesh 42.86, Maharashtra 29.46, Karnataka 37.14 and Rajasthan has the lowest at 1.67 percent.

The report observes that "the traditional norms and values of Indian society laid stress on giving respect and taking care of older persons. The family has traditionally fulfilled the needs of the elderly in respect to social, psychological and economic security. In turn the elderly have contributed acquired wisdom, accumulated wealth and maintained family harmony. In other words however, this relationship is facing headwinds in a modern day society."

Assessing the impact of the forthcoming social changes on the status of older persons, many experts apprehend that the transition from an agrarian to an urbanised society would certainly worsen the plight of older persons. Given this trend, the older persons face innumerable problems to adjust to in varying degrees. These problems range from absence of income to physical dependence and loss of social status and recognition.

The report says the definition developed by Action on Elder Abuse in the United Kingdom and adopted by the international network for the Prevention of Elder Abuse states that "Elder Abuse is a single or repeated act or lack of appropriate action occurring within any relationship where there is an expectation of trust which causes harm or distress to an older person."

Such abuse is generally divided into the following categories:

Physical abuse: The infliction of pain, or injury, physical coercion or physical or drug induced restraint.

Psychological or emotional abuse: The infliction of mental anguish or material abuse. It can also be described as the illegal or improper exploitation or use of funds or resources of the older person.

Sexual abuse: Non-consensual sexual contact of any kind with the older person.

Neglect: The refusal or failure to fulfil a care giving obligation. This may or may not involve a conscious and intentional attempt to inflict physical or emotional distress on the older person.

Financial abuse: Also known as financial exploitation e.g. illegal or unauthorised use of an elderly person's property, money etc.

Living arrangement

An overwhelming 74 percent of the respondents lived with the family compared to 8 percent who lived alone. 15 percent lived with spouse. An overwhelming 73 percent of the respondents were owners of the house in which they lived.

The above mentioned paragraphs bring out the status of the elderly with a magnitude of the various types of abuses. Growing industrialisation and urbanisation, and changes in the attitude of the youngster towards family relationship are held to be responsible for the growing abuse of elderly. It may be stated that these are the reasons which cannot be reversed. Urbanisation has to take place for development of the society and in turn the country. At the same time it is absolutely necessary to make the life of the elderly enjoyable. As human beings, it is the right of the elderly to be free from abuse of any kind and live old age with dignity. What are the cases for denying their right and what are the steps and remedies to bestow their rights and whose duty is it to assure this? It may be clarified here that in most of the abuse of elderly, the victims are poor elders, incapacitated due to failing health, a lack of sense of duty, and attitude conflicts among the members of the family; of course all these are mutually dependent on each other. It is necessary to examine each of these and possible remedies to amend the situation. The position of aged women, especially widows, needs special analysis.

Elder abuse does not take place only in the family. Elder abuse, especially financial abuse and sexual abuse, is committed by outsiders and antisocial elements. Aged couples or aged single widow/widowers are easy targets. They are robbed, sexually abused and even murdered not leave any evidence of their actions behind. In view of the fast changing family and social structure the state and NGOs have to step in a big way.

Abuse of the elderly takes place in all strata of society. Whether rich or poor, emotional attachment and family ties are the most important factors for a happy life especially in old age. The rich elderly during their active age would have had respect and authority in the family affairs. But when they become old, the young take over the charge of the house and due to gradual failing health the aged realise that they have lost authority in the house and are being neglected by the younger members of the family.

It is extremely necessary that the elderly, after retirement from active service, should immediately adjust to the changed circumstances which in most cases are natural. In their intergenerational relationship they should develop an attached and detached affiliation. If they do not adjust, youngsters tend to just ignore them and this has an adverse impact on their psychology.

Remedies

There is no doubt that during the last ten years or so there has been a growing awareness on the part of individuals, NGOs and the state on the necessity of evolving the actions to be taken to protect the interests of elderly as a matter of their human rights. This is evident from the deliberations and discussions of the social scientists. The media also plays a big role in exposing the bad elements and guiding the public. The following measures should be taken seriously to prevent elderly abuse.

i) All elder abuse whether physical, psychological or financial, and or neglect of elders should be recognised as major crimes, and the offenders and perpetrators of these heinous activities must be prosecuted within the quickest possible time frame strictly to be adhered to.

ii) General awareness of the problems should be created in the minds of people and authorities. It may be necessary to train the police, health, social service institutions, and spiritual leaders accordingly. Establish services for victims of abuse and rehabilitation arrangements should be made a part of such initiations.

iii) In every locality there should be young volunteers to keep a watch on the miscreants to prevent any abuse or elderly of the locality especially widows.

iv) Reviving the fast depleting moral values cherished and nourished traditionally through centuries. Urbanisation, industrialisation, growing inevitable nuclear family system should not be an excuse for loss of moral values like respecting and taking care of the elders. Everyone should set an example by his own behaviour. It is the moral responsibility of the spiritual leaders to awaken the humanity within. Our tradition of respecting elders, parents, and teachers is not outdated or redundant. It are as eternal as human life which is a continuous process. Disrespect of these values results in elderly abuse.

Crimes against the elderly

The cases of crimes against the elderly are rising fast in India, especially in metro cities. "Crimes against senior citizens on a rise" has become a common headline in the newspapers. But what is being done to prevent this? Are steps to prevent these crimes against the elderly being prioritised?

Today more and more people are resorting to anti-social means to earn quick money and senior citizens are becoming soft targets. Some of the most common crimes against the old are fraud, burglary, theft, exploitation and murder. Fraud and violence specifically are on the rise in crime graphs.

There is also a sense of hesitation on the part of the elderly in reporting crimes against them in fear of the consequences. They often also want to avoid a sense of shame in the community and to steer clear of unnecessarily legal hassles. Lack of support and no concrete action from the police further adds to their unwillingness to report crimes.

Police departments need to step up and reach out to the elderly community. They need to create a sense of security and support for senior citizens so that they can confidently approach them with their issues. Also, separate departments to deal specifically with issues concerning the elderly should be set up at the Central and state levels. The government has a responsibility to protect the elderly and must put more measures in place to ensure the security and safety of senior citizens.

Although some special safety programs have been started by the government and police, a lot more remains to be done in this regard. Some measures are listed below:

- Properly structured senior citizens security cells and dedicated senior citizens toll-free helplines.
- Each police station should have comprehensive

documentation of all senior citizens in its area whether living alone or in joint families.

- Surveying elderly persons living alone and assessing the kind of protection they need.
- If faced with the problem of shortage of staff, the police can hire volunteers from local communities and enrol them as special police personnel. Verification of antecedents of these volunteers should be mandatory.
- Regular visits by constables to the residence of the elderly, foot patrolling both during daytime and night, and reinforcement of beat police system. These activities will help provide a feeling of safety to the elderly.
- Police should not fail to keep a regular check on domestic help hired by senior citizens who are living alone.
- Security guards of the areas (if any) should be briefed to take special care of such citizens. These security guards should also be verified by the police.
- Police should examine the homes of elderly people and motivate them to install security systems for added safety.
- Create awareness among people/Resident Welfare Associations (RWAs) regarding various safety measures.
- Counselling drives for senior citizens.
- Encouraging the setting up of more senior citizens organisations.
- More regular interaction between residents of the area and the police.

The elderly themselves can contribute to their safety if they follow certain dos & don'ts and are alert and careful in their daily routines:

- Keep emergency medicines handy.
- Make a note of the phone numbers of police stations, hospitals, fire stations, family doctor's number or emergency medical services and special helpline numbers.
- If you are living alone, notify your neighbours and also the manager/in charge of your housing society.

• Never leave your doors unlocked.

• Install a spy-hole and safety bolt on the main entrance door and allow admission only to known persons.

• If possible, install a double door system. It is always safer to interact with strangers without opening the main door.

• If need be, install modern security gadgets like door alarm, electronic-eye bell, CCTVs etc. Consult professionals for setting up such gadgets.

• Notify neighbours and the police when going away on a trip. Cancel deliveries such as newspapers and arrange for someone to collect your mail for you.

• Don't hesitate to report crime or ignore any suspicious activities.

• Never let a stranger into your home.

• Ask for proper identification from delivery persons or claims to be from a utility company or other local business. If you have any doubts, call the utility company to confirm that they sent the person. Allow them access only after informing the security.

• When you admit a workman or a salesman into the house, do not leave him alone at any time.

• Do not give out personal information to anyone who calls you, especially bank account or credit card information. Your bank and credit card companies already have your account numbers.

• Never give out information over the phone indicating you are alone or that you won't be home at a certain time.

• If you are attacked on the street, make as much noise as possible by calling for help or blowing a whistle. Do not pursue your attacker. By fighting back you will get hurt. When talking to the police stay composed, cooperate and try providing maximum information.

• Don't carry any more cash than is necessary and do not display large sums of cash. Do not keep a lot of cash/jewellery/ valuables at home. Store valuables in a safe deposit box instead.

• Avoid wearing or exhibiting jewellery.

• Never discuss financial matters in front of domestic help or strangers.

• Avoid opening your cupboards/purse in front of domestic helps or strangers.

• Never leave spare keys or even the original keys in the open.

• Do not leave valuables in plain view in your car. Most thefts from cars occur when passers-by see a cell phone, purse or other item in your car and they break a window and steal it.

• Employ a servant after verifying his antecedents with the nearest police station.

• Do not encourage relatives or friends of your domestic help to visit your house. If at all he/she has any frequent visitors, get their antecedents checked from police.

• Don't walk in deserted or dark areas alone.

• Do not hesitate to ask for help in case of danger and always wait for the help to arrive.

• Stay alert to the surroundings.

In the wake of rapidly increasing gruesome crimes, the police and the elderly can together formulate a structure and coordinate in a manner such that they help each other and contribute towards a safe and secure society.

Reference:

http://www.mahapolice.gov.in/mahapolice/jsp/temp/seniorcitizen.jsp

http://www.baby-boomer-retirement.com/2013/09/crime-against-senior-citizens.ht

Chapter IV

OLD AGE HOMES

Until a few decades ago, the concept of old age homes was somewhat alien to India. It was considered a Western concept where the elderly preferred to live in old age homes either with their spouse or alone as in the case of widows or widowers. Western family structure and living portray old age homes as post-retirement living homes. During the active age itself they plan to acquire a place for living during old age and their financial planning for old age includes this arrangement too.

In India, the family structure and living to a large extent was, and still is to some extent, entirely different. The elderly after retirement continued to stay in the joint family system. It was considered the duty of the youngsters to take care of the elders in every respect. If they got an opportunity to serve the aged it was considered as a special blessing. It was immaterial whether the son, whose duty is to take care of the parents, was poor or rich. The aged in the house were treated with special attention.

Until the middle of the twentieth century, the thinking in the Indian society was that old age homes were *anathashrams* meant for the destitute with no support from the family members. But this thinking is fast changing due to various developments in the family structure due to growing urbanisation, fast eroding joint family system, growing preference for nuclear families, and changes in the attitudes of youngsters and also of the elderly. Economic security is also one of the considerations. As a result, more and more elderly people, whether poor or rich, feel that old age homes are a big solace as they can spend their twilight years with dignity and independence.

Retirement Homes in the West

With the elderly in India rapidly changing their acceptability towards the concept of retirement homes, it would be helpful to know something more about the concept of old age homes in the West.[41]

A retirement community in the West is invariably a specialised and thoughtfully planned undertaking.

In the West such projects are executed in a single-floor format or equipped with attended lifts and escalators. Wheel chair ramps and hand railings are evident throughout such townships. Bathrooms are equipped with specially designed fittings that give top priority to safety and ease of operation. Club houses are equipped with entertainment facilities that keep the physical limitation of the elderly in mind—in other words indoor games and sit-back entertainment systems are given primary importance.

Medical facilities include a project based, fully staffed emergency room or a small fleet of ambulances and paramedical staff to facilitate speedy medical care at a larger hospital. Moreover, retirement communities in the West are developed on the "everything within walking distance" format. Provisions are made to meet basic requirements of living such as groceries, laundry etc.

Industrial dwelling units are equipped with electronic alarm systems that can be used instantly to call for help in case of sudden distress. In other words, while we are witnessing a number of senior citizen oriented schemes coming up in India, we are nowhere near the Western benchmark in terms of quality and services.

The quality and services in the retirement homes are, no doubt, well planned. It is however wrong to presume that

[41] *Free Press Journal,* 5 November 2011

elders in the West automatically go to old age homes to spend their last phase of life.[42] A study of senior citizens in the United Kingdom, points to revealing statistics i.e. not more than 5 percent of elders live in old age homes. Even so, the need for old age homes with necessary facilities is growing fast in India for various reasons.

Old age homes are a necessity in the present day as the younger generation does not have the time and also in many cases, the resources, to meet their needs like medical expenses, special food etc. Old age homes are also good options for the betterment of the senior citizens by way of good facilities available for keeping them physically fit and encouraging social interaction.

The state-wise position of old age homes in different states/ cities is as follows:[43]

Andhra Pradesh	14
Delhi	4
Karnataka	6
Kerala	9
Tamil Nadu	10
Rajasthan	2
Mumbai	9
Pune	7
Gujarat	18
Kolkata	34
Uttar Pradesh	22
Uttarakhand	10
Himachal Pradesh	9
Haryana	24
Punjab	17

The above mentioned figures indicate that the necessity of old age homes is felt by people in all states of the country.

[42] *Times of India,* 8 September 2011

[43] www.pagindia.com/OldAgeHomes.pdf/

The number is increasing fast. Details such as location, postal address and other details can be obtained from their websites. You may also refer to the "Resources" section as the end of this book.

The growing involvement of government, NGOs, and philanthropic institutions and groups involved in serving the elderly is an encouraging factor. According to the Association of Senior Citizens Mumbai (1992), there were 655 organisations in India out of which 65 percent were old age homes, 18 percent senior citizens associations and 3 percent day care centres. Maharashtra had the largest number of these organisations (180) and the state also had the distinction of having the highest number of old age homes (76) as well as senior citizens associations.

The old age homes can be classified in three broad categories viz:

i) Category A:

These are the old age homes in the form of owning residential accommodation in the community centre. They are more or less colonies established for elderly citizens who are affluent.

ii) Category B:

These are the residential accommodation available in the community centre for the elders mostly on rental basis.

These two categories of residential accommodation are built on the lines of old age homes in the Western countries with a view to provide best facilities required to live with independence and dignity in old age.

iii) Category C:

These are the old age homes built by government, NGOs, and philanthropic institutions for the poor elderly and destitute. The inmates are provided shared accommodation in rooms. They are fully taken care of and provided with food, medical facilities etc. free of cost. In India, hundreds of such old age homes are available throughout the country and more are coming up. It is necessary to analyse the status of each category of old age homes.

Categories A and B

It may be reiterated that the concept of retirement communities or residential projects developed especially for the aged who are affluent in varying degrees is becoming more popular in and around the major cities like Pune, Bangalore, Chennai, Mumbai and Delhi.

The late emergence of retirement communities in India is due to various reasons. Until about 10-15 years ago, elderly Indians, either by choice or by the wishes of their family or by tradition, rarely left the fold of the family even in advanced old age. Very few senior citizens made financial arrangements for their golden years to the extent of buying or hiring retirement homes. However, now there is a growing feeling that as the younger generation starts building their own households independently the elderly need not be dependent on them and feel neglected. Hence the elderly have begun valuing their independence even after retirement. Serene, tranquil and calm—that is the kind of life most people desire post-retirement.

Retirement homes typically include enhanced features that make living for the elderly far more secure and comfortable. Advanced medical facilities in and around the area, high-tech security syndromes, recreational choices specially designed keeping the clientele in mind and other superior facilities are a part of these communities.

Some of the existing projects of this type are Dignity Lifestyle Township at Neral near Mumbai, Classic Kudumbams and Melur Meadows in Chennai, Ashiana Utsav at Saket, Athashri and Golden Nest Senior Commune in Pune, and Vishrant Dhama in Bangalore. It would be interesting to understand the thinking behind the establishment and the working of these homes.

Rajesh Shankar, sales director at Classic Kudumbam, a retirement village located at Sholinganallur says, "Some of the chores for the elderly would not have been a problem for them earlier, like cooking, cleaning and maintaining the house. These become more difficult as they get older; and this is where we step in. Our management handles all their needs and requirements. We have maids and cooks as well as care takers and trained medical staff for those with special needs."[44]

Vishal Gupta, managing director at Ashiana House says, "The idea of coming up with the retirement resorts has been taken from the countries like Australia and America where such services are quite common and easily available. Now this trend has geared up in India as well; comfort buying is a new phenomenon which has grabbed India socially now. The desire to live a comfortable retired life, till recently suppressed due to affordability factor, is no more a concern to senior citizens."

Gupta further said, "The necessity of providing long term luxurious living was felt, and taking cues from abroad, we ventured on this path. In India more than 60 percent of households are nuclear and 8.94 percent of the population is aged 60 plus indicating that the aged are in greater need of support than ever before. According to market estimates, the housing need in this segment has increased four to five fold. The estimated units in this segment are 4000 as of now but the way this segment is growing it can jump to 20,000 units in the next three years."

Ashiana, which specialises in this area, feels that demand is going up. The group is constructing a 200 crore project called Utsava Lavasa in Lavasa city near Pune, which will have about 500 retirement homes comprising villas and luxury Ashiana hopes to complete construction and hand over homes by next year. The company has constructed similar units in Bhivandi and Jaipur.

P. Sathyanaran , chief executive officer, Melur Meadows, says, "There is a growing need for such villages. We cater to senior citizens from all walks of life; there are NRIs, retired defence officers, as well as ordinary citizens looking for comfort in their twilight years. Most of our respondents stay here on a permanent basis as it is a full-fledged housing complex catering to the needs of senior citizens. However, residents can

[47] *The Indian Express* dated January 15,2011

also sublet or lease out their cottages to another person as long as they are willing to abide by the village rules."

He further added, "We are not a real estate company but a service company and understand that people have chosen to stay with us because of the package of services bundled with the user friendly cottages and service village atmosphere."

About the surroundings he said, "With nearly an acre of park area, Melur Meadows has already more than 80 Neem trees and a further 400 trees have been planted to ensure pure, pristine air and oxygen abounds in the village."

As stated before besides Ashiana Housing, there are projects such as Dignity Lifestyle Township at Neral near Mumbai, Athashri and Golden Nest Senior Commune in Pune, besides premium high-end projects such as Impact Senior Living at Amritsar. The price of Ashiana varies from location to location. While in Jaipur, it starts at ₹11.8 lakh, properties in Bhivandi are priced from ₹17.4 lakh onwards. While cottages at Melur Meadows start from ₹8.5 lakh onwards, studio apartments at Classic Kudumbam can be had for a refundable deposit of ₹12.5 lakh besides a monthly maintenance payment of around ₹10,000. Luxury projects can cost as much as ₹45 lakh. (Figures applicable in October 2013)

Mr. Shankar from Classic Kudumbam says, "Each apartment is bright, cheerful, and air-conditioned. All apartments have special non-slipping floor tiles in the bath. They are also fitted with guide rails. Apartments are intuitively furnished with even a rack for umbrellas and walking sticks. There are several cheerful and bright open central courtyards in the building."

The response of the elderly staying in the old age homes is interesting. Lt. Col. Vibhakar Chaturvedi who is sixty-seven years old and who is a long term resident at Ashiana Utsav at Bhivandi says, "I find this place wonderful for us retirees. It has a beautiful environment, people of the same age group, an activity centre to pass our time in a more useful manner, on site medical facilities etc. to name a few. It has everything which is required at our age. Life here in Utsav is very comfortable, healthy, pollution free, and safe breathing and much better than what it used to be in Delhi." (This is a representative response to indicate that elderly are happy to live in an old age home.)

For philanthropists and social workers, establishing an old age home without any commercial motive is a service to the elderly. This thinking is growing. Hema Malini, a former MP and a social worker is planning to establish an old age home. Hema Malini says, "I plan to invest a major portion of the money I earned from acting into an old age home. It pains me to see parents, when they need the whole hearted support of their kids, being left all alone. At times they are unable to get their medicines."

Elaborating more on her dream project, she says, "This old age home will be divided into three groups: poor, middle class and the rich. Residents here will be provided with the essentials that one needs for comfortable living. This old age home will have different sections where people can get together, talk, eat peacefully until they breathe their last."

Category C

It must be stated here that though the availability of modern facilities for the elderly in retired communities in increasing, the benefits of this can be availed of only by a small percentage of the elderly population whose financial position is comfortable. But we have seen earlier that a large section of the Indian population is educationally and economically backward, living on meager earning with no capacity to save for the old age. The concept of retirement community is rather a distant dream for them.

Fortunately the state, philanthropic institutions and NGOs are doing a good job in establishing old age homes in which the poor and destitute can spend their old age with no financial burden on them. They get good food, medical facilities and above all community living with social surroundings. Mention can be made of some such old age homes which are a boon to the needy and the distressed.

Niwara—old age home in Pune

David Sassoon Infirm Asylum, Niwara, is perhaps the oldest or at least one of the oldest old age homes. It celebrated 150 years in 2012. It is a public charitable trust solely devoted to the welfare of men and women above 60 years of age, without any source of livelihood, who are without any close family members to look after them. Once admitted into the institution they are looked after till their last day. All their necessities, like food, clothes, medical treatment, and shared living arrangements in comfortable rooms, are taken care of. At present nearly 150 elderly persons, both men and women, stay in Niwara.

The residents live as in an extended family, where everyone contributes and shares the responsibilities according to one's abilities and physical strength. Cleaning the campus, looking after the plants, helping in the kitchen are some items of work where they contribute.

From the press reports,[45] it is clear that the inmates are very happy to stay in the old age home. Some responses received from the inmates are listed below:

Vaishali Dongre, 72, says she found comfort in Niwara, "I have been here for the last two years. The discipline, sense of community belonging that I experience here is endearing. An in-house clinic, care takers, freshly cooked food, new clothes and entertainment facilities are provided to us."

Suresh Joshi, 62, said, "I was indignant and in need of support. My brother got me here and I have been happy since. It means a lot. I do not have to worry about the old age problems and illness."

I (author) had the opportunity to visit Niwara for the 150th year celebrations in August 2012 and talked to many inmates, both men and women. I found the rooms clean and well maintained. After asking questions about their physical and mental health before joining Niwara and after, I was

[45] *Pune Mirror*, 9 August 2012

convinced that they are absolutely happy. They truly think that their second life in Niwara is worth living. They were eager to express their joy, both in words and by gestures. They expressed their gratitude to the officials and volunteers who manage the working of the institution. My talk with some of the office bearers convinced me that involvement in social work with dedication and hard work can do wonders. It is an ideal institution in every respect and a boon to the needy.

Old age home in Thiruvananthapuram District, Kerala

A group discussion carried out by a group of research scholars at the old age home in Thiruvananthapuram is worth mentioning[46]. This home is meant for poor and destitute women and is run with the help of donations. The inmates are provided with food, clothes, and shelter. Medical care is also taken care of by the institution.

The six widows who participated in the discussion stated that their life became miserable after the death of their husbands. One of the widows narrated her own story reflective of the pitiable condition of widows in society. She has only one daughter. After marriage of the daughter the parents handed over all their property to their daughter and son-in-law. In the initial years, the son-in-law was very nice to them. Later, especially after her husband's death, the son-in-law's behaviour changed drastically. One morning he ordered his wife to send her mother out of the house and asked her to choose between him and her mother. After great difficulties the old lady managed to join this old age home. This is classified as both financial abuse and psychological abuse of the elders within the family.

Most of the inmates were very old. They shared their experiences and were engaged in some activities of the old age home. They expressed their happiness about the arrangements in the home and were happy to get the company of friends to share their feelings.

---

[46]*India's Elderly: Burden or Challenges?* S. Irudaya Rajan, P. Shankara Sarma, p.189-201

Admitting the elderly in the old age home without the consent of the concerned

It has been elaborated in the previous paragraphs that old age homes are the facilities meant for the comforts of the elderly. But there are instances where the widowed mothers are admitted in the old age home against their will even though the family is financially well off to look after their widowed mother, thus defeating the very purpose of old age homes—i.e. comfort of the elderly. This is clear from the feelings expressed by some ladies living in an old age home in Pune.

One lady narrated her story: "My son is a chemical engineer and my daughter is also highly educated. Even then I have become a burden to them. That is why they have kept me in this old age home." With tears in her eyes she said, "I expect that at least children and grandchildren should come and meet me often. But they are too busy and do not find time to meet me."

Another lady said, "Mother's day is the day when my children come and meet me."

One of the inmates was very angry and burst out: "I do not want to see the face of my son who attempted to kill me for the sake of property. I very often remember my only daughter and wish both my children were daughters."

Despite everything, all the women in the institution said that in spite of their sufferings, they will always pray to God for the welfare of the children. That is a mother's heart.

Changing nature of old age homes

The attitude that old age homes are meant for the old destitute is fast changing. More youngsters and also the elderly are looking at the old age homes with a positive attitude. Due to the fast changes in the nature of family and other social set up like nuclear families, separation of children from parents for various reasons like growing preference to stay independently both by young and old, the old age homes are getting more and more popular and they are considered as the best alternative to joint family system for living happily. Hence, old age homes are coming up to suit the financial position of the elderly with all modern facilities. However, the most important point is to preserve the sanctity of the family system with emotional attachment whether the young and old live under one roof or independently.

Chapter V

HEALTH

A. GERIATRIC MEDICAL CARE

~ Dr. Rajesh Jaria, MD

(Dr. Rajesh Jaria is a consultant physician with Hinduja Health Care Surgical Hospital Khar, Mumbai. He has an MD from Grant Medical College, Mumbai, and a post graduate qualification in palliative care from Singapore. He can be contacted at Life Link Health Centre, JP Road, Andheri West, Mumbai 400058 [beside Andheri Sports Complex] Tel: 9930-9940-74.)

Geriatrics is a branch of General medicine that is concerned with the clinical, preventive, remedial and social aspects of illness in old age. The challenges of frailty, complex co-morbidity, different patterns of disease presentation, slower response to treatment and requirements for social support call for special medical skills.

Many aspects to treating the aged patient require special training and care, with comprehensive assessment being a core. Therapy escalation is a key only if combined with accuracy in timing and preventing poor outcomes in the face of short term gains.

This science has received very little attention in India

primarily as it does not possess a potential for high returns on investment on one side, and does require a very significant investment on the other side. With the four ashrams being a foundation of Indian culture, high investment in the *sanyasashram* group would be against popular sentiment.

However, adoption of the Western culture has led to two significant changes that ensure older patients continue to possess enough value that demands investments into them. One, the mushrooming of nuclear families, with "both parents working" system creates a need for grandparents to ensure the grandchildren are well taken care of. Two, economic viability, stability and flexibility are greater with the presence of parents in a society with mushrooming figures of divorce and job losses.

Demographic changes having led to a rise in emergency admissions to hospitals with a significant focus on quality and cost-effectiveness, a need has arisen to define best practices with regard to acute medical care for older people.

The health issues faced by the elderly are numerous and the assessment categories unique to elderly patients are:

-Sensory perception and injury prevention, and

-Risk of falling.

In addition areas of special implications for older patients include

-Immunizations,

-Diet and exercise, and

-Sexuality.

Traditionally, the "Five I's of Geriatrics", include intellectual impairment, immobility, instability, incontinence and iatrogenic disorders—iatrogenic because it's important to know what *not* to do.

Assessment therefore is the key to the care of the elderly and also ensures the optimal use of resources. When does an older person require specialised geriatric medical care? A comprehensive geriatric assessment is a time-intensive evaluation of a patient, who by definition, has been previously identified as being at significant risk for imminent morbidity or mortality. It is a diagnostic instrument designed to collect data on the medical, psychosocial, and functional capabilities and limitations of elderly patients.

Sensory perception, injury prevention and the risk of falling

Incidence of falls in patients over the age of 65, is approximately 25 percent (more so in patients who live alone) but rises to 50 percent in patients over 80 years of age.

Factors that contribute to falls can be intrinsic such as:

-age-related changes in postural control, gait, and visual ability,

-acute/chronic disease that affect

- sensory input,
- the central nervous system, and
- musculoskeletal strength and coordination.

Extrinsic factors that contribute are:

-certain medications,

-furniture arrangements at home, and

-the availability of aids to over-come disability.

Medicines that affect the elderly patient making her/him more prone to falls are a dichotomous set being often the ones most needed to ensure appropriate treatment so there is reduced danger of loss of life from primary illnesses. A classic example is anti-arrhythmic drugs without which many an elderly patient would be at an increased risk of death, but which also increase the potential of a patient having a fall.

Osteoporosis is one notable intrinsic factor that leads to falls and a pathologic fracture may precede a fall. Risk assessment for osteoporosis and attempts to prevent the same need to start at an early age. How early does prevention start? For example a Bristol University study has reported that girls who drink a lot of milk till their late teens (read: eighteen) enjoy the benefits of having drunk milk in their eighties. Nevertheless a geriatrician will encounter a patient only at a late age and may need to bring in controls to prevent the effects of osteoporosis.

Extrinsic factors that contribute to falls include poor lighting, obtrusive furniture, slippery floors, loose floor coverings, and bathrooms without handrails or grab bars.

Mobility and dexterity play an important role in balance assessed with a simple evaluation of one-leg balance test (ability to stand unassisted on one leg for five seconds) or a more structured "Get Up and Go" test (patient observed as she/he rises from a sitting position, walks 10 feet, turns and returns to the chair to sit). The effectiveness of the test for predicting falls is enhanced by timing the process, with more than 16 seconds predictive of an increased risk of falls. Any observed changes need further evaluation.

Interventions that reduce the risk of falls in the elderly are amongst the most important of contributions to long term better outcomes of health in the elderly. These interventions can range from something as simple as furniture rearrangement and provision of a walking stick or walker to complex changes in hypertension medications to prevent postural hypotension (defined as a drop in systolic blood pressure of ≥20 mm Hg or to < 90 mm Hg on standing). Restricting use of sleep inducing agents and prescription medications to a maximum of four per day as also installation of grab bars or handrails on stairs and physiotherapeutic mobility improving exercises are additionally important useful changes.

Diet, immunizations and sexuality

Malnutrition/under-nutrition is a very common unaddressed problem in the geriatric population. A compromised nutritional state is responsible for numerous cost increases in the care of the elderly who not only require longer hospital stays with more complications, they also have poorer outcomes after hospital discharge. In addition, therefore, there is more demand on the caregivers who may be another person or group of people.

Again, few simple home remedies go a long way and are

universally applicable to all ages. Six small meals, low fat high protein diet, ensuring good, continuous and sustained diabetes control & mandatory daily physical activity are a few such examples. Specific to older age group is attention to dentition that often in general escapes attention and in specific is left unmentioned by the common stoic and non-complaining geriatric patient. Inability to chew is a common reason for poor nutrition that can be easily corrected.

Weight loss may reflect changes in appetite, dentition, taste, depression, comorbidity, poverty, isolation, constipation and other factors. Appetite and food intake often decline with ageing. Older people tend to be consistently less hungry than younger people (a hormonal effect), eat smaller meals, have fewer snacks between meals and also eat more slowly. Older adults on an average have a decrease in energy intake of approximately 30 percent and lose about 0.5 percent per year the function of many tissues and organs, manifested in the shape, needs and metabolism of the older person and regardless of cause, loss of lean body mass is an inevitable consequence of age. Physical activity declines with age, especially in the affluent group of society, depriving muscles of what is probably their most essential stimulus to maintaining their mass and function. Geriatric patients do not enjoy many things that earlier gave them joy—primarily as they are unable to achieve end points. An alternative must be sought and a hobby found which inculcates and sustains their interest and maintains activity and if such a hobby can incorporate increased mobility and exercise it will serve a higher purpose.

Changes in the gastrointestinal system besides loss of teeth, unsteady teeth, ill-fitting artificial dentures etc., are in the swallowing process being less synchronised due to changes in the pharyngeal structure and deterioration in neural control with a decrease in neural conductivity that affects neural response besides different neurological disorders like cerebrovascular accident (CVA), Parkinson's disease, and others.

An ounce of prevention goes a long way in compromised nutrition. Hence the basics must be done:

a) An assessment by a geriatrician who submits a summary, a laminated copy of which is maintained for ready reckoning.

b) A calorie charting with adequate vitamin supplementation (if needed in the form of injections) incorporated into the patient's meals. A common problem with geriatric patients is a tendency to repeat the same foods on a daily basis. This is more common when they live alone, as is eating of pre-cooked stored food over several mealtimes. This has a significant effect on overall nutrition in terms of quantity and quality.

A simple screening device for geriatric nutrition is the Nutritional Health Screen—a simple to administer assessment tool which can be graded by a family member, and may help to prevent nutritional problems in at-risk patients. (http://www.jblearning.com/samples/0763730629/Frank_Appendix10D.pdf).

It is important to remember that catabolic processes (processes in the human body that lead to breakdown of tissues) are easy to set in when there is nutritional deficiency because the body is designed to give preference to vital organs—a classic e.g. is calcium. Calcium is the component that gives bones strength. It is also the component that is used by muscles to bring about movement. The most important muscle in the body is the heart—a whole pump made of specialized muscle cells called myocardium. Myocardial cells do not die or regenerate and the same cells live through-out an individual's life. Myocardial cells need a constant source of calcium and in case calcium is inadequate in food consumed, the body will preferentially remove calcium from bone and maintain the level of calcium in blood even if it means severely weak bones—because a dead person has no use of strong bones. Once a catabolic process has set in it is difficult to reverse the same in older patients. In fact the process may be stopped but will not reverse—as in calcium loss from the bone may stop but the calcium already removed from the bone will not replace back unless therapy is used—therapy which is costly and prolonged.

The consequences of malnutrition are physiological, biochemical and psychological. They include reduced immunity, delayed wound healing and decreased muscle strength, which in turn have detrimental effects on recovery and rehabilitation. The psycho-social impact of malnutrition is also significant with changes in mood, attitude, self-esteem and reduced socialisation.

The following points may be checked for to detect if an older adults is at risk for under-nutrition:

- Little or no appetite.
- Problems with eating or swallowing.
- Eating inadequate servings of nutrients and fewer than two meals a day.
- Limited income may cause restriction in the number of meals eaten per day or dietary quality of meals eaten.
- Isolation and loss of desire to cook because of loneliness.
- Appetite of widow's decrease.
- Difficulty cooking due to disabilities.
- Lack of access to transportation to buy food.
- Chronic illness and chronic conditions can affect intake.
- Disability can hinder ability to prepare or ingest food.
- Depression can cause decreased appetite.
- Poor oral health.
- Antidepressants, antihypertensives, and bronchodilators can contribute to xerostomia (dry mouth).
- Change in taste (from medications, nutrient deficiencies, or tastebud atrophy) can also alter nutritional status.

Immunizations are a new aspect of science with regard

to the elderly. Traditionally, immunizations were a thing of childhood, most having been completed in the first few months of life. However medical science and doctors have always acknowledged that an ounce of prevention is worth more than a ton of cure. Immunizations are at the forefront of prevention.

The following is a list of vaccine-preventable infectious conditions which are recommended for use by elderly adults—if not already vaccinated:

- Influenza
- Tetanus,
- Diphtheria
- Pertussis
- Varicella
- Zoster
- Pneumococcal polysaccharide (PPSV23)
- Pneumococcal 13-valent conjugate (PCV13)
- Meningococcal
- Hepatitis A
- Hepatitis B

Although the above list is exhaustive, changes do occur and updates must be incorporated. Additionally, not all adults are suited for all of the above for various reasons and a doctor must be consulted prior to taking any of the above.

Certain circumstantial vaccines e.g.: Rabies Vaccine, can be taken if the indications are met.

Myths about sexuality in the older person

Sexuality remains a prominent part of the lives of older persons. Despite evidence to the contrary, many believe that older adults do not or should not have sexual activity. In fact, if an older person is physically able and has a partner, sexual activity and satisfaction with sex can persist well into the 90s. Sex, physical intimacy, and emotional intimacy are **lifelong** needs. Often physical or functional limitations may alter sex to include mutual masturbation, use of mechanical devices, or simply hugging and kissing. Libido and sexual needs decrease with age in males and females reducing the frequency, prolonging the excitement phase and requiring a longer period of stimulation in order to achieve orgasm in both men and women. The refractory period between orgasms is also longer in both men and women.

It should be noted that persons with healthy sex lives as younger adults will be more likely to have healthy sex lives carried on into their later years. A study of older persons showed that sexual activity declines from 73 percent to 26 percent among persons aged 57-64 and 75-85, respectively.

It is a myth that sexual problems are just part of normal ageing, with no solutions, so why bother talking to your doctor about it. Physicians are trained to be unbiased, empathetic, and non-judgmental especially in sensitive matters of a personal kind such as sex. Patients need to realise that they need not feel embarrassed discussing these issues during their routine appointments. Treatments, medications, alternative solutions may be available to improve or solve problems for e.g.: many medications contribute to reducing sexual drive and/or contribute to erectile dysfunction and changes in the same, may, at times; lead to dramatic improvements. Such medications include antidepressants (selective serotonin receptor antagonists are most important), narcotics, anti-hypertensives like alpha and beta blockers, diuretics etc. Except for mirtazapine and wellbutrin, most antidepressants impact libido.

Erectile function is the most important factor in a healthy sexual life in older men, with many chronic diseases contributing to its development. Surgical treatment for prostate cancer is a cause of untreatable and irreversible ED. Vaginal dryness and dyspareunia (pain with sexual intercourse) are the most important factors in reducing the sexual desire and frequency in women. Menopause also results in a marked decrease in libido, which does not always recover, especially now that few women take hormone replacement therapy.

Other risk factors for sexual dysfunction for older women include being unmarried, divorced or widowed; lack of a physically capable partner; past sexual problems; and lower educational level. As women outlive their husbands, lack of a physically capable partner is becoming more frequent a problem and women report significantly less sexual activity than men at all age groups.

Other medical conditions that contribute to a reduced desire for sex, include urinary incontinence, osteoarthritis (due to pain with intercourse), and changes in body mass and shape. Up to 50% of breast cancer patients report significant sexual problems due to alteration of self-image and self-confidence. A study assessing the sexual healthcare needs of older women reported that they had concerns similar to younger women, but were less likely to discuss these concerns.

In effect sexuality is an important part of the quality of life in older persons and due to physical and functional limitations, sexual activity may need to be adapted to bypass limitations. Physicians are open to discussing these issues with their patients, initiating conversations and being sensitive to the comfort level of the patient. It is required that older patients also have such an open attitude.

The effects of age are truly in the mind. What determines the effect of ageing is highly dependent on the attitude that one takes towards it. Nobody can defy time but one can defy the effects of time. Science today allows such defiance to succeed far greater than one could hope for in earlier times. It also allows many patients to live longer than they were genetically programmed to. Nobody wishes to live long and unhealthy—and health is an ounce of prevention, a ton of cure but a whole lot of attitude—so that one can live long and healthy.

B. MENTAL HEALTH IN OLD AGE

~ Dr. Dhananjay Chavan, MD (Psychiatry)

(Dr. Dhananjay Chavan is a geriatric psychiatrist with an MD from BJ Medical College, Pune [1991] and Fellowship in Geriatric Mental Health from KGMU, Lucknow. He is a volunteer with Dignity Home Foundation which is a charity for senior citizens. He has a private practice in Pune and Nashik. He is an honorary consultant at Jehangir Hospital and Aditya Birla Hospital in Pune. He enjoys drinking tea, reading, meditation, long walks, Pali study and history. He can be contacted on 94235 78087 or 94235 74592. Email: geropsychiatrist@gmail.com)

"Mind comes first, mind is foremost." ~ *The Buddha*

Introduction

Today, many elderly enjoy excellent physical and mental health. Therefore, it is often said that in this era, the sixties is the new middle age. Many senior citizens live a productive life, enjoy their newfound leisure after retirement or stay actively involved in their work, indulge in hobbies, and use their experience and wisdom to serve society. Still, old age remains a vulnerable time for both physical and mental health.

Mental health at any age is important and is influenced by many factors. But at no other time is it as important and as susceptible to various physical, personal and social factors as in old age. Mental health is a broad subject that encompasses diverse fields—from medicine to philosophy and spirituality. Though we will discuss overall mental health as well, we will focus more on psychiatric problems among the elderly including what are called the three Ds of old age mental health: depression, dementia and delirium. Some important topics such as elder abuse are discussed elsewhere in this book.

Elderly in India

India has made significant progress in the field of health.

Life expectancy has increased in India from less than thirty-five years at the time of independence to more than sixty-five years today. We now have about ten crore senior citizens. This number is growing, and because of the falling birth rate, the proportion of the elderly is growing even faster. In India, as in most eastern cultures, the elderly are respected. But often this is only in theory. In practice, the elderly are often lonely and helpless due to migration of youth in search of livelihood, changing family structure, materialism, poverty, etc. This contributes to the increased incidence of psychiatric disorders in the elderly. It is estimated that about 20 percent of the elderly suffer from a psychiatric disorder.

Ageism

Society has a stereotypical perception about old people and looks upon the elderly as debilitated, incompetent and unworthy of attention. Ageism is prejudice and discrimination on the basis of age. It also involves policies and practices that perpetuate and strengthen the stereotypes of the aged.

In geriatric mental health, ageism is compounded by the stigma attached to mental illnesses.

Ageism goes beyond simple age discrimination (where old people are treated differently, unequally, and unfairly). It is a broader term that includes the negative attitudes towards ageing and the aged which in turn contributes to discrimination.

One major misconception is that decline in mental abilities, even when it interferes with professional or social functions, is normal in old age.

Active ageing

More and more elderly are living an active life. They remain physically and mentally active. Physical exercise and remaining engaged in meaningful intellectual work are perhaps the best insurance for a happy old age. With age, people lose muscle mass and gain fat tissue. Therefore, they benefit from resistance exercises (weight training) along with aerobic exercises, but it must be done in consultation with a doctor. Tai-chi and some yoga postures are suitable for the elderly. Proper nutrition goes a long way in keeping the mind healthy.

There is an expectation of self-denial among the elderly in the eastern cultures. Though this is a laudable aspiration in theory, in practice the elderly find much fulfilment in humour, entertainment, tourism, and general enjoyment of life's pleasures. The number of senior citizens who flock eagerly to laughter clubs is a testimony to their zeal for life.

Anubhai is seventy-four. He travels for an hour each day to his business in Mumbai. He leads an active social life. He takes morning walks and does *pranayam* regularly. His ability to regale both the young and the old with jokes makes him a very popular and a sought after man in social circles!

Mental changes with age—What is normal and what is not

Most elderly have intact mental faculties well into their eighties. Sometimes they may have difficulty remembering a name. They may also be slightly slower with tasks that require mental speed or shifting attention and are a little more likely to forget incidents. However, this is compensated by their overall fund of knowledge, which does not decline with age, and by practical wisdom that comes from experience. Elders retain most linguistic skills and vocabulary. In conclusion, it is important to remember that any decline in mental faculties that interferes with professional, social or personal life is not normal and should be brought to the attention of a psychiatrist or a neurologist.

Prof. Deshmukh, a dandy even at seventy-eight, often competes with his grandson in solving mathematical puzzles. But on computer games, his grandson is way too fast for him. He is sometimes not able to recall the name of a relative. Having seen dementia in a friend, he worried whether he was also developing dementia but found his doubt without basis on psychiatric consultation. He now engages his grandson with greater vigour.

Mental changes may not be just in the mind

Ageing is associated with many physical health problems. Several medical problems lead to behavioural and psychological problems in the elderly. Here is a list of some common causes:

- Infections
- Constipation
- Pain
- Dehydration
- Malnutrition
- Medication related
- Hearing and visual impairment
- Electrolyte imbalance
- Heart and kidney disease
- Severe anaemia
- Gastroesophageal reflux disease

Hypertension (high blood pressure) increases risk of stroke (cerebrovascular accidents that sometimes cause paralysis of limbs) and vascular dementia. In India, hypertension often remains undetected and there is need for increased awareness about hypertension as well as for proper treatment.

Jacob Pinto was a successful architect but, in spite of doctors' warnings, often neglected to monitor his blood pressure saying it was borderline and that he felt just fine. He was also a diabetic but often took liberties with his diet. He developed depression in his early sixties (his psychiatrist concluded that it was due to changes in brain due to hypertension and diabetes) and later fell victim to vascular dementia.

Medical diseases are far more likely to cause psychiatric problems in the elderly but unfortunately far less likely to be suspected. Most people think, "It is just old age!" Because the medical basis of many psychiatric problems is not appreciated by society and looked upon as normal mental changes due to ageing, elderly are not brought to doctors.

Ram Kishan, a sixty-two year old farmer, was brought to me by his son, Sanjay, who reported that his father had been losing his memory for almost three years; was often despondent and was finding difficulty with most mental tasks. Laboratory tests revealed very low level of Vitamin B12 in blood. With vitamin supplements, Ram Kishan showed rapid improvement in mood and his memory improved but he didn't return to his level of mental ability. This could have been due to irreversible damage to brain due to long standing vitamin deficiency.

Medication side effects

The elderly are more prone to side effects of medicines. They are also likely to be prescribed multiple medications. Informing physician about ALL medicines helps the physician help the elderly. Since many medications have the potential to cause psychiatric problems in the elderly, it is a good practice to ask the doctors specifically about it.

When psychotropic medicines are prescribed for elders, they are often started on low doses and slowly increased.

Three Major Psychiatric Disorders in the Elderly

Dementia

Dementia is a brain disease. In addition to forgetfulness, there is impairment in language; orientation; motor skills and capacity to conceptualise, plan, execute, evaluate and modify an action. Social and occupational functioning suffers. It is essential to identify dementia early because one can treat, if present, reversible causes of dementia. Early treatment is helpful, even in irreversible progressive dementia, in maintaining functional independence for a longer period.

Some warning signs of dementia:

- Becoming forgetful. Often unable to find the right word.
- Forgetting to take medicines.
- Frequently losing or misplacing things in house.
- Not remembering names of relatives and friends.
- Asking the same question again and again.

- Difficulty following conversations.
- Forgetting conversations.
- Getting lost in the neighbourhood.
- Unable to keep track of time.

Psychiatric consultation should be sought when these warning signs are present.

Bapu Mali was an orator of some repute who had given hundreds of public talks over forty years. But in his seventies, he started finding it difficult to give public speeches, often losing the thread of his argument during speech. His talks became rambling. His family noticed that he forgot names often, repeated questions and conversations. Otherwise a restrained man earlier in life, he became more and more irascible. He was seen by a neurologist and put on medication for more than a year that led to significant improvement.

Depression

Depression in elderly is a group of clinical conditions that require a broad intervention. Late life depression is often under-recognised and under-treated. Some of the features of late life depression are:

- Lack of feeling
- Complaints of forgetfulness or intellectual disability
- Preoccupation with bodily functions such as bowel habits
- Constant health worries
- Frequent visits to doctors
- Unexplained functional decline
- Social withdrawal
- Loss of interest and apathy

Loneliness is so common and causes so much suffering that many experts advocate that loneliness be recognised as a disease. Losing a spouse in old age makes one vulnerable to depression. An elderly person may be dependent on the spouse not only for emotional support but also for assistance in daily activities. Though grief is normal reaction to the loss of a spouse, it is important to recognise when grief becomes pathological and may need therapeutic intervention.

Late Yashwantrao Chavan, former CM of Maharashtra and Deputy PM of India, was a freedom fighter, an able administrator and an exceptional politician with a clean track record. He was known as a strong, stable, sensitive, caring, happy and wise person. But when he lost his wife, he became extremely depressed and never recovered. He died heartbroken within two years.

In addition to various medical conditions (such as cancer, heart disease, lung disease, alcohol dependence, dementia, etc.) chronic pain and physical, verbal or emotional abuse by relatives or caretakers are often associated with depression. Those living in a nursing home may also be more prone to depression. These days, many elderly couples live alone. When one of them becomes disabled, the spouse is the caregiver. This can be very stressful and may lead to depression.

Reliable statistics are not available about Indian elderly but in the West elderly are more prone to commit suicide. Better care of mental illness, especially depression, in the elderly diminishes risk for suicide but it is important to remember that suicide in the elderly is not limited to those with a mental illness.

Proper treatment of depression in the elderly, with both medication and psychotherapy, helps not only in relieving depression but also in improving overall health and reducing the burden on their caregiver/s.

Delirium

Elderly are particularly prone to delirium, which is an acute impairment in consciousness and higher mental functions. There is inattention, distractibility and often disturbance of sleep-wakefulness cycle. Visual and auditory hallucinations are common. Delirium is a life threatening medical emergency that is reversible. There are several conditions that predispose and precipitate delirium. Multiple medications are a common cause of delirium.

Though we have discussed these three disorders, the psychiatric problems of the elderly are not restricted to the above three.

Caregivers: a valuable and vulnerable pillar in care of the elderly

The elderly, especially those with disabilities including functional impairment due to dementia, are often cared for by family members or professional caregivers. Among family members the spouse, daughters, and daughters-in-law are common caregivers.

Caring for a disabled elderly, especially one with dementia, is an extremely demanding and stressful task.

Many caregivers give up their jobs, completely or partially, to care for a parent or a spouse. Many of their leisure activities are curtailed due to caring duties. This leads to considerable burden on the caregivers. Depression is common among caregivers. Therefore, it is important to take care of the caregivers, to ensure that they get enough rest, enough counselling and suitable intervention when needed.

Advance Directive or Living Will

Government of India is in the process of enacting a law that allows one to make an "advance directive" about how one would like to be treated if one develops an illness that impairs decision-making capacity. "Living will" allows one to influence the end of life decisions to doctors or relatives. This may give the elderly a sense of empowerment as also a preparedness and acceptance about death. Giving clear advanced instructions is helpful because sometimes family members and relatives are confused or may have conflicting views.

At eighty-five, Sudha Apte was as sharp and alert as ever. But she was getting very frail physically. She had given clear instructions to her only son and friends that if she is hospitalised, she should not be put on any life support such as a ventilator, pacemaker etc. To avoid any confusion, she also left clear written instructions. Her son, friends, and doctors followed her wishes and made her last hospitalisation, during which she passed away, peaceful and comfortable.

Some important issues that affect mental health of the elderly

Hearing and visual impairment

Problem with eyesight is noticed early and treatment sought by most elderly. We all know the importance of good eyesight. However, good hearing is equally, or even more, important in maintaining a good quality of life. Hearing difficulty is often ignored by senior citizens and their family members. Decline in hearing causes isolation and feeling of loneliness. Social contact is a basic need for humans. Decline in hearing leads to lack of or poor quality of social contact and may also cause depression, illusions, hallucinations and paranoia.

Cataract surgery and prescription lenses are relatively straightforward solutions to most visual problems of the elderly. For hearing impairment, on the other hand, the solutions may not be simple and results may not be as miraculous. But understanding that good hearing is important for good mental health helps the elderly and their family in giving a patient trial to hearing aids or other interventions advised by their doctors.

Bhanu Pratap Singh, a retired accountant, had lived a perfectly healthy life until he developed partial deafness at the age of sixty-five. He was advised use of hearing aid. But he was ashamed to use it. "Anyway, it doesn't make that big a difference to my hearing," he claimed. He became increasingly isolated in his own big joint family as he couldn't participate in family discussions. Gradually he became suspicious and depressed. His family persuaded him to see a psychiatrist. He and his family were counselled about hearing aids. They agreed to try one that was relatively unobtrusive and gave better results. His recovery was remarkable.

Sleep

There are certain changes in the sleep pattern in old age. Sleep is more fragmented. One may go to bed earlier and get up earlier. Day time naps increase. Some tips for good quality sleep are:

- Keep a regular bedtime and wake time.
- Go to bed only when sleepy.
- Don't lie in bed for long if unable to fall asleep.
- Do not watch TV while in bed.
- Keep daytime nap short—less than thirty minutes.
- Exercise regularly; but avoid strenuous exercise for four hours before bedtime.
- Avoid tea/caffeine, smoking, alcohol in the evening and at night.
- Develop relaxing routine before bedtime.

Many elderly take sleeping pills without consulting their physician. Improper use of such pills further increases sleep problems.

Pain

Pain plays an important role in the psychological life of elders. This is all the more important because they often suffer from painful chronic conditions such as arthritis, fractures, neuralgia, neuropathy, etc.

Uma Shah, sixty-six, told me, "Of late, I am very irritable." On questioning she reported constant pain due to arthritis of knee that also curtailed her favourite pastime of walking. She was prescribed medicines by her orthopaedic surgeon but didn't take them as she was worried about side effects. Counselling, adequate pain medication in consultation with the orthopedic surgeon and alternative exercises helped her bounce back.

Pain, like depression, is an under-treated condition. This is further exacerbated by a culture of resistance to pain medication, often due to exaggerated fear about the side effects of pain medication.

Spirituality and meditation

Spirituality helps in achieving a sense of purpose and a sense of well being for many elderly. It is an inner dimension of life that goes beyond the mundane material pleasures or desires and involves positive ethical values, aspirations and actions that create peace and harmony in the society. Meditation helps in living a balanced and contented life.

Religious faith may lead to a healthier lifestyle and a more cohesive family life. Membership of a religious group is often important for the elderly.

Therefore, the elderly should be given an opportunity to involve themselves in spiritual or religious activities of their choice. Often due to their physical problems, they are unable to participate in activities of their religious group. This leads to a feeling of alienation. Family members and physicians should keep this in mind.

Retirement homes, nursing homes and assisted living facilities

Many elderly require help in day to day activities due to their health problems and disabilities.

The elderly find themselves isolated. In spite of their best intentions, family members are often not able to look after senior citizens who are no longer able to live independently. Though caring for older adults in the community gives better results, there is a role for retirement homes, nursing homes and assisted living facilities. Such facilities will increase in India in coming decades:

- Retirement homes for those who are able to live independently.
- Assisted living facility combines independent living with nursing help. No special medical monitoring equipment or specialized nursing staff is present. But trained staff provides

various services such as managing medication, help in dressing, cooking, getting in and out of bed or chair etc.

- Nursing homes provide more specialised help.

Some elderly get depressed when they are transferred to a long-term care facility. However, if it is planned beforehand, it can be a welcome change for the elderly as they get help in basic activities of daily living and it also offers them an opportunity for socialisation.

Lastly, it is important to note that the fatalistic attitude of our society to mental health issues of old age deprives elders of the care they deserve. Even when cure is not possible, early detection and intervention for psychiatric problems of the elderly leads to significant reduction in suffering and improvement in quality of life.

Old age alone does not produce mental illness.

~ Dr. Felix Post (a pioneer in old age psychiatry)

C. ALTERNATE THERAPIES FOR FITNESS AND GOOD HEALTH

~ Dr. Arundhati Govind Hoskeri

(Dr. Hoskeri is an educationist and a freelance journalist contributing to leading newspapers and journals. She is a soft skills trainer, with stress management being her forte. She conducts workshops for corporate and private groups. She has published a book of poems titled Mindscapes. Her interests include reading, writing short stories, poetry, painting, dramatics, astrology, yoga, homeopathy, naturopathy, and alternative medicine.)

Introduction

Modern scientific age with its innovations and research in the field of medicine has no doubt increased human longevity and made our life comfortable with everything available at our fingertips but at the same time, too much dependency on the machines without any physical strain has also created health hazards. The so-called lifestyle diseases like hypertension (high blood pressure), diabetes, and heart attacks have started targeting the younger generation.

Everybody is chasing something or the other in life! Too much stress at the work place, junk food, irregular eating habits, smoking, alcohol, drugs, lesser number of sleeping hours, and mechanical and sedentary life are taking a heavy toll on health. This has lead to people taking Allopathic medication that acts faster, fixes the problem quickly but not always without side effects. With modification in lifestyle and by practising age old Indian wisdom of alternative medicine or alternative therapy, we can lead a healthier and happier life.

I. Health Management Using Home Remedies

For minor health problems, our kitchen is an excellent store house of medicine. All the consumable food ingredients have a lot of curative property, which when taken helps to cure the ailments without any harmful effect on the human system. Some very effective remedies which are tested and have given best results will be discussed. Readers can apply and follow these remedies for ailments like hypertension, diabetes, rheumatoid arthritis and heart conditions or any other such illness that has dependency on prescribed medication. These natural remedies are effective and harmless, but do not try to stop or alter your medication without consulting your physician. The following are some common ailments in the elderly:

ACIDITY/ACID PEPTIC CONDITION (APD)

When pungent, hot and spicy food is consumed or when sour food is consumed, there is a burning sensation in the stomach, which can lead to ulcers of the digestive tract (usually stomach and intestines). This condition is called acidity.

Precaution: It is better to habituate yourself to sober food with less oil, less salt and less spices, which is recommended in Ayurveda and known as *satvik ahara*. Avoid chillies in any form, green/red/powdered. It is better to divide your meal into short meals, eat something every two hours, rather than eating two heavy meals in a day. Chew your food properly.

The gastric glands in the stomach produce hydrochloric acid which is necessary for digestion of food. When this acid is produced more than necessary, it leads to acidity. This is also known as Acid Peptic Disease (APD).

Symptoms

- Discomfort and burning sensation in the stomach.
- Heart burn, burps, nausea
- Sour belching

Causes

- Acidity occurs due to stress and mental tension.
- Irregular eating habits, improper chewing, poor digesting capacity.

- Consuming hot, spicy pungent food.
- Improper digestion and malfunctioning of digestive organs
- Smoking and alcohol consumption.

Remedies

1) Sipping two spoons of cold milk very slowly, every hour, gives good results.

2) After meals keep a small piece of jaggery in your mouth and suck on it gently.

3) Boil two glasses of water with two tea spoons of aniseed (*saunf*). Cover and leave it overnight, strain, add one spoon honey and drink in the morning.

4) Avoid foods such as pickles, vinegar, fried foods, hot spicy foods, chocolate, pastries, and raw salad vegetables like onion, radish, cabbage, chilli and peppers.

5) Sucking a piece of clove after meals relieves acidity.

6) Eating a banana daily after dinner reduces acidity and heartburn.

7) Drink tender coconut water in the morning; it helps to reduce acidity.

8) Eating alkaline fruits like watermelon and cucumber also relieves acidity.

9) Do not skip meals. Do not keep large gaps between meals. This produces gas.

10) Eat dinner 2-3 hours before going to bed.

PEPTIC ULCER

Peptic ulcer refers to eruptions/erosions on the inner lining of the stomach and the duodenum (first part of the intestine). When ulcers are located in stomach they are called gastric ulcers and those related to digestion are called peptic ulcers .When they are located in Duodenum they are called duodenal ulcers. The home remedies suggested here are good enough for all the three types. If the ulcers are in advanced stage, please consult the doctor.

Symptoms

- Classic symptom of duodenal ulcer is pain appearing when the stomach is empty usually between meals. This pain is relieved after eating something or taking cold milk.
- Gastric ulcer pain occurs usually an hour after meals and it may not occur at night.
- Peptic ulcer causes severe pain in the upper abdomen.
- When the disease progresses, symptoms like insomnia, stress, weakness and lot of flatulence may be experienced.
- In severe cases blood is detected in the stool.

Causes

- Emotional disturbances, stress and nervous tension.
- Food poisoning or certain type of infections.
- Hyper acidity and long term consumption of hot and spicy food.
- Chronic alcoholism

Home Remedies

1. Consuming lime juice in diluted form thrice a day.
2. Boil 100 gm cabbage in 250 ml water, reduce the quantity to half, and let it cool. Strain and drink this twice a day
3. Eating banana at least three to four times a day is an excellent remedy; it provides a soothing effect as well as nutrition.
4. Soak two teaspoons of fenugreek seeds (*methi*) in two glasses of water for some time and then boil it. Cool the solution and add little milk (optional) and drink it along with the seeds. This gives a kind of mucilaginous coating to the intestines and helps in healing.
5. Regularity in diet, exercise, sleep and staying relaxed are very important.

ARTHRITIS/RHEUMATISM

Arthritis is derived from Greek word *arthron* meaning joint and *itis* meaning inflammation.

Arthritis is a disease, causing painful inflammation (swelling) and stiffness of the joints. It generally occurs as a chronic condition, persisting for a long time worsening gradually with time. It occurs in different forms, the most common being, rheumatoid arthritis and osteoarthritis.

Rheumatoid arthritis (RA) is an autoimmune disease causing chronic inflammation of the joints and the surrounding tissue, also affecting other organs in severe cases. It affects the joints in fingers, wrists, elbow, toes, feet, ankle, knee, hip joint and so on.

Autoimmune disease is an illness that occurs when the body tissues are attacked by their own immune system, by mistake. Our immune system is a beautifully designed complex organisation of cells and antibodies meant to seek and destroy the attacking enemies or invaders in general and infections in particular. Unfortunately when an autoimmune disease strikes the antibodies in the blood which are supposed to guard the body, inadvertently target and attack the body tissues of the patient, causing inflammation. Rheumatoid arthritis is also called a systemic illness as it affects the different organs of the body in severe cases. RA is a chronic, progressive illness likely to cause joint destruction and functional disability. The exact cause of rheumatoid arthritis is unknown. Even though infectious agents such as viruses, bacteria, and fungi have long been suspected, none have been proven to be the cause. Smoking is said to increase the risk of the disease.

Symptoms

- Lack of energy, fatigue, low grade fever, pain and swelling in the joints (Redness in severe condition)
- Inflammation of multiple joints in a symmetrical pattern (both sides of the body are affected).
- Swelling in the small joints of both the hands and

wrists.

- Difficulty with simple tasks of daily living, such as turning door knobs and opening the lids of jars etc
- The small joints of the feet can lead to painful walking, especially in the morning after waking up.
- Pain and stiffness in the joints usually increases after physical exercise/exertion.

Causes

- Osteoarthritis is a degenerative joint disease associated with old age.
- It results from structural changes in the particular cartilage in the joints, usually those which are weight bearing such as spine and knees.
- The possible causes are constant physical stress, obesity and calcium deficiency

Home Remedies

1. Grate a raw potato and extract its juice, consume two teaspoons of this before meals. This helps in eliminating toxic matters from body and gives relief from joint pains.
2. Lemons are beneficial in the treatment of rheumatism. The patient should take the juice of two or three lemons each day diluted with warm water and a pinch of rock salt (*saindhav lavan*).
3. Applying heat packs on affected area gives instant relief from pain.
4. Avoid meat, eggs, fat-rich food, sour food, aerated drinks, all purpose flour (*maida*) and bakery items. Eat lot of fresh fruits, raw and boiled vegetables.
5. A cup of bitter gourd (*karela*) juice extracted freshly mixed with two teaspoons of honey, can be taken every day first thing in the morning for 3 months.
6. Eat a few cloves of garlic fried in butter daily.
7. A glass of raw carrot juice daily is helpful.
8. Eating a banana daily is also good for joint pains.

BACKACHE

Backache is a common problem faced by all, especially the elderly. The pain may be concentrated either in the lower part or upper part of the back.

Symptoms

- Pain in the back while bending, squatting down.
- Pain while lifting weight, while stretching hand.
- Constant pain in severe cases.

Causes

- Degeneration of tissues, obesity and poor posture.
- When the skeletal system is burdened with more body weight than it can hold, result is back ache.
- Injury to back/spine due to accident or fall.

Home Remedies

1. Take some lemon juice, dilute it with warm water and add a pinch of salt. Have this solution before lunch and dinner for at least a month. It provides relief.
2. A good body massage, followed by hot water bath improves the blood circulation and relieves pain.
3. Overweight individuals have to lose weight, take some moderate to light exercise and maintain good posture.
4. Boil 5 grams of fenugreek (*methi*) seeds along with five dates in water, cool and drink that water and later eat the boiled fenugreek seeds (*methi*) and dates. It cures lower back pain.

INSOMNIA

Insomnia or sleeplessness is a disorder when an individual is unable to get sound sleep, has a very disturbed sleep pattern and as a result he/she does not feel fresh in the morning. Instead of taking sleeping pills you may try out the following remedies and lead a relaxed life by de-stressing yourself.

Causes:

- Over physical or mental exertion

- Chronic health conditions
- Worry, stress and personal setbacks or losses

Home Remedies

1. Eating raw white onion with dinner helps induce good sleep without any side effects.
2. Consuming plenty of curds or buttermilk is a good remedy.
3. Take two teaspoons of juice of fenugreek (*methi*) leaves mixed with one teaspoon honey every day before going to bed for at least two months. This helps regularise your sleep pattern.
4. Massage the feet and soles with warm coconut oil before going to bed (do not forget to wear old socks).
5. Lightly massaging the scalp with fingertips, with or without oil, induces sleep.
6. Have early dinner and drink a glass of warm milk with a pinch of turmeric and a teaspoon of honey before going to bed

KNEE PAIN

The knee joint takes most of the weight of the upper body, during any kind of movement like walking, running and jumping. Pain in the knee could be very annoying as well as troublesome while walking, bending and squatting.

Causes

- Swelling or tear in the ligaments (ligaments are short bands of connective tissue that connects two bones or cartilages and hold a joint together).
- Any injury to knee due to fall or accident.
- Too much of strain on knee joint (eg. athlete's knee) can also lead to painful condition.

Home Remedies

1. **Ice:** This is a common remedy used to alleviate pain and swelling in most instances. Ice can be very effective in relieving pain, soothing the inflammation and reducing the swelling in the knee. For best results, you need to place a huge ice pack

on your knee in a manner such that the entire knee is covered. However never apply ice to a particular spot for more than 10 minutes, as it could damage the skin and the nerves in that area. Do not apply ice directly on the skin. Put the cubes in a plastic bag, then wrap this bag in a thin cotton cloth/towel and apply on the affected area.

2. Steam: Heat therapy is as effective in dealing with pain, as cold therapy is. Therefore, you could go in for a steam bath so that your knee soaks up the warmth from the steam, which is excellent for alleviating the pain. Or take a towel (not a turkish towel), dip it in boiling water, wring it and apply it on affected part—it supplies the necessary steam. Alternately, you could apply a hot water bag on your knee too.

3. Massage Therapy: This technique is very effective in soothing aches and pains all over the body. Gently massage your knee area with medicated oil two or three times a day. Make sure that the massage lasts for at least 5 to 10 minutes at each time.

4. Elevation: You could reduce the swelling in your knee by keeping it raised. Prop your affected leg on a couple of pillows, or sit on a recliner chair, which allows you to keep your legs elevated.

5. Diet: In your diet include, oranges as they are high in vitamin C, apples, onions, red grapes and leafy greens-especially spinach, Soybean and other Soy products, ginger, garlic which are helpful when you suffer from Knee pain.

COMMON COLD, COUGH AND INFLUENZA (FLU)

Common cold, as the name itself suggests, is very common among all age groups. It is a viral infection that affects the upper respiratory tract. It takes generally from a week to ten days and sometimes even three weeks for cold to subside, depending on the severity of infection and type of virus that has caused it.

Symptoms

- Sneezing, runny nose, sore throat.
- Mild to severe head ache and fever.

Causes

- The virus is transmitted through infected air (air borne disease).
- Physical contact with a person suffering from cold.
- Poor hygiene and low immunity.

Home Remedies

1. To clear a blocked nose, inhale steam from boiling water to which a teaspoon of common salt is added. Do this every two hours for relief. As far as possible do not add any medicinal drops to the water. Do not take a steam bath as there is a risk of overheating your body.
2. Take plenty of rest as cold makes you feel tired.
3. Wash your face and hands as often as possible with germicidal soap to avoid re-infection.
4. Drink a glass of warm milk with a pinch of turmeric powder to control throat infection.
5. Salt water gargling provides relief from sore throat. Salt in the water draws out mucous and reduces the swelling. You may add a tea spoon of honey to salt water for extra soothing effect.
6. A glass of warm water with one teaspoon of honey and two teaspoons of lemon juice boosts immunity.
7. Take 3-4 cloves of garlic, burn them lightly on flame, peel the burnt skin and chew and eat them. This gives quick relief from cough.
8. Add a tea spoon each of cumin (jeera), coriander (dhania) and fennel (*saunf*) seeds in half litre of water and boil. Drink this decoction (warm) to get relief from body pain.
9. Add a fistful of common salt and neem leaves to (hot) bathing water to get relief from body pain.

CONSTIPATION

Constipation is a kind of disturbance in the digestive tract due to which bowel movements (stools) become irregular or they are not removed completely. Constipation produces toxins in the body and affects vital organs leading to various diseases.

Symptoms

- Difficulty in passing stools
- Painful and hard bowel movements
- Irregularity in motion cycles
- Coated tongue, ulcers in mouth, bad breath, loss of appetite, dizziness, and nausea

Home Remedies

1. Eating one pear a day after dinner helps.
2. Guava is another effective remedy for constipation. When eaten with seeds, it provides roughage to the diet and helps in the normal cycle of the bowels. One or two guavas should be consumed every day.
3. Bael fruit is an excellent laxative. Eating one bael fruit regularly before dinner, for two to three months helps cure constipation.
4. Orange is also beneficial in the treatment of constipation. Eating one or two oranges before bedtime and again after waking up is an excellent way of stimulating the bowels. The general stimulating influence of orange causes peristaltic activity and helps prevent the accumulation of food residue in the colon.
5. Eat four to five fresh figs or dry figs soaked in water for few hours. This acts as an excellent laxative.
6. Eating ripe papaya daily during the day helps to relieve constipation

INDIGESTION

Indigestion is a common condition often associated with psychological upset and stress. It may sometimes signal problems connected with ulcers or swelling on intestines.

Symptoms

- Abdominal bloating, flatulence.
- Nausea, vomiting.
- Heart burn.

Causes

- Over eating, eating in a hurry without proper chewing
- Eating rich fat food or very spicy food.
- Eating under stressful conditions.

Home Remedies

1. A glass of pineapple juice after every meal helps digestion.
2. Take a glass of warm water and squeeze a lemon in it and drink it before meals. Lemon juice fights against bacteria and helps the condition.
3. Eating plenty of fresh grapes and oranges is good for digestion.
4. Applying cold compression/ice bag over the stomach for 20 to 30 minutes after meals gives good results.
5. Chewing a small piece of fresh ginger with salt, six to twelve minutes before meals, stimulates digestion.

DIABETES

Diabetes Mellitus is a metabolic disease in which a person has high blood sugar either because the body does not produce enough insulin or because cells do not respond to the insulin that is produced. Insulin is a hormone secreted by pancreas that helps in absorption of sugar by the body cells.

The most common types of diabetes are:

- Type 1 Diabetes: when the body fails to produce insulin and the patient needs to inject insulin.
- Type 2 Diabetes: results from insulin resistance a condition in which cells fail to use insulin properly.

Symptoms

- Polyphagia or increased hunger
- Polyuria or increased urination
- Polydipsia or increased thirst
- Fatigue

Causes

- Type 1 Diabetes is partly inherited and then triggered by certain infections.
- Type 2 Diabetes is due to faulty and stressful lifestyle and genetic factors.

Home Remedies

The following home remedies are safe but if you are under allopathic medication, **please do not stop** it without consulting your diabetologist. You may try the remedies along with your medication and gradually try to reduce the dosage as per medical advice.

a) Bitter gourd (*karela*) is a well known remedy for diabetes. Eat this vegetable as often as you can. Consuming one table spoon of fresh bitter gourd juice is very helpful to reduce sugar in blood and urine.

b) Soak two table spoons of fenugreek seeds (*methi*) over night. Eat them first thing in the morning and drink the water in which they are soaked. Then do not take anything for the next one hour. Do this for 3 months to notice improvement in sugar levels. Fenugreek seeds contain the alkaloid Trogonelline, nicotinic acid and Coumarin. This remedy helps in managing Triglyceride and Cholesterol levels.

c) Eating a medium sized raw white onion and three cloves of raw garlic daily helps the condition.

d) Avoid white sugar, sweets, chocolates, soft drinks, alcohol, and bakery products totally. Reduce the intake of rice.

e) Another popular folk remedy is to eat four to five leaves of white Vinca Rosea plant popularly known as *sadafuli*, daily along with some basil leaves.

f) Jamun fruit is very good for controlling diabetes. The seeds can be dried, powdered and stored (or this powder is easily available in ayurvedic stores, if you have no patience to make at home). One tea spoon of this powder mixed with either water or milk or curds can be taken daily to control diabetes.

g) Leading a relaxed and disciplined life is very important and daily exercise or walking for at least an hour daily will help control diabetes.

II. Health Management Using Psychological (Mind Control) Techniques

a. Therapeutic touch and Reiki healing

Therapeutic touch and Reiki healing are thought to help activate the self-healing processes of an individual and help in curing certain physical and mental ailments. These "energy-based" techniques do not require actual physical contact but they work better when there is a close physical proximity between the practitioner and the patient.

Dr. Mikao Usui is the founder of Reiki system of natural healing. Reiki is derived by two Japanese words, "*Rei*" which means "God's Wisdom or the Higher Power" and "*Ki*" which is "life force energy". So Reiki is actually "spiritually guided life force energy".

Reiki

Reiki is considered as a holistic treatment of mind, body and spirit. It relaxes the body and mind leading to emotional stability and induces a feeling of security. Natural method of Reiki is safe and simple, without any internal or external medication. Reiki is considered as an effective treatment for almost all mental as well as physical maladies and alleviates the pain in cancer and other terminally ill patients.

Reiki and Pranic healing, which works on the same principle, can easily be learnt by all, under the guidance of a Reiki Master. Please note that self learning through books or recorded tapes is not advisable.

b. Meditation

Deep breathing and meditation helps body to relax, and eases pain by releasing tension and tightness from muscles. Although there are many ways to meditate, the soothing power of repetition is at the heart of some forms of meditation. Focussing on the breath, ignoring thoughts, and repeating a word or phrase relaxes the mind and body. It is not a religious practice.

Repetitive sound has a soothing effect on mind; it can be any word you choose. Sit comfortable with eyes closed and repeat a word continuously and quickly without stopping so that your mind does not wander. If you don't like chanting then you can choose a quiet type of meditation.

One can choose a quiet place without any disturbance and harsh light, close the eyes to avoid distraction and just sit erect or lie down comfortably and focus on one's breathing and try to avoid thoughts. Initially lots of thoughts disturb the mind; let them just pass off, don't try to curb them but at the same time don't pick up one thought and start weaving around further.

By daily practice one will be able to concentrate better. Meditation strengthens our discriminating power and lets us weed out poisonous fodder that we keep feeding our mind. Life becomes more peaceful then.

III. Chinese Wisdom

a. Acupuncture

Acupuncture originated in China and is one of the oldest healing therapies in the world. Various sensitive points on the meridians of human body are identified for stimulating them by gently piercing the skin with very fine needles using different techniques. Earlier it was done only manually but nowadays electric stimulation method is also used. When needles are applied with a proper technique of controlled pressure on the identified points, endorphins (a group of hormones released in the body that help in controlling pain) are released and pain is blocked.

Acupuncture is good for getting relief from any kind of pain such as headache, lower backache, menstrual cramps, Carpal Tunnel syndrome, Tennis Elbow, Fibromyalgia, Osteoarthritis etc.

Note: One must consult a qualified doctor who has also learnt the science of acupuncture, or else it may cause nerve damage and lead to complications.

b. Acupressure

It is science of balancing the body's energy by applying pressure to specific points along the energy channels. The points are located in the palms, feet and all over the body. Acupuncture and Acupressure use the same pressure points and meridians, but Acupuncture employs needles, while Acupressure uses gentle to firm finger pressure.

When certain points are stimulated, they release muscular tension, promote circulation of blood, and enhance the body's life force energy to aid healing. Acupressure is used to relieve pain, detoxify the body and tone muscles. When pressure is applied to the points in the palm, either using fingers or a blunt back of a pencil, it helps in regulating the system. For example, for getting relief from sinus headache and cold, all the five finger tips should be pressed three times a day for about 5 minutes. To get relief from backache, pressure needs to be applied on a point located at the angle of thumb and fore finger. There are many books and charts available on Acupressure. One can refer to the specific points according to their health problem and apply pressure. This has no side effects at all.

IV. Healing by Balancing the Chakras or Energy Centres in the Human Body

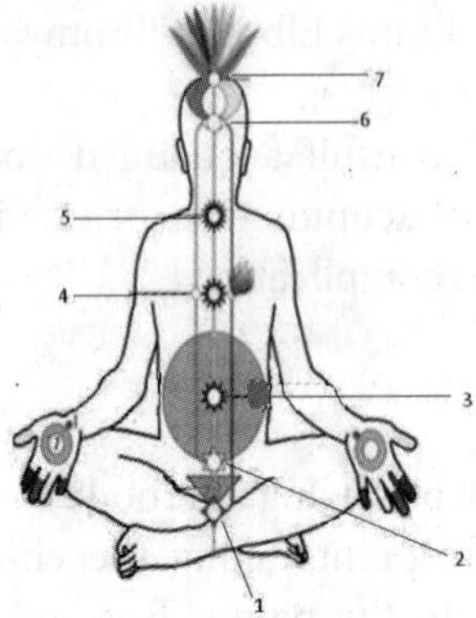

Key:
1. Mooladhar Chakra
2. Swadhisthan Chakra
3. Manipura (Nabhi) Chakra
4. Anahat ChakraVishuddhi Chakra
5. Vishuddhi Chakra
6. Agya Chakra
7. Sahasrar Chakra

Chakras are subtle energy centres placed along the Sushumna Nadi nerve, a subtle body channel in the spinal column. Each of them is represented as a lotus with specific number of petals. There are seven major Chakras in the human body directly connected with higher centres of the brain. The brain monitors, coordinates, regulates and controls the functions of the body through nerves.

The seven main Chakras are:

***1. Mooladhara* Chakra or Root Chakra**: It is situated at the base of the spinal column, below the tail bone (Coccyx). This is the seat of *Kundalini* the great dynamic energy, which lies dormant in a coiled form (snake like). The function of this chakra is to provide energy, support and balance the body. This is connected with creativity.

***2. Swadhisthan* Chakra**: It is situated two fingers above the

Mooladhara, this chakra is concerned with elimination of waste materials as well as reproductive activity.

3. *Manipura* Chakra or *Nabhi* Chakra: It is located at the navel and corresponds to the solar plexus. It controls the process of digestion of food, assimilation of food and maintains the body temperature.

4. *Anahata* Chakra or Heart Chakra: It is found behind the base of the heart. It controls the functions of the heart and the lungs. It promotes the virtues like truth, non-violence, love, compassion and forgiveness.

5. *Vishuddhi* Chakra or Throat Chakra: It is situated at the level of throat pit and controls the thyroid gland, vocal cords and discriminates the knowledge of the external world.

6. *Agya* Chakra or Brow Chakra: It is situated in between the eyebrows and corresponds to the pituitary gland and pineal glands in the brain. This acts as the command centre and has control over all the functions of human life.

7. *Sahasrara* Chakra or Crown Chakra: It is represented by a lotus having 1000 petals as the name suggests. It is believed to be situated at the very top of the head which is the culmination of *Kundalini* power, the seat of higher awareness and is physically connected with pituitary gland and the life system. This is the crown of expanded awareness.

Apart from above seven important chakras there is another major chakra called *Bindu* chakra, located at the back of the head where Brahmins grow a tuft of hair. This is considered a centre of Nectar (*Amrit*). This nectar secreted by *Bindu* chakra spreads throughout the body through *Vishuddhi* chakra making the body radiant and provides the energy for procreation.

Interestingly most of the Hindu rituals are scientific and some of them help in activating the energy centres or chakras, for instance women applying vermillion (*Kumkum*) on forehead in between the eye brows and men applying Tilak (red mark) activates the *Agya* chakra. Men and women pulling up and tying up the hair/tuft activates *Bindu* chakra.

a. Crystal Healing

Crystal Therapy is the ancient art of laying of gems, stones and crystals on the body over the chakras (energy centres).

Each chakra resonates to a particular colour, so by laying a stone of that colour over the chakra, the chakras open, align and blend with one another. When the chakra system is balanced, the physical body is able to innately self-correct and heal. This is practised by Reiki masters and spiritual healers. This is a harmless practice and has no side effects.

Crystal healing helps in relieving stress, sleeplessness and depression. Again this is an excellent therapy for the elderly as it involves neither internal medication nor any kind of invasive procedure.

b. Cosmic Ray Therapy

Cosmic Ray therapy is a method of rectifying the shortage of a certain colour radiated by planets, causing effects on living beings. This treatment is closely linked with astrology. Depending on the position of the planets in an individual's birth chart (horoscope) the gems are selected and used.

For example:

For curing general headache, Amethyst is used.

Coral water is used for headaches induced by anger. A piece of coral is left in a glass of water over night and that water is consumed the next day morning. As the age advances, the level of tolerance decreases and irritability increases. This simple treatment can help the elderly to control their temper to a reasonable extent.

For getting relief from cancer pain: Amethyst and Cat's eye are worn either in a ring or a locket letting the stone touch the skin.

The stones are also set against electric lights to emit rays on the body of the patient.

V. Healing Through Music Therapy

Music has the power to soothe, inspire, energise, uplift, and heal. Research shows it can also help in chronic pain management, cures depression and insomnia. Music has been used in medicine for thousands of years, but emerged as a formal means of care in the USA in the 1940s, after doctors learned that music helped restore World War II soldiers who were suffering from shell shock. Listening to music provides sensory stimulation that evokes a response in the patient and has a therapeutic effect on mind and body. Research has found that music when used as a clinical intervention can help patients by reducing the amount of pain they perceive. Promoting relaxation, rhythmic breathing, rest, alleviating anxiety and stress in patients, music gives their mood a positive boost. In chronic pain management, therapists often use music therapy as a means of conditioning the patient to relax and release pain and stress. Soothing music is paired with relaxation techniques, and eventually the patient learns to relax automatically when listening to music.

a. Western Music therapy

In general Western music therapy techniques seem to fall into categories of using sympathetic vibrations and/or harmonics to achieve desired mental states of activity or to use the emotional responses of music in the mind as a form of therapy or to explore the relationship of the ear, brain, and mind. The therapy uses more of instrumental music with soft vocal rendering. This is not yet popular in India. The practitioners need to be well trained in classical Western music, vocal and instrumental and also have a medical background. It soothes the mind, cures sleeplessness and helps in relieving stress.

b. Indian Music Therapy

Indian music had its origins in the Vedas (4,000 BC to 1,000 BC). Indian Music has a very highly developed melodic and rhythmic structure with complicated poly-rhythms, delicate nuances, ornamentations, and microtones. *Samaveda* explains seven notes of music, that later culminated in "*Karaharipriya Raga*".

The seven chakras of the human body vibrate and activate with a particular raga as shown below.

Chakra	*Raga*
Muladhara	*Vaghadisvari, Shyam kalian*
Swadhisthana	*Kanakanji , Yaman*
Manipura	*Vachaspati, Abogi*
Anahata	*Curukesi , Durga, Bhairav*
Vishuddhi	*Jaijayawanti, Dwijavanti*
Ajna	*Kamavardhini, Bhoopali, Bhoop, bageshwari*
Sahasrar	*Darabari Kanada, Jhinjoti Bihag*

Hearing is physical and listening is psychological. Both are vital to our communication skills, establishing good relationship, socialising with everyone and learning intuitiveness. Out of the 12 cranial nerves, 10 are linked to the ear, indicating the importance of the musical sounds to our nervous system. The sound we utter and hear creates vibrations in the body that affects our nervous system. Right syllable/sound uttered has a protective as well as curative effect on the body. This concept explains the chanting of *mantras* (Vedic hymns) used not just as a protective shield but also to cure physical as well as mental ailments by ancient Indians.

In India, on the outskirts of Mysore, in Karnataka, there is Ragragini Chikista Kendra established by Sri Ganapaty Sachhidanand Swamiji, who has identified ragas for treatment of diseases and has composed the music accordingly. For example, *Raga Bageshri* arouses a feeling of darkness, stability, depth and calmness. This raga is also used in treatment of diabetes and hypertension. His compositions are in Carnatic music.

Some of the Ragas and their effects have been stated below:

Raga	Effects
Raga Bageshri, Ganamurte, Bhupali, Todi and Ahir-Bhairav (Chakravakam)	Reduces Hypertension and Diabetes
Raga Bhupali/Mohana	Provides relief from Migraine
Raga Todi	Helps reduce cold and headache
Raga Natabhairavi	Cures headache due depression
Raag Ananda Bhairavi	Suppresses stomach pain
Raga Hemavati, Rohini	Helps relieve back pain and joint pain
Raga Madhyamavati	Relieves pain in legs and hands
Raga Hemavati, Rohini	Helps relieve back pain and joint pain
Raga Darbari Kanada	Helps reduce asthama
Raga Neelambari	Helps with insomnia
Raga Brindavani Sarang	Helps in recovering from depression

VI. Health Management Using Yogic Techniques

The word "Yoga" finds its root in "*yuji*" in Sanskrit, which means to unite or combine. Through various techniques using mind, body, and breath yoga brings about the union of human consciousness with divine consciousness.

Maharshi Patanjali is considered as the father of yogic science. He compiled, collected and de-codified the principles of yoga and wrote a treatise around 300 BC which is popularly known as *Patanjali Yogasutras*. These aphorisms are an integrated system as they address to both gross and subtle body on physical, mental, emotional and intellectual levels. They can be practised by anybody irrespective of age, sex or religion.

The science of Yoga and Yogasanas is very vast. Here a few important sections of practical utility are explained.

A. *Mudra* Therapy

Mudras are hand gestures, using specific fingers, to activate the nerve centres and get rid of disease. *Mudra* therapy is gaining popularity as it is harmless, requiring no supervision, and can be practised by anybody at any age. In fact some of the *mudras* are included in "*Sandhyavandan*", a daily ritual supposed to be practised by Brahmins along with breathing exercises. The science of *mudra* is a part of yoga and is based on the five fundamental elements of life namely: Ether/Space (*Aakash Tatva*), Air (*Vayu Tatva*), Fire (*Agni Tatva*), Water (*Jala Tatva*), Earth (*Prithvi Tatva*) and five *Pranas—Prana, Udanan, Samana, Apana* and *Vyana*. It also connects with three *doshas* mentioned in *Ayurveda: Vata, Pitta* and *Kapha. Hatha Yoga Pradeepika* and other tantrik texts consider *mudra* to be a part of yoga (Yoganga). "*Kularnava Tantra*" traces the word *mudra* to "*Mud*" meaning joy or happiness and "*Dravya*" meaning to draw forth. The basic meaning of *mudra* is thus to draw forth the divine bliss latent in all of us which is called *Satchitananda*.

Mudras are practised as gestures by fingers, hand positions and also with yogasanas, bandhas and breathing techniques (*Pranayama*), and eye techniques (*Trataka*) to create and maintain equilibrium in the body elements to lead a healthy, happy life. While performing yogic exercises (yogasanas) senses are primary and the life force (*Prana*) is secondary; while practicing *mudras*, life force (*Prana*) is primary and senses are secondary. *Mudras* have been a part of Indian culture for thousands of years and are incorporated in Indian dance, worship and daily Vedic rituals. Some of the useful *hasta mudras* (hand gestures) that are easy to follow are explained below:

Finger	Element (*Tatva*)
Thumb	Fire (*Agni*)
Index Finger	Wind (*Vayu*)
Middle Finger	Space (*Aakash*)
Ring Finger	Earth (*Prithvi*)
Little Finger	Water (*Jala*)

Hasta mudras are formed with fingers of each hand and each finger represents a particular natural element. "*Agnid bhutaanaam adhipatih*" proclaims Jayadi Homa mantras, meaning: *Agni* or Fire is supreme among all the five elements and it controls all the remaining four elements. Fire is represented by the thumb which is most important among all the five fingers of the hand. It supports the remaining fingers to function as we desire. It is responsible for balancing, increasing or decreasing the other elements while performing the *mudras*.

General rules:

• Touching the tip of the thumb and tip of the finger balances the element represented by that finger.

• Touching the finger tip at the base of the thumb decreases the element represented by that finger.

• One should not apply too much of pressure or tense fingers while performing *mudras*. A tender, light touch is all that is required.

• *Mudras* can be practised any where any time, while travelling, while watching a television or while relaxing.

• Therapeutic *mudras* have specific time durations and cycles, the time can be split into smaller durations. For instance, if a *mudra* needs to be practised for 45 minutes and one is not able to do it at a stretch, one can do it three times, 15 minutes each time. The benefit will be the same.

1. Varun Mudra **:**

Almost 70 per cent of human body is water. *Varun mudra* keeps water balance in the body, affects the water metabolism, and rehydrates cells, tissues, muscles, joints, cartilages and skin. *Varun* means water, so this *mudra* helps in curing the diseases caused due to water imbalance in the body.

Method: Bring the little finger and thumb together, gently touch without applying any pressure and keep the remaining fingers straight. Practice this 3 times a day, each time for 25 minutes, using both hands.

Benefits: It relieves the pains of gastroenteritis, menstrual Cramps, dysentery, vomiting, dryness of eyes, dry cough, osteoarthritis, sun stroke, loss of taste and inadequate urination.

2. Vayu Mudra :

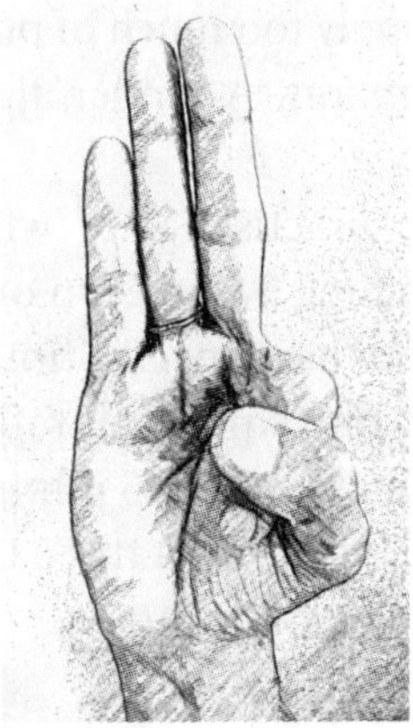

Vayu means air; this *mudra* helps cure ailments caused due to imbalance of air in the human body. This has to be practised for 45 minutes every day for two months to get best results, but the positive results will be noticed within 10 days of regular practice. It removes excess air in the body, improves blood circulation and relieves body pain.

Method: Place the tip of index finger at the base of the thumb and place the thumb on the back of the index finger gently. Keep other fingers straight.

Benefits: *Vayu mudra* helps to cure, rheumatism, arthritis, gout, Parkinson's disease and paralysis. It is useful for cervical spondylosis, paralysis to face and a catch in the neck, tension headache, and muscle sprain. It also corrects the disorder of

headache, and muscle sprain. It also corrects the disorder of gas in the stomach. Convulsions can be cured by a regular practice of *Vayu mudra* daily for 15 minutes.

3. *Shunya Mudra*

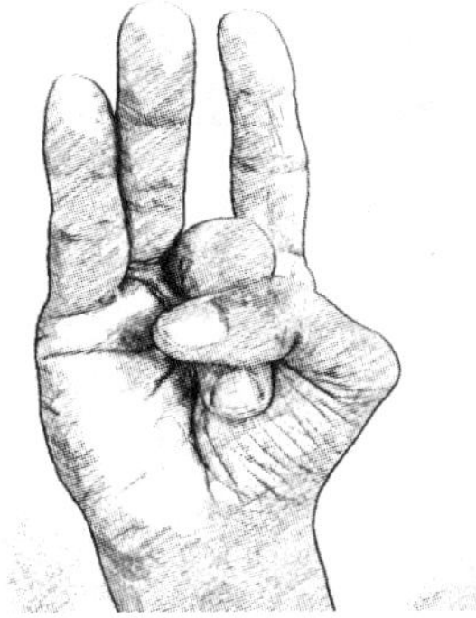

Middle finger represents space or *Aakash tatva* or ether. The disturbance due to excess ether elements causes the diseases like ear problems, vertigo and cardiac weakness. *Shunya mudra* controls and reduces ether element.

Method: Bend the middle finger and press it gently with thumb.

Benefits: It helps in curing partial deafness by increasing hearing capacity, ear ache, sleeplessness and vertigo. This *mudra* helps control an earache in around 5 to 7 minutes.

4. *Surya Mudra*

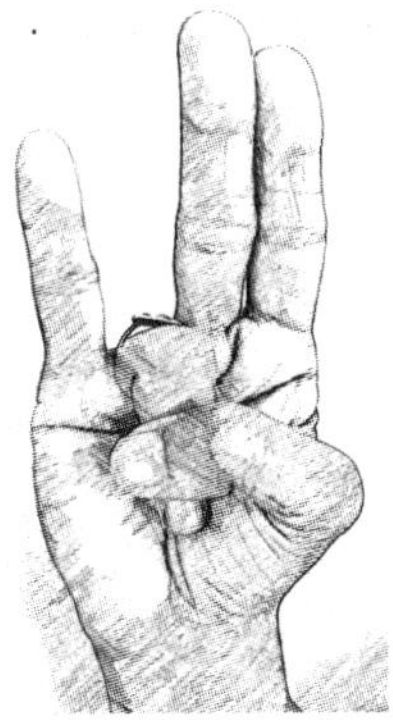

Surya means sun and thus this *mudra* is supposed to generate heat in the body by activating fire element. This *mudra* helps sharpen the centre of the thyroid gland. It should be practised daily twice daily for 5 to 15 minutes.

Method: Bend the ring finger and press it gently with thumb.

Benefits: It helps reduces cholesterol in body, corrects indigestion problems, reduces anxiety, and helps in reducing weight.

5. Pran Mudra (Mudra of Life)

This has a reference to oxygen or pran vayu which is breath itself. As it is the mudra of life, it improves the power of life. Weak people become strong. It reduces the clamps in blood vessels. If we practice it regularly, we will become active. One can practice it any time.

Method: Bend ring finger and little finger and touch the tip of thumb with their tips gently without applying any pressure while keeping the remaining two fingers stretched.

Benefits: This *mudra* improves immunity, improves eyesight and reduces eye related diseases. It also helps reduce vitamin deficiency and fatigue.

6. Apan Mudra (Excretion)

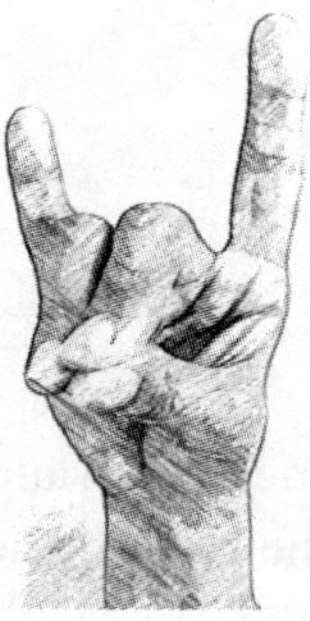

The *Apan mudra* helps regulate the excretory system by helping to expel waste materials like sweat, urine and undigested food. It can be practised daily for 45 minutes but longer duration can yields better results.
Method: The tip of middle finger and ring finger touch the tip of the thumb, while the other two fingers are stretched out.
Benefits: It helps regulate the bowel movements and cures constipation and piles. It also helps control diabetes. It soothes toothache and regular practice of this mudra for 10-15 minutes helps in maintaining healthy gums and teeth.

7. Vyan Mudra (Energy)

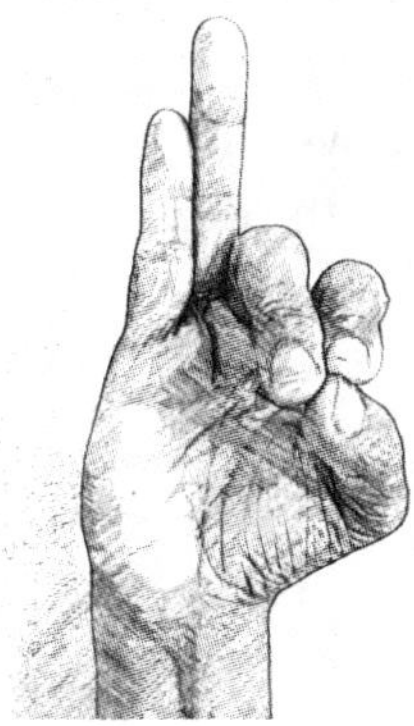

The Vyan mudra balances the energy in our body. It can be practiced daily for 20 minutes.
Method: Join the tips of fore finger and middle finger with the tip of thumb while keeping the ring finger and little finger straight.
Benefits: It strengthens the whole nervous system and helps regain the heat energy in the body. It controls excessive thirst, urination, loose motion and sweating. It helps in controlling hypertension (high blood pressure) practicing this mudra 3 times a day for 45 minutes each time followed by Prana mudra for 15 minutes. This is especially useful for the elderly.

8. Samaan Mudra (Digestion)

This *mudra* helps control the digestive system. It can be practiced daily for 20 minutes.

Method: Join the tips of all fingers with the tips of the thumb.

Benefits: It helps digest food, nourishes body, enhances the function of the digestive system, and prevents and cures many problems associated with the digestive system.

9. Hakini Mudra

This *mudra* helps improve memory power. It can be practiced for 15 minutes daily.

Method: Touch the tips of the corresponding fingers of each other.

Benefits: It helps to improve concentration. It promotes the cooperation between the right and left brain hemispheres. For children suffering from autism, *mudra* of knowledge (Gyan *mudra*) and this *mudra* can be very helpful. (Autism can be partially cured by *mudras* and some *asanas* in yoga. But for permanent cure you have to follow other methods prescribed by doctors.)

B. *Pranayam* or Breathing Techniques

In Sanskrit *prana* refers to cosmic energy or breath and *ayama* means "to control" so the literal meaning of *Pranayam* (*Pranasya Ayamaha*) is "controlled breathing". Breathing is a necessity for all living creatures. *Pranayam* in fact cleans up body, mind and spirit and hence promotes good health.

> "The pure soul, cleaned through the control of
> Breath and Meditation soon attains salvation
> and becomes one with God through Yogic Samadhi"
>
> ~ *Atharva Veda* (6.51.1)

Breathing is an art and systematic breathing alone controls the entire human body system. Normal rate of human respiration is about 16 to 20 cycles per minute in a wakeful state, 10 to 12 cycles per minute during sleep, and it can come down to 4 to 6 cycles per minute in deep meditation. *Pranayam* helps in slowing down the breath, conscious awareness of breath, and balancing of breath. It supplies sufficient quantity of oxygen for slow combustion of food and removal of gaseous wastes from the body and helps in release of energy, thereby curing physical and mental ailments. It cleans up Ida and *Pingala Nadi* and opens up all subtle energy centres (chakras) and balances *Sushumna Nadi*.

The word *nadi* has originated from a Sanskrit word *nad* meaning vibration or motion or path for flow. These are energy channels facilitating good health. Tantric texts say that there are 72000 *nadis* in the human body out of which 3 are most important namely *Ida* that lies to the left of spinal cord and *Pingala* that lies to the right of spinal cord and "*Sushumna*" that runs along the spinal cord and balances both *Ida* and *Pingala*.

Pranayam should be learnt under a proper practitioner who can teach the correct ways. However here are a few breathing techniques that can be self taught and are harmless. While practising these techniques, sit in any comfortable position on the floor or on a chair but make sure that the spine, back and neck are kept erect, and do not exert or do vigorous breathing.

a) Right Nostril Breathing

- Exhale completely, and then close the left nostril.
- Breathe in slowly with the right nostril.
- Breathe out slowly with the right nostril.
- Begin with 5 cycles and gradually increase it to 15 in one session.

b) Left Nostril Breathing

- Exhale completely, and then close the right nostril.
- Breathe in slowly with the left nostril.
- Breathe out slowly with the left nostril.
- Begin with 5 cycles and gradually increase it to 15 in one session.

c) Alternate Breathing

- Exhale completely.
- Close the right nostril, inhale through left nostril.
- Then close the left nostril and open the right nostril.
- Breathe out slowly through the right nostril, then slowly breathe in through the right nostril.
- Close right nostril, breathe out through the left nostril.
- This completes one cycle. Begin with 5 cycles and gradually increase up to 20 cycles per session.

d) Abdominal Breathing:

- Breathe in deeply and see that the stomach/ abdomen is extended.
- Do not hold your breath, slowly exhale completely.
- This breathing concentrates on the lower portion (lobes) of the lungs.
- This completes one cycle, begin with five and then gradually increase.

e) Thoracic Breathing:

- Sit erect and breathe in and slightly raise the shoulders and push your chest (rib cage) out.

- Slowly breathe out and come back to normal position.
- This breathing concentrates on the middle portion of the lungs.
- This completes one cycle. Begin with five and then gradually increase.

f) Upper Chest Breathing:

- Breathe in slowly lifting your shoulders slightly backwards.
- Breathe out slowly coming back to normal position.
- This completes one cycle. Begin with five and then gradually increase.
- This breathing concentrates on the lower portion of lungs.

g) General Benefits of Breathing Exercises:

- For general good health the above breathing exercises are sufficient.
- Help to regulate blood pressure.
- Control blood sugar levels to some extent.
- Help in burning calories/fat.
- Regulate digestion and excretion.

C. Yogasanas or Yogic Exercises

Yogasanas or yogic exercises are different from other exercises as they involve breathing techniques. These again need to be learnt under expert supervision.

Here is a list of some Yogasanas with their health benefits as per Therapeutic Yoga.

	Yogasanas (Yogic Exercises)	Health Benefits
1	*Ardhakati Chakrasana*	Fat reduction in abdomen area, cures liver disorders, cures stiff neck and back pain
2	*Trikonasana* (Triangle Posture)	Strengthens ankles, knees, shoulder, tones up muscles. Cures back pain, shoulder pain and joint pain

3	*Utkatasana* (The Chair Posture)	Cures stiff neck, pain in knees and strengthens heart
4	*Vrikshasana* (The Tree Posture)	Muscles of legs and hands get toned up. It improves mental concentration.
5	*Garudasana* (The Eagle Postures)	Cures pain in ankles, shoulders and removes cramps in calf muscles.
6	*Ardha Chandrasana* (The Half-Moon Posture)	Improves digestion, cures gastric trouble, indigestion. Strengthens muscles of legs and hands.
7	*Padmasana* (The Lotus Posture)	Strengthens nervous system, cures leg pain.
8	*Siddhasana*	Improves concentration, strengthens spine.
9	*Vajrasana* (The Diamond Posture)	Provides youthfulness, vigour. Strengthens heart and improves digestion.
10	*Veerasana* (The Warrior Posture)	Strengthens legs, hands, wrist, heels, and feet. Cures heel pain.
11	*Sukhasana*	Cures pain in legs, ankles, joints. Improves concentration.
12	*Matsyasana* (The Fish Posture)	Cures neck pain, gives relief from Asthmatic attacks. Cures back ache and spinal disorders.
13	*Parvatasana* (The Mountain Posture)	Strengthens legs, knees, shoulders. Reduces rheumatic pains and shoulder stiffness.
14	*Gomukhasana* (The Cow Head Posture)	Helps to cure pain in all the major/minor joints in the body.
15	*Bhujangasana* (The Serpent Posture)	Exercises all the muscles in body. Corrects menstrual disorders.
16	*Shavasana* (Corpse Posture)	Complete relaxation of the body and mind. Calming effect, cures hypertension

VII. Other Remedies

a) Aromatherapy

This technique uses volatile plant materials (essential oils) and other aromatic compounds for the purpose of altering a person's mind, mood, cognitive function or health. Aromatic oils are recommended for spraying around, for mixing with bathing water, for application or use in oil lamps. They affect the olfactory senses and are soothing to the mind.

b) Body Massage :

By applying adequate pressure on the aching part, muscles get relaxed and this relieves pain. Masseurs are trained in treating ailments and know their job well. It is always better to go to a masseur with medical/paramedical background if you are seeking cure to any disease. The popular types of massages are Chinese body and foot massage, Kerala oil massage and Thai massage. Different *Ayurvedic* and herbal oils having medicinal properties are used for the purpose.

Significance of alternative medicine for health management for all ages

Any practice claiming to heal that does not fall within the realm of conventional medicine is called alternative medicine. Alternative medicine does not administer any internal medication, hence it is safe from side effects. Alternative medicine caters to "holistic healing" of mind and body (to help the mind's ability to affect the functions and symptoms of the body). It is very effective for psychosomatic disorders (physical problems triggered by emotional or mental disturbances). The field of alternative medicine is very vast and has numerous branches. All these branches cannot be dealt with in detail. Hence some basic information has been given and few important ones that are easy to follow and practice have been explained in detail. For more information or treatment, one may read books on the relevant therapy or contact a practitioner.

Disclaimer: Persons with medical conditions are advised to consult their physician before trying any of the therapies mentioned in this article.

References:

- *Yoga for Health* by RN Ravishankar, Pustak Mahal publication (2002)
- *Art of Yoga* by Amey S Parulekar, VMP Publications (2004)
- *Health in your Hands* by Devendra Vora, Gala Publications

(1982)

- *The Acupressure Handbook* by Shizuko Yamamoto, Patrick McCarty, Pustak Mahal Publication (2002)
- *Mudras and Health Perspectives* by Suman Chiplunkar, Abhijit Prakashan (2011)
- *Hands of Light* by Barbara Ann Brennan, Bantam Books (1987)
- *Home Remedies for Common Ailments* by Dr. Arundhati Govind Hoskeri
- Wikipedia (Music Therapy)
- *Practical Hypnotism* by Dr. Narayan Dutt Shrimali, Pustak Mahal Publications (1985)

Chapter VI

FINANCE

(Kaushik Ramachandran, CEO & Research Director, Dyota Solutions Pvt Ltd., has over twenty years of experience in finance industry in various roles. After his MBA from IIM Lucknow, Kaushik worked in the software industry for several reputed companies in India and abroad. He is visiting Faculty and subject matter expert on Finance and conducts workshops in PSU's like Hindustan Petroleum, Bharat Petroleum, RCF etc., and leading MBA Institutions and Institutes promoted by Regulators like SEBI. He can be contacted at: 09819124890 kaushik@imoneyplant.com)

Most important savings of your life

While retirement for twentieth century employees happened by default i.e. every one retired by the time they were 60 years of age, retirement for twenty-first century employees has to be by design. This is because companies no longer retain people by age but rather by their contribution. So the moment an employee stops contributing to the organisation he/she may be forced to retire. Also, sometimes companies may shut down and employees may find it difficult to get another job because their skills are obsolete and not needed by other organisations. It is therefore essential to start planning your finances at an early stage in your life, in fact from the time one starts earning, to ensure a financially comfortable post-retirement life.

During working life it is possible that salary might grow in line with inflation (This is not guaranteed—of late, many organisations are not able to give salary hike in line with inflation due to competitive business environment), but when working life is over, inflation becomes a monster taking all savings away faster than one can imagine.

The following table is an indication of how our average monthly expenses have been increasing in the past and a projection of the future. Based on the above pattern we can estimate that expenses are growing at the rate of 12% every year.

Year	Monthly amount required by average families to live a happy life
1920	₹1
1940	₹10
1960	₹100
1980	₹1000
2000	₹10000
2020	₹100000 (Some middle class families are already exceeding monthly expenses of ₹100,000)
2040	₹1000000

Today, the choice of retirement age is with us. We can choose to retire by the time we are 50 or 55 or 60 years of age. Depending on the age we choose to retire and the number of years left for retirement the following table provides us a factor to estimate Retirement Corpus required on the day of retirement. For e.g. if expected retirement age is 50 and current age is 30, there are 20 more years to retire. Using the column 50, and selecting the row for 20 years, the retirement factor becomes 78.1. Multiplying this factor with current annual expenses gives the amount needed to protect from post retirement inflation impact. The calculations are based on the following assumptions:

1) current expenses growing at 7%,
2) Real Return after retirement is 3%
3) life expectancy is 80 years

Number of years left for my retirement________________________

Years left	Retirement by			
	60	55	50	45
6	23	26.9	30.3	33.2
7	24.6	28.8	32.4	35.5
8	26.3	30.8	34.7	38
9	28.2	33	37.1	40.7
10	30.1	35.3	39.7	43.5
11	32.3	37.8	42.5	46.6
12	34.5	40.4	45.5	49.8
13	36.9	43.2	48.7	53.3
14	39.5	46.2	52.1	57.1
15	42.3	49.5	55.7	61.1
16	45.2	52.9	59.6	65.3
17	48.4	56.7	63.8	69.9
18	51.8	60.6	68.2	74.8
19	55.4	64.9	73	80
20	59.3	69.4	78.1	85.6
21	63.4	74.3	83.6	91.6
22	67.9	79.5	89.4	98.1
23	72.6	85	95.7	104.9
24	77.7	91	102.4	112.3
25	83.2	97.3	109.6	120.1
26	89	104.2	117.2	128.5
27	95.2	111.4	125.4	137.5
28	101.9	119.3	134.2	147.2
29	109	127.6	143.6	157.5
30	116	136.5	153.7	168.5

Although the figure may look big, we will find if we start saving from today and every month regularly, the amount can be easily accumulated, even if we postpone by one day, even this small monthly savings can grow to a big amount. Next step is to find out how much to save every month so that the required corpus can be accumulated. You may choose to invest in EPS, NPS, or any Index Mutual Funds for the purpose of accumulating corpus.

My Retirement Factor from Table below (1)	
My Current Annual Expenses (Income-Savings) (2)	₹
My Retirement Corpus (1)*(2) = (3)	₹

Everyone may be saving some amount through company sponsored schemes. Estimating accumulated value of retirement benefits till date:

EPF / PPF Balance	₹
Gratuity Balance	₹
Value of Real Estate Investment allocated for Retirement	₹
NPS Balance	₹
Value of company sponsored Super Annuation Fund	₹
Value of Mutual funds/ Equity Allocated for Retirement	₹
Total Value of already Accumulated Retirement Investments	₹

The above investment is most likely to grow at a tax adjusted rate of 9% provided it is not withdrawn. Based on the number of years left for retirement, estimate how much these investments will grow to using the future value table below. For example if 20 years is left for retirement, the retirement savings will grow by a factor of 5.60, and if 30 years is left for retirement, the amount will grow by a factor of 13.26.

Future Value Factor of Current Retirement Savings					
Years left	FV Factor	Years left	FV Factor	Years left	FV Factor
1	1.07508	11	2.58043	21	6.10881
2	1.18810	12	2.81266	22	6.65860
3	1.29503	13	3.06580	23	7.25787
4	1.41158	14	3.34173	24	7.91108
5	1.53862	15	3.64248	25	8.62308
6	1.67710	16	3.97031	26	9.39916
7	1.82804	17	4.32763	27	10.24508
8	1.99256	18	4.71712	28	11.16714
9	2.17189	19	5.14166	29	12.17218
10	2.36736	20	5.60441	30	13.26768

Future Value of My Current Savings	₹
My Required Corpus	₹

Already Available	₹
Balance to be accumulated	₹

Monthly savings towards retirement corpus

No of Years left for retirement	Investments through EPF/PPF	Investments through NPS
6	0.0104	0.0101
7	0.0085	0.0082
8	0.0071	0.0068
9	0.006	0.0057
10	0.0051	0.0048
11	0.0044	0.0042
12	0.0039	0.0036
13	0.0034	0.0031
14	0.003	0.0027
15	0.0026	0.0024
16	0.0023	0.0021
17	0.0021	0.0019
18	0.0019	0.0017
19	0.0017	0.0015
20	0.0015	0.0013
21	0.0013	0.0012
22	0.0012	0.001
23	0.0011	0.0009
24	0.001	0.0008
25	0.0009	0.0007
26	0.0008	0.0007
27	0.0007	0.0006
28	0.0007	0.0005
29	0.0006	0.0005
30	0.0005	0.0004

Using the above table for e.g. if the balance retirement corpus to be accumulated is ₹80 lakhs, and 20 years is left for retirement, the Monthly savings factor if invested through NPS is 0.0013, or if invested through EPF the factor is 0.0015. Multiplying ₹80 lakh by 0.0013 or 0.0015 the monthly savings to be done is ₹10,400 or ₹12,000 per month. But if only 10 years left and ₹80 lakh is to be accumulated then monthly savings required is ₹38,400 (factor is 0.0048 if invested through NPS).

10 years delay means the savings required has become 4 times.

Making your savings plan

Savings cannot be increased by controlling expenses; savings can be improved only by:

- Measuring Savings as % of Income
- Following Rule : 30-30: 40-50: 50-100
- Treating Savings as the first expense

Measuring savings as % of income

Fix an amount to be saved as percentage of Monthly Net income. For example if monthly post tax income is ₹70,000/- then 10% of monthly income is ₹7000/-. The ratio is called savings ratio. Increase savings ratio by at least 2% every year.

Saving by 30:30-40:50-50:100 rule

By 30 years, save 30% of net income after tax; by 40 years, save 50% of net income; and by 50 years, save 100% of the income.

My age today	
How much % of Net Income am I saving?	
Am I saving more or Less?	

Treating savings as the first expense

Automate Savings and set up ECS to transfer on salary day to a liquid mutual fund or recurring deposit.

3 bagged approach successful investing and building wealth during working life

Bag No	Financial Products	How much?	Remarks
	FD RD Liquid Mutual Fund	At least one year Annual Income	Until this bag is full, do not put money in other bags If money is withdrawn from this bag refill on priority

	EPF Employer NPS Index Funds	Estimate monthly investments required to achieve corpus	If the bag one is full, divert monthly savings, to this bag. Until monthly savings are not enough, do not go to bag 3
	Real estate Diversified Mutual Funds Gold Savings Fund	Monthly savings left after filling bag 1 & 2	

3 bagged approach successful investing and building wealth during working life

Bag No	Financial Products	How much?	Remarks
	FD	Next 3 years Expenses	FD attracts 30% Income Tax and does not protect against inflation
	Fixed Maturity Plans	Expenses from 3rd to 10th year	2 year Fixed Maturity plans provides lot of tax benefits and they are safe
	Index Funds	Any balance left after protecting your 10 year expenses	Index funds provides tax free returns and is a good tool for protecting against inflation, but requires at least 10 years of patience

Insurance

Life risk

S. No	Description	Amount
Are you Married?	If not married , no need for Insurance unless parents/brothers/sisters are dependent on your income,	
A	Current Annual Income (if current annual Income from job is 0, which is true for most Retired Persons, then there is no need for Insurance)	₹
B	Your Existing Risk (From Table below)	
C	Recommended Insurance Cover (A) * (B)	₹
D	Insurance Cover Required = Networth – (C)	₹
E	Insurance Cover Already available	₹
F	Balance Insurance Needed (D)-(E)	₹

In the table below, first row refers to number of years of working life left and the second row refers to Insurance Factor

1	2	3	4	5	6	7	8	9	10	11	12	13	14	15	16	17	18	19	20	21	22	23	24	25	26
1	2	2	3	4	4	5	6	6	7	8	8	9	10	10	11	11	12	12	13	13	14	14	14	15	15

Assumptions: Insurance Factor by Income replacement method, assuming investment return same as inflation and salary growing 3% more than inflation accounting 20% towards personal expenses.

Post-retirement, you may need only health insurance, and vehicle insurance if you own a vehicle. Most likely you can ignore the life insurance and need not take any life insurance policy. Only if you have not secured your cash flows and your family is dependent on your post-retirement job for monthly expenses you may need to consider cheapest term insurance policy.

Most government employees are blessed with medical facility even after retirement; unfortunately those who have worked in private sector don't always have the benefit. We recommend a 3 pronged strategy to manage unexpected expenses that are likely to happen to because of old age and ill health.

Insurance premiums become very expensive once you are over 60 years. Hence it is recommended that a contingency plan be worked out to manage some expenses on your own.

My health insurance policy

Company Name	
Available cover	
Premium Amount	
Renewal Date	
Exclusions this year (Expenses not covered by Insurance if any)	
Co-Payment if any	
Nearest Cash Less Network Hospital	
Call Centre No for Pre-Authorization and Approvals Admission	

Strategies to manage unexpected medical expenses

1. 1.Have a Health Insurance Policy for about ₹3 lakh sum Insured for self and spouse (Likely to cost around ₹20000 depending on your current state of health) – Recommended Insurance Policies – Apollo Munich, Oriental Insurance (go for TPA services for faster claims settlement)
2. Have a Contingency Fund of ₹15 lakh allocated specifically for medical expenses. Invest this in a Debt Mutual Fund or FD to protect against inflation
3. Do regular exercises. Practice Yoga, Reiki, meditation or any other self healing techniques to lessen the burden on Medical expenses (Research indicates that Self healing is more powerful than modern Medicine)

Managing children's education

Even if you have accumulated money for your children's education it is always beneficial to take education loan to fund higher education. This is how it works. For e.g. let's say

Cost of Education	₹10 lakh or ₹2.5 lakh per year
Interest Rate on Education loan	13% (Interest rates on Education loan varies from 12.75% to 18%, so it is worthwhile doing a search on the education loan rate before finalising)
Interest Rate available on Fixed deposits	9.5%
Number of Years of Education	4 years

Suppose if you deposit of ₹10 lakh and an Education loan of ₹2.5 lakh per year this is how it will look at the end of 4 years.

₹10 lakhs at 9.5% for 10 years will grow to ₹14,37,661/=	The Education loan outstanding at the end of 4 years at the interest rate of 13% will accumulate to ₹11,95,000/=

Further, if we invest the ₹14,37,661 in a monthly withdrawal scheme giving us 9% interest for 5 years, we will receive ₹29,844 per month and if we want to repay the Outstanding education loan in next 5 years, the monthly EMI is ₹27,190/- giving us a additional monthly income of ₹2654/= per month.

Further, we get tax benefits on the interest component of Education loans.

Principal out standing	EMI	Interest Payment	Principal payment
1195000	27190	12946	14244
1180756	27190	12792	14398
1166357	27190	12636	14554
1151803	27190	12478	14712
1137091	27190	12318	14872
1122219	27190	12157	15033
1107187	27190	11995	15195
1091991	27190	11830	15360
1076631	27190	11664	15526
1061105	27190	11495	15695
1045410	27190	11325	15865
1029545	27190	11153	16037

Total Interest Repaid in the first year for Education loan is ₹144,789. This interest repayment is eligible for Tax Benefit and if the tax bracket is 30%, Total tax saved will be ₹43436/=.

Similarly for the next 4 years tax savings works out to:

	Interest Repaid	Tax Saved	Annual Savings on Repayment of Education loan from Investment withdrawals	Total Annual savings
Year 1	144789	43436	31848	75284
Year 2	119737	35921	31848	67769
Year 3	91227	27368	31848	59216
Year 4	58782	17634	31848	49482
Year 5	21859	6557	31848	38405

If the total savings is invested in an Index Mutual Fund giving 12% return, the annual savings will grow to ₹304968 by end of the 5th year when education loan is completed as illustrated in the table below, so by taking an education loan of ₹10 lakh, we stand to benefit ₹3 lakh.

	Investment This Year	Value at the end of 5th year growing at 12%
Year 1	75284	118461
Year 2	67769	95210
Year 3	59216	74280
Year 4	49482	55420
Year 5	38405	38405

Other points to consider while taking education loan

- The loan need not to be taken in the name of student, loan can be taken by any relative in the family
- Tax benefits on repayment is available for 8 years from the first year of repayment
- Although the processing time is more with PSU Banks, it is worthwhile to take loan from PSU's only since their rates are much cheaper than Private Banks
- It is preferable to take the loan through the Education Institute directly, this can cut down the process time greatly.

Reverse mortgage

(*consider only if you don't have any option*)

The reverse mortgage is a kind of financial instrument that allows an individual to use his/her housing equity (own residential property) to generate the income streams, post-retirement, while continuing to use the property as a residence and retaining its ownership.

The reverse mortgage is the inverse of the normal mortgage arrangement. As we all know, in the normal or forward mortgage, the borrower gets a lump sum payment against the property mortgaged and regularly pays the EMIs (covering Principal and Interest) to increase own equity of the property, till the time entire loan is paid off.

In the reverse mortgage mechanism, however, an individual agrees to avail of steady cash streams against a housing property without any encumbrances, based on the valuation of the house, till the time he / she or the spouse is alive. The borrower continues to occupy the property till the time of death or till the house is sold or the borrower moves out permanently, whichever happens earlier. In which case, the borrower(s) or the heir(s) (whichever applicable) have to pay off the loan to the lender, to claim back the property. This is a non-recourse loan arrangement which means that it protects other assets of the borrower(s) from being used as collateral, other than the house that is mortgaged.

Following are the features of this scheme:

i) The primary lending institutions (PLIs) are the Scheduled Commercial Banks (SCBs) and Housing Finance Companies (HFCs).

ii) The eligible borrower must be at least 60 years old. In case of married individuals, the other partner has to be at least 55 years old. The property owner is the primary lender and the other partner is the joint borrower. In case of joint ownership of property, the choice of the primary lender and the co-borrower is that of the borrowers.

iii) The property should be used as a primary residence and must be free of any encumbrances (i.e. must not be willed out to anyone or held as a collateral elsewhere) and must have a residual life of at least 20 years.

iv) The PLIs value the property and determine the eligible loan quantum of the property. Generally, the maximum Loan to Value ratio (LTV) is between 60% to 75%, varying directly in proportion to the age of the borrowers.

v) The lender (borrower) values the property and the cash streams are paid on a monthly, quarterly, half-annually or annual basis, as per the agreed mode with the borrowers.

vi) As the cash stream received by the borrower is actually loan proceeds, the same is not taxable at the hands of the borrowers.

vii) In case either of the spouses (in case of married borrowers) passes away, the spouse (borrower or the co-borrower) continues to receive the inflows, till his / her demise.

viii) Upon the death of the borrower or both the borrowers, the principal value of the cash streams already paid by the PLI, along with the applicable interest becomes payable. The settlement of the loan also becomes due in case the borrower wishes to sell off the property or permanently move out of the property.

ix) In case of the death of the borrowers, the legal heirs of the borrowers have the first right to settle the loan and claim the property. Else, the borrower can sell off the property to settle the loan. Any excess amount, realized after sale of property is payable to the heirs of the borrowers.

x) These days, many banks have also tied up with the Life Insurance companies (generally in case of the Bank promoted Life Insurance companies) to work out Reverse Mortgage Loan Enabled Annuity (RMLEA) schemes. In this case, however, the periodic annuity payable to the beneficiaries is treated as income at the hands of the annuitants, under the applicable sections 17, 56 and 80 CCC of the IT Act, 1961.

Pros and cons of reverse mortgage

Pros	Cons
Allows the owner(s) of the property to use own housing equity (primary residence) to generate cash streams, till death, without compromising on dignity and self-respect	The valuation of the property, along with the Loan to Value ratio, is at the discretion of the lender. Considering that the real estate sector is largely unorganized (with huge gap between the official registration rates and the market rates) in India, the borrowers may get less valuation (than what they may expect) for the housing property. Usually it is only 60% of the Market Value. Because of this difference Reverse Mortgage has not taken off in India. May be after 10 year when we people don't have a choice they will be forced to sell the property at 60% of the valuation for taking reverse mortgage
The borrower(s) could continue to reside in the property reverse mortgaged, giving them the psychological satisfaction and comfort of continuing to reside in own property in the golden years of life	The re-valuation of the property, along with enhancement of the amount mortgaged, may not happen before 5 years. This means that the borrowers may feel that they did not get the best deal
The cash streams, in case of Reverse Mortgage Loan arrangement, are tax free as the same are loan instalments	The annuity streams received in case of a Reverse Mortgage Loan Enabled Annuity (RMLEA) are taxable just like any other source of income

A very useful arrangement especially where the children of the retired individuals are well settled or where there are no liabilities (social or moral) to take care of	In our society, the social and cultural traditions are to pass on the property, upon death, to the progeny. As the heirs will be supposed to settle off the loan taken and 'buy' the property of their own parents upon their death, this may not be appreciated by the heirs and therefore, act as one of major obstacles for retired individuals not appreciating the reverse mortgage arrangement

Summary

While in the developed countries, the reverse mortgage arrangements have been well established and accepted means for planning for arranging post retirement cash flow streams, the concept has started catching up in India. However, the absence of a well-organized real estate sector, along with the social and cultural factors as well as low awareness levels, have been few factors that have impacted the whole hearted acceptance of these schemes.

However, with the changing social order and increasing regulation as well as developments in the Banking and Insurance sector, new concepts like Reverse Mortgage Loan Enabled Annuity Schemes are getting introduced and the gradually increasing awareness is making the retired people consider this arrangement in their retirement plans.

Make your will and revise it every year

The moment you have created wealth for more than what you want in your lifetime, it is recommended that you have plan on how you want to distribute your wealth. If you don't have plan, most likely your wealth will be useless. There are many cases we have seen, in the absence of proper estate planning, how the hard earned wealth get wasted

Ways to transfer wealth to your next generation (or means of "Estate Planning")

During Life Time	Post-Death
• Trust • Power of Attorney • Partition • Gift	• Will • Succession • Insurance

A will is the simplest and least expensive way of transferring your property to the next generation.

Notes on will

- A will need not be written on stamp paper, it can be written in your own hand on plain paper.
- Preferably registered, can be done through a notary for less than ₹2000/=
- Review your will every year, to add additional assets created by you.
- A will requires one executor and two witnesses.
- A will cannot be made by spouses jointly. Husband and wife must have separate wills. If the asset is owned jointly, then each spouse must mention only their share of the asset in their individual wills.

Sample Will

I __________________ inhabitant, residing at __________________being in a sound and disposing state of mind, hereby revoke all former Wills, Codicils and other Testamentary dispositions heretofore made by me and declare this to be my last Will and testament.

1. I appoint __________________and __________________to be the Executors/Executrices of this my Will, to act jointly and severally.

2. I direct that the following personal belongings owned by me shall be distributed amongst the persons named as follows:

3. I direct that my last illness expenses, the funeral and religious ceremony expenses / legal expenses of probate, etc.

unpaid taxes, other liabilities, if any, and such other expenses shall be paid from the followings:

4. I direct that the following movable and immovable properties owned by me shall be distributed as per their respective shares amongst persons named as follows:

5. I give, devise and bequeath all the rest and residue of my property, whether movable or immovable of whatsoever nature and wheresoever situate to my absolutely.

Dated this ___ day of ____ 20__

Signed by the said Mr./Mrs./Miss.

(Signature of the Testator)

The Testator, in the presence of us present at the time, who in his presence and in the presence of each other subscribe our name as witnesses:

1) Signature of the Witness: Name: Occupation: Address:	2) Signature of the Witness: Name: Occupation: Address:

Frequently accessed financial information

Bank Account Details

Note on passwords: Most passwords can be recovered through email. Please let your spouse know how to recover passwords for online accounts.

	Bank A/c 1	Bank A/c 2	Bank A/c 3	Bank A/c 4
Bank Name				
A/c No				
IFSC CODE				
MICR CODE				
Online User id				

PAN Details

Assesse Name	PAN	On line User id	Password

Mutual Fund Accounts

	MF 1	MF 2	MF 3	MF 4
MF company				
Folio No				
User id				

Credit Card

Issuing Bank	Bill due date	Credit limit	Cash Back benefits on	Cash Back %

Insurance Accounts

Insurance Type and Company (Life / Health / Motor)	Policy No	Insured amount	Annual premium	Maturity Date / Validity date	Online user id	Password

Bill Payments

Bill provider	Identification No	User id	Password	Bill due date

Fixed Deposits

Bank	Deposit Amount	Interest Rate	Date of Investment	Date of Maturity	Monthly/ Quarter ly/ Annual Interest Income

Mutual Fund Investment Details

Scheme Name	Investment Amount	Current Value	Wt. Avg. Days of Holding	Annualized Return	Dividend Received

Stock Investment Details

Company Name	Investment Amount	Current Value	Wt. Avg. Days of Holding	Annualized Return	Dividend Received

Real Estate Investment

Property Location	Purchase Cost	Current Estimated Value	Annualized Return till date	Property Tax Amount if Applicable	Property Tax Due Date

Investment in Gold

Description	Avg Purchase Cost	Current Estimated Value	Annualised Return till date	Wealth Tax Applicable ?	Wealth Tax Due date

Loans

Loan taken from	Interest Rate	Amount of Loan	Monthly Repayment Amount	Expected date of Loan closure

Vehicles

2/4 wheeler	Reg No	Purchase Date	Insurance Premium Amount	Insurance Company	Premium Due Date

Lockers

Bank	Location / City	Locker id no	Locker Key No	Annual Charges	Contents

PPF

Bank	Balance Amt	Date of Maturity	location

Disclaimer

This publication contains collective opinions and ideas of core team of Dyota Solutions Pvt Ltd. It is intended to provide helpful and informative material on the subject matter covered. The authors/ publishers specifically disclaim any responsibility for any loss, liability, or risk, personal or otherwise, which is incurred as a consequence, directly or indirectly, of the use and application of any of the contents. If you need investment or tax advice upon which you intend to rely in the course of your financial or business affairs, consult a competent, independent financial adviser.

APPENDICES

A. DEMOGRAPHIC TRANSITION OF POPULATION IN INDIA

The demographic changes in the twentieth century, more so during the second half of the twentieth century i.e. the post independent era are important in order to gauge the magnitude of the population problem in general and the growing population of older persons in particular to plan suitable solutions at all levels i.e. at individual, social, and state level.

In the first half of the twentieth century, birth, death and growth in the population of the country were not studied. Demographic studies were not a common feature of the planning policy of the country. A scientific study of high mortality and yet enormous growth in the population of the country and their impact on the health of individuals and on the health of the country was also not taken seriously and studied, though this aspect was taken up by some of the developed countries much earlier. It is therefore necessary to study and analyse the available statistical data in all its aspects to plan the course of action needed on the part of individuals, society and the state.

Growth of population in India (1901–2011)

The population of India at the turn of the twentieth century was around 238.4 million (23.84 crore). This has increased by more than four-fold in a period of one hundred and ten years to reach 1210 million (121 crore) in 2011. Interestingly the population of India grew by one and half times in the first half of the twentieth century, while in the later half it recorded a phenomenal three-fold increase.

The following statement gives the decadal growth of population since 1901.[47]

Census Year	Population (Million)	Decadal growth absolute	Percent
1901	238.4		
1911	252.1	13.7	5.75
1921	251.0	(-)1.1	0.31
1931	279.0	28.0	11.00
1943	19.0	40.0	14.22
1951	361.0	42.0	13.31
196	439.0	78.0	21.64
1971	548.0	109.0	24.80
1981	683.0	135.0	24.66
1991	846.0	163	23.87
2001	1029.0	183.0	21.54
2011	1210	181.0	17.64

From the details given above, it may be seen that the percentage of decadal growth during 2001-11 registered a sharp decline since independence. For 2001-2011 the decadal growth was 17.64 per cent, a decrease of 3.90 per cent for the period 1991-2001. The only earlier exception was the census year 1921 when the population actually decreased by 1.1 million. The position of 2001-2011 also implies that as a result of the combination of population momentum and somewhat impeded fertility, although India continue to grow in the size of population, its pace of net addition is on the decrease which can be considered as a good sign.

Another interesting feature of the population in India is that its population of 1210 million (2011) is almost equal to the combined population of six countries (1214) viz. USA (308.7),

[47]Census Report Series 1 (p. 41)

Indonesia (237.6), Brazil (190.7), Pakistan (184.8), Bangladesh (164.4) and Japan (128.1). Again, according to United Nation's estimation, the world population grew at an annual rate of 1.23 per cent during 2000-2010 as compared to India (1.64 per cent during 2001-2011).

Gender composition of the population

Gender composition reflects natality, mortality and migration character of a given population. Distribution pattern of male and female in a population affects relative roles in the society and economic relationships. Sex ratio is defined as the number of females per thousand males in the population. In India, out of a total population of 1,21,01,93,422 persons, 62,37,24,248 are males and 58,64,69,174 females. As per this, the sex ratio in India is 940 in 2011 as compared to 933 in 2001.

The following table displays the sex ratio in the world, India and other selected countries.[48]

Sr. No	Country	2001	2011
1.	World	986	984
2.	India	933	940
3.	China	944	926
4.	USA	1029	1025
5.	Indonesia	1004	988
6.	Brazil	1025	1042
7.	Pakistan	938	943
8.	Russian Fed.	1140	1167
9.	Bangladesh	958	978
10.	Japan	1041	055
11.	Nigeria	1016	987

It can be seen from the above table that the composition of population by gender is not uniform. The world has 984 females against every 1000 males. In USA, Brazil, Russian Federation and Japan, females outnumber the males. In the other six countries, the males are more than the females.

A little detailed analysis of the position of sex ratio in India

[48]Census of India (p.78)

in the twentieth century and the beginning of twenty-first century brings out the following picture.[49]

Census Year	Sex Ratio (Females per thousand males)
1901	972
1911	964
1921	955
1931	950
1941	945
1951	946
1961	941
1971	930
1981	934
1991	927
2001	933
2011	940

It may be seen that throughout the twentieth century and even in the twenty-first century, the statistics do not favour the females. The variation plus or minus has also been marginal from decade to decade. It is common knowledge that for whatever reasons—good or bad—the Indian society has been traditionally in favour of men. Birth of a girl child is not welcomed and the birth of a male child is considered a boon. Of course, this trend has wider social implications.

Demographic status of elderly in India [50]

Important aspects of growth in population in India during the twentieth century and the first decade of the twenty-first century have been analysed in depth in the earlier paragraphs with a view to throw light on the growth of population from decade to decade, highlighting the composition in two main age groups, one up to the age of six and another over six years of age. This brings out a comparative position of the status of the society in India and in some other countries. This should

---

[49]Census of India (p.81)

[50]Demographic Profile of Elderly in India, Tara Kanitkar, Sharari Shukla (International Longevity Census India, Pune)

serve as background material to understand, analyse and find possible solutions to the problems of the elderly. Again, to understand the magnitude of the problem of old age, statistics and analysis of the growth in elderly population and its effects on the lifestyle of the elderly of sixty years and above is required. As a basic data, it is necessary to know the age-wise and gender-wise break up of the total population.

Since this book deals with planning and living old age, it is imperative that one must study the demographic pattern of the elderly in India. According to data obtained from the Census Report 2001, an aged person is one who is of 60 years of age or above. The table below shows the number of aged persons in the households in India:

Number of Aged Persons	Households
None	132,852,466
1	41,117,035
2	16,216,488
3	763,059
4	92,776

The size of the elderly population is fast growing although it constituted only 7.47 percent of the total population at the turn of the new millennium, since a majority of the households do not have any elderly member in the family. Hence there are inadequate services and facilities for them. With the rise in the number of nuclear families, the elderly have a growing problem of whether they are accepted by their family members. Acceptability by the younger family members is an important factor for them.

A study was also made of the number of elderly members in rural and urban households. The table below indicates the decreasing number of elderly members i.e. more than 4 in a family.

No. of elderly	Rural	Urban
None	94,035,577	40,816,889
1	30,317,317	10,799,718

2	12,501,423	3,792,601
3	574,151	188,908
4+	66,792	25,984

We see that very few urban households have 4 or more elderly members. In such a scenario, who will address their problems and try to solve them? With a growing urban young population, policies will also favour only them. There is, hence, a need to identify the particular problems of the elderly and address them not only on a local level but also on a national level. The attitude should not be one of complacency or to cross the river when one reaches the bridge. Policies have to be framed so that the elderly, however small in number they may be, may lead their lives peacefully and happily.

The Indian Government declared the year 1999 as the International Year of the Older Persons with the National Policy for Older Persons. This policy highlighted the urgent need to understand and deal with the medical, psychological and socio-economic problems faced by the elderly. The government concerns for the elderly began with India's participation in the World Assembly Conference in Vienna in 1982 where India adopted the United Nations International Plan of Action on Ageing. From the government's point of view, various policy oriented programmes were introduced but these ignored the rural-urban divide.

Life expectancy is growing at alarming rate with better health facilities and technological advancements. With the rapid progression in medical science, it has now become easier to control various diseases which were earlier the cause of high mortality. This has resulted in a steady rise in the expected length of one's life leading to a growing greying population. With the improvement in socio-economic conditions, female life expectancy is higher than that of men. The life expectancy at birth for females has been rising continuously and during 2002-2006, it was 64.2 years for females as against 62.6 years for males. In urban areas, the life expectancy of both men and women is 68.8 years whereas in rural areas, it is 62.1 years. This gives us an idea about the general improving health status of the elderly in India.

The table below illustrates major changes in the share of broad age groups projected up to the year 2050.

Age groups	1960 Male/ Female	2000 Male/ Female	2020 Male/ Female	2050 Male/Female
0-14	39.8-39.6	34.2-34.1	26.2-26.0	18.9-18.3
15-59	27.0-27.0	29.4-28.9	31.0-31.1	31.4-30.2
60+	2.4-2.8	2.0-2.3	3.0-3.8	6.3-7.1

(Source: UN World Population Prospect (1998 Revision and 2002 Revision, Vol. II)

The above statistics reveals that the first two age categories are likely to grow at a very slow rate in response to possible reduction in fertility levels. The population in the last category is likely to grow substantially and increase over the years.

As seen earlier that the total population of elderly in India was 1029 million. This total population can and needs to be projected in various age groups and requires further break up gender-wise. Since the position under these categories cannot be uniform in all the States and Union Territories, it is necessary to know the comparative position at least in some major States and some Union Territories to understand the magnitude of the problems.[51]

a) Percentage distribution of population of India by broad age groups (2001).

	Broad age group			Total
	0-14	15-59	60+	
Percent	35.35	57.21	7.44	100
Numbers	363,610,812	589,377,195	76,622,321	1028,610,328

[51]Census of India (p 73)

The proportion of elderly persons in relation to total population was 7.4 percent. There are and there have to be inter-state variations in the level of elderly with reference to the total population of the state. The following table illustrates the percentage of elderly in some major states, smaller states and union-territories.[52]

S. No.	Major State	Percentage	Smaller State	Percentage	Union Territories	Percentage
1	Punjab	9.0	H.P.	9.0	Chandigarh	5.0
2	U.P.	7.0	Sikkim	5.4	Delhi	5.2
3	Bihar	6.6	Nagaland	4.5	Dadra & Nagar Haveli	4.0
4	Orissa	8.3	Meghalaya	4.6	Pondicherry	8.3
5	Madhya Pradesh	7.1	Goa	8.3		
6	Gujarat	6.9				
7	Maharashtra	8.7				
8	Karnataka	7.7				
9	Kerala	10.5				
10	Tamil Nadu	8.8				

The variation can be attributed to the professional opportunities in one's own state, migration of the youth to other states or abroad for jobs leaving the elderly behind.

The longevity of each person or in different age groups also varies as brought out in the following table:

Age Group	Proportion among elderly	Proportion to total population
60-64	35.9	2.7
65-69	25.8	1.9
70-74	19.2	1.4
75-79	8.6	0.6

[52]Census of India (p.18)

80+ (oldest old)	10.5	0.8
All elderly	100	7.4

In other words the proportion of elderly in the age group of 60-69 is 61.7 percent; in the age group of 70-79 is 27.8 percent; and in the age group of 80 and above is 10.5 percent. More than 10 percent of the elderly population live beyond the age of 80. There is steep increase in longevity with the result that living beyond 60-70 has become a normal feature whereas some years back living beyond the age 65-70 was considered rather rare.

Position in some bigger states

The statement above gives an idea of the age-wise composition of the elderly on all-India basis. It is also necessary to know the age-wise distribution of some major states in analysing the problems of old age. The following statement gives the age-wise break-up.[53]

State	Young old 60-69	Old 70-79	Very Old 80+	All Elderly
India	4.60 (61.79)	2.07 (27.78)	0.78 (10.47)	7.45 (100.00)
Punjab	5.15 (57.22)	2.62 (29.07)	1.22 (13.56)	9.00 (100.00)
Rajasthan	4.15 (61.57)	1.90 (38.19)	0.69 (10.24)	6.74 (100.00)
U.P.	4.33 (61.77)	1.92 (27.39)	0.76 (10.84)	7.01 (100.00)
Bihar	4.17 (62.90)	1.78 (26.85)	0.68 (10.25)	6.63 (100.00)
West Bengal	4.28 (60.01)	2.00 (28.09)	0.84 (11.80)	7.12 (100.00)
Orissa	5.09 (61.62)	2.37 (28.69)	0.80 (09.69)	8.26 (100.00)
Maharashtra	5.54 (63.46)	2.39 (27.38)	0.80 (09.76)	8.73 (100.00)
Karnataka	4.64 (60.34)	2.18 (28.35)	0.87 (11.31)	7.69 (100.00)

[53]Census of India (p.23)

Kerala	6.07 (57.98)	3.18 (30.37)	1.22 (11.65)	10.48 (100.00)
Tamil Nadu	5.49 (62.17)	2.45 (27.75)	0.89 (10.08)	8.83 (100.00)

It may be seen from the above table that Punjab and Kerala have the highest percentage of very old persons.

Gender pattern in different age groups

It is well known that female constitute nearly 50 percent of the total population. It is important to understand the comparative position in different age groups, especially elderly group as female and elderly are more dependent on others and their old age problems need special attention.

The following table gives the actual position:[54]

Age	Male	Female	Sex Ratio (for 1000)
0-14	35.6	35.1	919
15-59	57.0	56.9	930
60+	7.0	7.8	1029
Number	532,156,772	496,453,356	933

It may be seen that in the elderly group (60+) the percentage of female is more than male but in terms of number with reference to the total population it is less as it works out to 933 females to 1000 males.

The position of male and female elderly in some of the major states in comparison with all of India is as under:[55]

State	Male	Female
India	7.01	7.8
Punjab	8.06	9.5
Rajasthan	6.2	7.3
U.P.	7.1	7.0
Bihar	6.8	6.5
West Bengal	6.7	7.5
Orissa	8.1	8.5
Maharashtra	7.8	9.7
Karnataka	7.2	8.2

[54]Census of India (p.24)

[55]Ibid.,p.26

Kerala	9.6	11.3
Tamil Nadu	8.7	8.9

From the above table it is clear that except Uttar Pradesh and Bihar the percentage of female elderly is higher than the male in other states.

Sex ratio in terms of the number of females per 1000 males in the above mentioned states is as under:

State	Persons of age 60+	Total Population
India	1029	933
Punjab	971	876
Rajasthan	1083	921
U.P.	887	898
Bihar	883	919
West Bengal	1047	934
Orissa	1022	972
Maharashtra	1150	922
Karnataka	1112	965
Kerala	1247	1058
Tamil Nadu	1013	987

Decadal trends in ageing

In India the elderly population is growing from year to year. The challenge before the society and government is how to make the life of elderly a happy and contented one. In order to understand the magnitude of the problem, it is necessary to have statistical information on the growth of elderly population. The following table gives decadal growth in the elderly population from 1961.[56]

	1961	1971	1981	1991	2001
1) Percentage of population of age 60+ in total population	5.6	6.0	6.5	6.8	7.04
2) Number of people of age 60+ (million)	24.7	32.7	43.2	56.7	76.6

[56]Census of India (p.28)

It can be seen from the above table that the elderly population is increasing rapidly every passing decade. In 1961 we were required to give attention to the problems of elderly population of 25 million. We are now required to give attention to the elderly population of more than 77 million.

Distribution of population[57]

Age groups	Rural	Urban
0-14	37.42	30.64
15-59	54.84	62.36
60+	7.74	6.70
All ages	100	100
Old dependence ratio	141	107

The percentage of elderly and ratio of dependency is more in rural areas which has its own implications. Following is the position in some of the major states:[58]

State	Rural	Urban	Total
India	7.74	6.70	7.45
Punjab	9.82	7.34	9.00
Rajasthan	6.99	5.95	6.74
U.P.	7.31	5.88	7.01
West Bengal	6.59	8.44	7.11
Orissa	8.58	6.43	8.26
Maharashtra	10.24	6.68	8.73
Andhra Pradesh	8.13	6.16	7.59
Karnataka	8.28	6.53	7.69

Large variation between rural and urban elderly population is found in the states of Uttar Pradesh, Orissa, Maharashtra, Andhra Pradesh and Karnataka. This might be due to migration of the younger generations to the cities for jobs, professions etc.

Literacy status of the elders in India

Literacy and education play an important role in the life of an individual and, in turn, in society for progress during one's youth and middle age and to live a life with positive attitude

[57]Census of India (p.29)
[58]Census of India (p.31)

in old age. Literacy is an important tool for the development of the country. Following is the position of literacy of elders in rural and urban area and also gender-wise for India and some important states: (2001):[59]

State Rural Males	Illiterate	Primary	Secondary	Graduate & above
India	54.51	13.90	4.61	1.28
Punjab	66.33	4.82	8.22	1.01
Rajasthan	67.45	9.33	2.46	0.81
U.P.	61.87	11.99	4.39	1.27
Bihar	61.87	11.99	4.39	1.27
M.P.	58.79	10.12	1.54	0.82
Maharashtra	47.83	15.11	3.72	0.95
A.P.	63.61	14.90	3.39	0.94
West Bengal	38.76	13.49	5.94	1.9
Kerala	20.60	22.53	7.65	2.21
Tamil Nadu	49.66	20.21	4.24	0.77
Rural Females				
India	86.99	4.00	0.48	0.10
Punjab	88.21	5.10	0.82	0.13
Rajasthan	95.02	1.17	0.09	0.02
U.P.	91.74	3.08	0.29	0.07
Bihar	90.58	3.97	0.60	0.11
M.P	92.49	1.49	0.11	0.04
Maharashtra	87.55	3.07	0.30	0.07
A.P.	88.76	4.96	0.33	0.06
West Bengal	82.15	3.55	0.42	0.12
Kerala	44.56	15.83	2.69	0.54
Tamil Nadu	85.28	5.48	0.67	0.14
Urban Males[1]				
India	25.02	16.40	16.10	12.25

[59] Ibid., p.40

Punjab	33.49	14.03	21.16	9.96
Rajasthan	28.08	15.89	14.78	11.80
U.P	35.89	12.68	11.63	12.42
Bihar	28.31	15.49	16.13	16.45
M.P.	27.76	15.71	10.70	12.48
Maharashtra	19.91	17.95	18.83	11.68
A.P.	32.55	17.98	13.54	12.67
West Bengal	17.17	11.67	19.59	16.70
Kerala	12.49	22.52	13.80	7.93
Tamil Nadu	24.64	20.03	15.69	6.02
Urban Females				
India	58.20	13.12	5.32	2.70
Punjab	63.18	13.82	5.53	2.58
Rajasthan	69.51	9.43	3.08	1.63
U.P.	67.59	10.20	4.28	2.83
Bihar	66.50	13.78	4.31	1.82
M.P.	67.24	9.43	2.98	2.32
Maharashtra	55.30	13.22	6.88	3.45
A.P.	67.01	14.25	3.43	1.59
West Bengal	44.82	12.95	6.63	4.15
Kerala	34.55	19.14	6.57	2.25
Tamil Nadu	58.75	13.38	5.28	1.39

It may be seen from the above table that 54.51 percent rural elderly males are illiterate. Excluding Maharashtra, West Bengal, Kerala and Tamil Nadu, the percentage of illiterate elderly is higher than the national average in other states.

The position of rural females is worse than the males on all-India basis—86.99 percent of the elderly females are illiterate. The percentage of illiterate females is very high except in the case of West Bengal, Kerala and Tamil Nadu. In the case of urban males the position is much better than the rural one. On all-India basis the percentage of illiterate urban males is only 25, whereas in rural males the percentage is more than double i.e. 54.5. Again in the case of urban states , except in the case of Maharashtra, West Bengal, Kerala and Tamil Nadu, the percentage in other states is higher than national percentage.

In the case of urban females the percentage of illiterate is only 58.20 which is lower in comparison with the rural females which is almost 87 percent. Even in respect of each state the percentage of illiterates in rural areas is much higher, giving an indication of a wide gap. Only in the case of Kerala, the percentage of gap in the rural and urban areas, both in the case of males and females, is much less which is rather a good sign.

Life expectancy and longevity

The general life expectancy has increased considerably during the last five or six decades. In the early 40s, average life expectancy was 30 years or so which increased rapidly from decade to decade. In the 80s, it rose to more than 50 years and at present it is more than 60 years; this is increasing rapidly due to various factors. Again the longevity of females is more than the males, thus needing special attention to their problems.

The following statement gives the position of life expectancy for males and females for India and some major states (2001-2005).[60]

State	Male	Female
India	63.8	66.1
Punjab	67.7	70.4
Rajasthan	64.1	67.2
U.P.	62.0	61.9
Bihar	65.6	64.7
M.P.	60.5	61.3
Maharashtra	66.4	69.8
A.P.	63.4	67.9
West Bengal	66.7	69.4
Kerala	70.8	76.0
Tamil Nadu	66.1	69.1

It may be seen from the above table that in the case of males except in the states of Uttar Pradesh, Madhya Pradesh and Andhra Pradesh, the life expectancy is more than the national average.

[60]Registrar General, Indian Population Projections for Indian States 2001-2005

A comparative position between males and females indicates that except in the case of Uttar Pradesh and Bihar, life expectancy for females is more than the males in other states. Female elderly living more years than the male elderly have their own personal and social implications.

Projected growth in the elderly population

It is a matter of common knowledge that the rate of growth of the elderly population is higher than the growth of the total population. The following statement gives the projected position:[61]

Years	2001-05	2006-10	2011-15	2016-20	2021-26
Growth in elderly population (annual)	3.65	3.56	3.99	4.25	4.18
Growth in total population	0.6	1.4	1.3	1.1	0.9

It is clear from the above that during 2001-26 the annual rate of the growth of the elderly population would be larger than the growth of the total Indian population at each point. In 2021-26 however the growth of elderly population would be lower (4.18 percent) than the previous period 4.25 percent (2016-2020). The growth of total population in 2021-26 is also less (0.9 percent) than the 1.1 percent in the previous period (2016-20).

Following statement gives the anticipated position i.e. number of elderly female to 1000 males.[62]

Age elderly	Years					
	2001	2006	2011	2016	2021	2026
60+	1023	1051	1046	1032	1029	1047
80+	1083	1026	1155	1264	1346	1363

A numerical excess of elderly females in the age group of

[61]Census of India (p. 79-80)

[62]Office of the Registrar Government & Census Commission – Population Projections for India and States 2001-2026

60+ during the coming years is a matter of concern. A still greater matter of concern is the high proportion of difference in females in the age group of 80+. It would be 1264 in 2016, 1346 in 2021 and as high as 1363 in 2026. The majority of these females would be widows who would be entirely dependent on others, often making their old age rather an unhappy one.

Marital status of the elderly

In assessing the quality of life of the elderly, especially in their old age, the marital status is an important factor. Togetherness and mutual support are much needed in one's old age for mental peace and for quality life. This is not possible in the case of all elderly people. As females live longer than males at least by five or six years, the women end up having to spend the last years of their lives as widows. Even in certain cases of males, many elderly men have to spend some years of their lives as widowers. In old age, both are deprived of their life partners making it necessary to know the magnitude of the problem to work out the possible solutions and responsibility thereof the person concerned of his/her family and the government. The following statistics indicate the actual position:

Percent distribution of elderly–males-females (2001)[63]

Age Group	Rural Males				
	Not married	Married	Widowers	Divorced	Total
60-69	1.90	86.18	11.58	0.35	100
70-79	2.51	78.03	19.12	0.34	100
80+	4.96	65.30	29.37	0.36	100

Age Group	Rural Females				
	Not married	Married	Widowed	Divorced	Total
60-69	0.92	56.98	41.57	0.53	100
70-79	1.27	36.37	61.94	0.42	100
80+	3.23	25.64	70.75	0.38	100

Age Group	Urban Males				
	Not married	Married	Widowers	Divorced	Total

[63]Census of India (p.46)

60-69	2.14	88.64	8.95	0.27	100
70-79	3.5 2	79.16	17.03	0.29	100
80+	6.87	65.24	27.55	0.34	100

Age Group	Urban Females				
	Not married	Married	Widowed	Divorced	Total
60-69	1.76	53.89	43.79	0.55	100
70-79	2.51	33.10	63.93	0.46	100
80+	4.28	23.55	71.75	0.43	100

Percent distribution of elderly (60+)

The subject matter of our study namely the problems of old age and possible solutions makes it necessary to know the percentage of the elders who are with spouse (married) and who are without spouse (widows or widowers) in India and some other major states.

Following statement gives the required information:[64]

State	Rural Males		Urban Males	
	With spouse	Without spouse	With spouse	Without spouse
India	81.64	18.36	83.66	16.34
Punjab	76.59	23.41	79.89	20.11
Rajasthan	81.00	19.00	83.10	16.90
UP	75.27	24.73	78.53	21.47
Bihar	79.83	20.17	81.50	18.50
MP	79.13	20.87	81.93	18.07
Maharashtra	86.96	13.09	85.60	14.40
AP	86.04	13.96	87.77	12.23
West Bengal	86.29	13.71	84.53	15.47
Kerala	87.44	12.56	87.47	12.53
Tamil Nadu	83.13	16.87	84.08	15.92

State	Rural Females		Urban Females	
	With spouse	Without spouse	With spouse	Without spouse
India	48.18	51.82	44.84	55.16
Punjab	61.36	39.64	56.60	43.40
Rajasthan	49.73	50.27	49.14	50.86
UP	57.76	42.24	52.11	47.89
Bihar	55.93	44.07	51.45	48.55
MP	50.61	49.59	46.60	53.40

[64] Census of India (p.47)

Maharashtra	49.91	50.09	43.69	56.31
AP	41.60	58.40	41.65	58.35
West Bengal	36.25	63.75	40.20	59.80
Kerala	37.79	62.21	33.21	66.79
Tamil Nadu	45.55	58.45	42.26	57.74

It may be seen from the above mentioned statement that there is a large variation in the all-India percentage and rural/urban percentages in some states in respect of both males and females.

In the case of rural males the percentage of widowers in the age group of 60-69 is 11.58, while in the case of urban males it is 8.95 percent. In the case of rural females, the percentage is 41.57 and in the case of urban females in the same age group it is 43.79 percent.

A comparative study of the position in states also reveals that in the case of Punjab the percentage of rural females with spouse is 61.36, in the case of Rajasthan it is 49.73, West Bengal 36.25 and Kerala 37.79. In the case of urban females without spouse, Punjab has a percentage of 56.60, Rajasthan 49.14, West Bengal 40.20 and Kerala 33.21.

From whatever angle we study the position, it may be considered that by and large the females outnumber the males, thus requiring greater attention to be paid to their problems in old age.

Work force in the Indian society

The following statements should give a clear picture of the work force participation of the elderly (India 2001):[65]

Males

Age Groups	Total workers Males	Non-workers	Total
60-69	69.73	30.27	100
70-79	49.30	50.70	100
80+	34.63	65.37	100

Females

Age Groups	Total workers	Non-workers	Total
60-69	26.30	73.70	100
70-79	13.32	86.68	100

[65]Census of India (p 58)

80+	8.57	91.43	100

Rural Males

Age Groups	Total workers	Non-workers	Total
60-69	76.04	23.96	100
70-79	54.12	45.88	100
80+	36.76	63.24	100

Urban Males[66]

Age Groups	Total workers	Non-workers	Total
60-69	51.13	48.87	100
70-79	34.37	65.63	100
80+	27.83	72.17	100

Rural Females

Age Groups	Total workers Males	Non-workers	Total
60-69	31.36	68.64	100
70-79	15.77	84.23	100
80+	9.97	90.03	100

Urban Females

Age Groups	Total workers Males	Non-workers	Total
60-69	10.98	89.03	100
70-79	6.17	93.83	100
80+	4.68	95.32	100

It is clear from the above statistics that the national average of male workers in the age group of 60+ is 60 percent and 40 percent are non-workers. In the case of females the total workers are 21 percent and 79 percent are non-workers. Difference between males and females is nearly 40 percent.

In the case of rural males in the age group of 60+ the total workers are 66 percent and in the case of urban it is only 44 percent, i.e. comparatively the percentage of rural workers is more than that of the urban workers. That means that in rural areas, the elderly male workers work for more years because of the nature of their duty of mostly working in the agricultural lands. In the case of urban males, after retirement, nearly 56

[66]Census of India (p 59)

percent remain without work opportunities even though most of them may be physically fit.

Even in the case of females, for the same reason, non-workers in the rural areas is 75 percent against the higher percentage of 89 in urban areas. Thus, both rural males and females work for longer years than their counterparts in the urban areas.

Work force participation in some major states (60+ - 2001)[67]

Urban Males

State	Total workers	Non-workers	Total
India	44.13	55.88	100
Punjab	50.91	41.09	100
UP	37.97	62.03	100
Bihar	54.47	45.53	100
MP	46.24	53.76	100
Gujarat	39.26	60.74	100
Maharashtra	35.69	64.31	100
Karnataka	43.09	56.90	100
Kerala	32.78	67.22	100

Urban Females

State	Total workers	Non-workers	Total
India	8.96	91.04	100
Punjab	6.77	93.23	100
UP	7.69	92.31	100
Bihar	7.55	92.45	100
MP	11.63	88.37	100
Gujarat	6.16	93.84	100
Maharashtra	8.50	91.49	100
Karnataka	10.23	89.77	100
Kerala	7.00	93.00	100

Rural Males

State	Total workers	Non-workers	Total
India	65.60	34.40	100
Punjab	57.94	42.06	100
UP	74.50	25.50	100
Bihar	72.61	27.39	100
MP	69.40	30.60	100
Gujarat	57.39	42.61	100
Maharashtra	64.77	35.23	100
Karnataka	64.19	35.81	100

[67]Census of India (p. 62)

Kerala	43.09	56.91	100

Rural Females[68]

State	Total workers	Non-workers	Total
India	24.94	75.06	100
Punjab	16.92	83.08	100
UP	21.22	78.78	100
Bihar	19.78	80.22	100
MP	33.64	66.36	100
Gujarat	22.71	77.30	100
Maharashtra	36.65	63.35	100
Karnataka	26.69	73.31	100
Kerala	9.45	90.55	100

In the case of literacy of elderly both in respect of rural and urban males and females, Kerala occupies the highest position compared to other states. On the other hand, in the case of elderly workers, it has the distinction of being the lowest both in the case of males and females and also urban and rural. This might be perhaps due to the fact that the working facilities are less because of availability of less agricultural land and also industries.

Again, it may be noted that in the case of urban females the percentage of non-workers is abnormally higher than that of workers. It is almost 90 and 10 percent respectively. The percentage is slightly better in the case of rural females again except in the use of Kerala where the percentage of workers is as low as 9.45 while in the case of many states it is more than 20 and 30 percent. This aspect needs to be critically examined to find out the ways and means to make the life of elderly an enjoyable one.

Ageing in China and United States

We have seen in the earlier paragraphs the position of ageing in India from different aspects both in respect to males and females. Naturally, the question arises as to what is the position of ageing in some other countries especially China and USA as these are the two countries with the most ageing population.

According to the United Nations estimates (2005)[69] China

[68]Census of India (p. 63-64)

[69]Census of India (p.55)

is the most populated country with 132 crore population followed by India with 110 crore population. USA has only 30 crore population. Together China and India constitute 42 percent of the world population.

The following statement gives a comparative position of ageing in China, India and USA from 1950 to present day and future trends till 2040.

China	2050	1950	1960	1970	1980	1990	2000	2010	2020	2030	2040
%age of aged 60+	31.0	7.5	7.2	6.8	7.4	8.6	10.0	12.5	17.1	24.0	28.2
%age of aged 80+	7.2	0.3	0.4	0.5	0.4	0.6	0.7	1.4	1.9	2.8	4.5
India											
%age of aged 60+	20.7	5.6	5.7	6.0	6.5	6.8	7.5	8.5	10.6	13.6	16.8
%age of aged 80+	3.3	0.3	0.3	0.3	0.3	0.5	0.7	0.9	1.2	1.6	2.3
USA											
%age of aged 60+	26.4	12.5	13.3	14.1	15.6	16.5	16.2	18.1	22.0	24.7	25.4
%age of aged 80+	7.3	1.1	1.4	1.8	2.4	2.6	3.2	3.7	3.7	4.09	6.7

If one looks at the above figures the percentage of elderly (60+ and 80+) has been increasing from decade to decade in all the three countries. The increase is significant since the decades from 2010 onwards. It has almost more than doubled. This requires special planning to make the old age healthy and happy.

Ageing indicators in China, India and US in 2050

Parameters	China	India	USA
Percentage of children 0-14	15.7	18.3	17.3
Median age	44.8	38.7	41.1
Percentage of 60 and above	31.0	20.07	26.4
Percentage of 80 and above	7.2	3.3	7.3

Life expectancy (Years)			
Males	76.6	73.8	79.9
Females	80.9	78.1	85.0

Based on the above data it can be said that the elderly population (60+ and 80+) constitute a sizable chunk of the total population and that in all the three countries, life expectancy of females is more than males by five years. This necessitates special attention to the elderly population regarding their health and quality of life.

B. SENIOR CITIZENS SPEAK FRANKLY

Questionnaire - A

Introduction

The subject of the book is "Planning and Living Old Age". Growth is a natural process and one has to go through all the four stages of life which have been elaborated in the book. Needless to say that proper planning of every stage of life makes a qualitative difference in the living pattern and enjoyment in each stage of life. Without planning, life automatically drifts from one stage to the other.

The senior citizens in this piece are witnesses to the first half of the twentieth century i.e. during pre-independence period. They had to plan their lives in an age of strife and according to the then prevailing political and social structure. From the second half of the twentieth century there have been evolutionary and revolutionary changes in the demographic, family and social structure as a result of growing industrialisation and urbanisation. These changes affect both young and old of the present who have to adjust to the present-day challenges.

In order to understand their views of living their young age and also challenges to be faced in the present times, a questionnaire was sent to about sixty-five senior citizens who are well educated and are more than seventy years old. About sixty senior citizens have responded with their frank views which reveal many important aspects of life. The following is a brief analysis.

The table below gives an age-wise break-up of the respondents and their marital status:

Sr. No.	Age Group	Both Husband and wife living	Widowers	Widows	Single		Total
					Men	Women	
1	70-80 yrs	33	8	-		1	42
2	81-90 yrs	8	6	-	-	-	14
3	90+ yrs	-	1	1	-	-	2
	Total	41	15	1		1	58

Following are the responses by the senior citizens

Q1. During your student age did it ever occur to you that old age is bound to come and whether you thought that you should be physically and mentally fit in your old age. If so, did you follow a time table of daily exercise/yoga to keep the body and mind healthy.

From the responses it is seen that most of them did not think that they would one day face old age and need to prepare for it. 23 senior citizens however exercised regularly in their youth age to keep themselves physically fit without any deliberate thought of its benefit in old age.

Q2. During your young age whether your elders and parents imbibed in you or impressed upon you that the young men's duty and most obligations are to respect the mother, father, teacher and other elders.

In 80 per cent of the cases it was parents who taught them values, and respect to elders etc. In 8 out of 56 cases this came, through their cultural background, though none was taught this. In another 8 cases also none was taught, but values were imbibed in them naturally. Only in one case from a rural background, it was imbibed in school.

Q3. When you started your own career after education by joining some service or by starting own business/profession and after marriage, did you have a clear concept about your responsibilities and moral obligations towards your own family members –

wife, children and parents and other dependents, if any. Did you actually fulfil these obligations – if not, reasons therefore:

Here also 80 per cent of the respondents fulfilled their responsibilities to their families but these were the common responsibilities which every family man had to fulfil. One respondent stated that being the youngest member of a joint family, he had no responsibility at all.

Two respondents stated that they realised their responsibilities only after marriage or even later; but they fulfilled them.

There is one special case of a daughter who remained unmarried and who started earning to look after her sick brother and widowed mother. She worked as head mistress and was awarded the President's Medal as Best Teacher and was deputed to UK for further study. After the death of her sick brother and mother she has remained a spinster but has kept fully engaged in social work. Her life is indeed a role model.

In another similar case, the elder brother had to fulfil the needs of the education of two younger brothers and the marriage of his one younger sister. These two cases reflect the realisation of family responsibility in India.

In one case the elder brother took care of the education of his younger brother. This brother lost his wife early and had no children. He remained unmarried and fulfilled his obligations to his elder brother's family.

The last three cases depict the sacrifice undergone for the needs of the family. This is the true Indian culture where "family" comes before "I".

Q4 During your active age–earning age–did you have proper financial planning for meeting the expenses on your daughters/sons education, marriages? Did you have plans of financial security during old age–answer in brief.

During their active life 43 (74 per cent) were in service either with Government or private organisations; one was in agriculture and allied business, one was self employed, 9 were in the academic profession like professors and headmistress, 2 had their own business, One each was a musician and journalist. Those in services, of course with their limited income had saved in Provident Fund and insurance and all had fulfilled their obligation of children's education and marriage and now most of them are settled in life either with family or separately. But all of them are financially independent which shows proper planning for the future. Further some (8 to be exact) are still working and other (12) are working voluntarily in social welfare organisations. 28 persons are retired and have not reported any financial stringency. This shows either proper planning or that their offspring is looking after them well.

> Q5. Did you as a part of positive utilization of spare time during service/profession/business and with a view to remain occupied during old age get involved in some social work, useful hobbies like writing, painting, teaching etc (Any others)

Lack of hobbies, perhaps except reading fiction, among Indians in service is seen from the replies given to this question. Perhaps, the burden of their work may also be the cause. As many as 22 people (36 per cent) have reported that they had no time for anything but their jobs during their service. Other items of hobbies were reading, writing, teaching, research work, gardening, painting and social activities. From these, 15 were involved. Some had to do part-time work as teacher in night school, one managed a UTI agency and others did farming, wrote articles for magazines and papers either to augment their income or because of their liking for the job. There were 6 such cases. One respondent has mentioned her achievements in job such as "President's Award" or deputation to UK for study. Others in social work such as tree planting, research etc was also one of the aspects which kept about 3 respondents busy while in service and could be carried over to the post retirement period also.

Q6. Actually after retirement from service/profession/ business did you get proper opportunities to make use of these qualities? If so, how? If not, how are you spending your time (daily routine)?

There is a good tendency among the senior citizens is to work for the welfare of the other similarly placed citizens. As many as 12 respondents work for the organisations helping senior citizens. In addition, there are some engaged in helping parents of NRI children in reading and writing (1) in existing magazine or acting in play as a hobby (1). Some 6 senior citizens are still working, some to maintain family, (2) as a means to manage (1) to be self-employed (2) or in schools or institutes of handicapped (2) there are 5 connected with music, either in teaching or listening. Four are keeping themselves fit by yoga, morning walks and household work. One works in an educational institution as honorary director. One person is researching in Marathi ancient classic Jnyaneshwari and, adding value to present day Marathi research. Two people spend time travelling. One is a member of both Giant International Club and Gandhi Smarak Nidhi, while another is the Principal of a night school and guides underprivileged students. One established the "Prabhat Mandali" to organise collective prayers and another is a founder member of a school and is fully engaged as chairman in honorary capacity. Some keep busy doing consultation, teaching, writing books and research papers. Some 12 or 13 people just read and attend to household work. It is worth noting but everyone keeps busy in one or the other activity.

Q7. Do you agree that after retirement from your active service/profession/business your role and status in the family gets changed and that you are required to make a lot of adjustments in your behaviour with and towards family members? Please narrate in brief your own personal experience and suggestions, if any.

Though the joint family is still a prominent feature of Indian society, the lack of sufficient accommodation and attitudinal differences are slowly making the joint family a rarity. Though majority of the senior citizens live in a is with joint family, either out of choice or compulsion—both sons and daughters-in-law working or lack of cheap accommodation, one cannot be sure it will continue. At present 35 respondents stay with joint families as against 14 who stay in nuclear families. In one case, the daughter-in-law has to look after her 102 year old mother-in-law. Also there is one joint family with parents, 3 sons with their wives and grand children living under one roof. There are 3 families where only parents live because their sons and their families have shifted abroad. There are two cases of senior citizens (widowers) staying alone. One keeps himself busy with household work and another a journalist writes three articles a week and also works for a private foundation which has provided him with residential accommodation. One widower who has no sons, but only daughters has to keep shuttling between the houses of relatives at the age of 80+. Almost all senior citizens have stated that they have to adjust and make a lot of changes in their living style when they get advanced in years.

> Q8. Joint family system is fast disappearing. The attitude of the youngsters is also fast changing for various reasons. How the old people (aged) or surviving widows or widowers should plan their life? Did they prefer staying separately or live in old age home without any friction or ill will of the family members—sons and daughters?
>
> Q9. How actually you are spending your old age either with the family or separately? Was it willingly or out of frustration, quarrels and dislike for daughter-in-laws will etc. Please feel free in narrating actual facts.

These three questions are interlinked.

The answers also showed that family tradition is not breaking up as fast as it is made out to be and that children take care of their old parents.

But with more and more young people going abroad and families becoming smaller and smaller, in the very near future, a situation may arise where there will be more old parents to be looked after because their children are abroad or are staying away from them. Then the old age home will be the only alternative. Old people with independent incomes (as in the case of specimens selected) may not find it difficult to stay separately. But senior citizens with no or insufficient income will face the greatest of the problem and they will then be a burden on society and government It is more so with the sick and invalid. This has been dealt with in the earlier chapters.

Q10. How do you like the idea of live in relation for the widows and widowers? Will the children of both sides cherish this idea? Why live-in relation and not in marriage?

The responses vary on this highly sensitive issue from outright rejection to conditional acceptance. Nineteen persons are not in favour and four are totally favourable to live-in relationships. Six respondents are of the view that live-in relationship should have the consent of the children also.

Q11. Do you personally experience that the next generation has been planning properly for their old age—both financially and emotionally?

Q12. Do you personally experience that the youth though living away are caring for their parents and other elders properly? And, what is your experience of youth staying with parents and elders in the family?

It is heartening that to the above questions respondents have overwhelmingly given a positive response. It would mean that present day senior citizens are looked after well by their offspring.

To the question whether the younger generation plans for its future, the overwhelming response, of 33 to be exact is Yes. 10 have said a definite No. One respondent has said that they follow the Western method of "earn and spend". Some have described them as cautious, thoughtful, mature and quite conscious. So the overall feeling is that the younger generation, more or less, is on the right path.

In case of question 12, a good majority (62 percent) of the parents have agreed that the young people care for their parents whether living away or in joint family. Those whose parents are not cared for at all is in a negligible minority of less than 10 percent. 2 respondents have not replied at all and one has said that he has no experience. For some, the experience is mixed; there is no emotional bondage but the children provide financial help. One parent says that it is difficult to adjust with the youth because in these days of competition, they have less time for parents. Parents should also cooperate with sons and live without interfering in the son's affairs. One respondent has said that daughters are more caring. One says his son is caring for him now; but he is not sure of tomorrow. From these replies it is clear that relationships are individually different and don't adhere to any set pattern, but what is clear is that extreme cases of neglect are few and are the exceptions rather than the rule.

Q.13 Your personal views and suggestions for a happy and constructive old age life.

Though above 70 years of age, the respondents are still alert in mind and thought. They are active in life and capable of having their own view of life. So when asked to give their views on the life of senior citizens they have given interesting views and useful tips. A well-known journalist who is still active at the age of 90 has said that, other than the government servants who get a pension, the senior citizens have to fall back on the love and care of the younger members of the family which may not be coming forth in many cases. In such cases he says that the government should collect extra tax and make arrangements. He has brought forth the seriousness of the matter with the words, "It cannot be brushed aside." Another respondent of around 80 years of age who is somewhat financially comfortable but affected partially by paralysis has stated that persons should plan for old age much earlier, say from the age of 40 years onwards by spending less and keeping away from vices like drinking and gambling. He is voluntarily staying separately from his son and his family. But they keep visiting him at regular intervals. There are 13 more such couples among the respondents staying independently either of their own choice or because their sons and daughters are out of India. The rest of the respondents stay with their families and have not spoken about any rift or fight.

Q.14 Do you think that the government is doing enough for the senior citizen population in the country? If no, why do you think so?

Old age schemes are not receiving proper attention and priority. In 18 cases the senior citizens have stated that government is not doing anything. Even others have stated that government is doing nothing but have given some suggestions that at least medical check-up, better implementation of "Below Poverty Line" schemes etc should be implemented. Mumbai Police visit to senior citizen's homes was started but the scheme has not achieved the desired results. One has pointed out the menace of middle men, who pocket whatever little money that is sanctioned by the government. The general impression that one gets from the replies is that government is not serious about the welfare of senior citizens and the old are left to their own means and fate.

Q.15 Do you think that old-age homes are a good idea for senior citizens? Please explain your opinion, whether Yes or No, in detail.

The response of old men to the question was varied. One respondent said that old age homes are good and four have said "No" or "not good". There are, of course, a few who have really appreciated old age homes as good where old people can spend a cheerful life, away from family strife and by enjoying the company of similarly placed people. One respondent has simply said it is a "good idea" and another has conditioned his remark as "where there is none to look after or for those disowned by youngsters or children away in foreign countries".

Some others have said that old-age homes are good, when not expensive and are well run, when there is financial backing if there is none-else to look after, for widowers, widows and single, for those who do not get on well with children or those who can adjust to circumstances. Against these sober responses, one respondent has said, "they are refined jails" and against such a view, one respondent has said "for those who are alone they (old age homes) give company" and "by adjusting old men can lead a contented life", another has said it is "a good idea where one has money to spend."

Questionnaire – B

Introduction

Questionnaire A was intended to ascertain the views of elderly on various personal and social issues arising out of increase in longevity in general and more so in respect of ladies resulting in increase in the number of widows with attendant problems as explained in the previous chapters. The respondents were expected to elaborate their views. The present questionnaire is more personalised in the sense that the respondents were expected to give answers in Yes or No terms indicating their personal status in the various issues which arise in different stages of life.

Sixty-six elderly—54 males and 12 ladies responded. Nearly thirty-two percent of the elderly were above seventy years of age.

Position of their family size and occupation was as under: Family size: 13.5 percent respondents had children up to two, 31.5 percent respondents had children up to four and 45 percent of the respondents had more than four children. Occupation: Before the age sixty, 12 percent were in business, 66 percent in service, 7.5 percent were housewives. After the age of sixty, 10.5 percent continued to be in business, 50 percent in service, 4.5 percent took to consultancy, 4.5 percent housewives and 24 percent retired.

Response to questionnaire:

After studying replies to the various questions generalised percentage has been worked out and is indicated in the questionnaire itself.

A)	Childhood & Health:-			
1	At what age did you start to exercise? 30% 20% 45% 4.5% 10.5%	3%	15%	15%
	Age 10 15 20 25 30	40	50	60+
2	Whether family members prompted you to exercise	Yes 34.5%	No 16.5%	Own 43.5%
3.	Whether friends encouraged you to exercise	Yes 46.5%	No 24%	
4	At what age was fitness in old age the aim? Age 20, 25, 35, 45, 55, Above 65% 1.5% 10.5% 3% 21% 3%	-	-	-
5	Was there time-table for exercise/yoga?	Yes 73.5%	No 22.5%	
6	Do you spare time for physical fitness now?	Yes 87%	No 4%	
7	Are you physically fit now?	Yes 88.5%	No 7.5%	
8	Do you have any chronic complaints now?	Yes 30.5%	No 69.5%	
9	Have you any fixed diet for health?	Regular 79.5%	No 15%	
B	Responsibilities:-			
1	Whether your parents socialised you for respecting Mother/Father/Teacher/ Sisters/Brothers/Elders?	Yes 84%	No 2%	
2	Whether your parents were taking responsibilities of their family of origin/ or elderly persons?	Yes 95.5%	No 1.5%	
3	Actually, when you started sharing family responsibilities?	Not required 4.5%	From Child-hood 9%	Only after earning 88.5%

4	If you could not share the responsibilities, why?	Age-Wise no need 16.5%	Not earner 4.5%	Meagre income 4.5%
C)	Financial Position			
1	At what age you started earning i) Below 16 yrs ii) Between 20-25 yrs iii) After 25 yrs } iv) After marriage }	9% 48% 37.5%		
2	Was career making/earning forced?	Yes 48.5%	No 39%	
3	You had to earn for meeting family expenses?	Yes 60%	No 31.5%	
4	Could you plan financially for old age security?	Yes 81%	No 7.5%	
5	Could not plan security because of my limited income Obligations towards parents Nuclear family responsibilities	7.5% 7.5% 7.5%		

D) Emotional Attachment

1	Are you emotionally attached to your family of origin?	Yes 84.5%	No 7.5%	
2	Whether emotional attachment to the family prevented career making	Yes 50.5%	No 7.5%	
3	Could not develop your hobbies like: Social involvement Writing/painting/teaching Own business/travel	40.5% 9% 3%	1.5% 3%	3%
4	Whether prior to your retirement could you develop your hobbies?	Yes 59%	No 30%	
E	Family life and involvement			
1)	Whether your hobbies helped you for remaining active?	Yes 75%	No -	
2)	Could you spare money and time for desired goals?	Yes 83.5%	No 7.5%	
3)	Is role in the family changing after retirement?	Yes 56.5%	No 34%	
4)	Whether impartment changes you have made afterwards?	Yes 31.5%	No 19.5%	

5)	Are you happy with the changes made?	Yes 60%	No 3%	N.A 13.5%
6)	Are you spending retired life with spouse only?	Yes 66%	No 19%	N.A. 3%
7)	Do you live now with your son/ daughter?	Yes 46.5%	No 46.5%	
8)	Should widows/widowers plan their life?	Yes 75%	No 4%	
9)	Is planning impossible for widows/ widowers?	Yes 37.5%	No 45%	
10)	Should widows/widowers be in old age home/ashrams?	Yes 36%	No 36%	
11)	Is spending your old age with son or daughter-in-law comfortable? Or daughter and son-in-law comfortable?	Yes 48.5% 19.5%	No 18% 10.5%	
12)	Can senior citizens help the family of children and be useful?	Yes 83%	No 3%	
13)	Whether you are all alone or member of joint family?	Yes 58.9%	No 24%	N.A. 2.5%
14)	Is it fair to help needy children if you are stable, of financial assistance will affect your security?	Yes 85.5%	No 9%	N.A. 4.5%
15)	Whether your financially able children help you?	Yes 64.5%	No 3%	
16)	When you don't need money, should children physically help you?	Yes 82.5%	No 7.5%	
17)	Whether separate living affects taking care by children?	Yes 50%	No 35.5%	
18)	Your impression about youngsters planning for their old age.	Physical Fitness 36%	Financial Security 58%	Emotional Life 36%
19)	Is Government taking enough care for the age old people?	Yes 15%	No 67.5%	
20)	Whether old age homes ideal for senior citizens? If yes, in what way If not, Why Not?	Yes 32.5%	No 22.5%	
21)	Are you happy with life and would like to continue still?	Yes 78%	No 1.5%	

Observations

Following observations are made on the responses on the major aspects contained in the questionnaire.

A. Childhood and health:

Exercise is a must during childhood and young age to have a sound health throughout life. From the responses it is seen that only about 30 percent started exercise at the age of 10 and 20 percent at the age of 15. Though by and large—88.5 percent are keeping fairly good health at the age of sixty or more about 30.5 percent have some chronic complaints. However, the present younger generation should understand the importance and necessity of starting exercise at the age of six or so.

B. Responsibilities:

Respecting and taking care of the elderly is a traditional way of life. This mindset is passed on from generation to generation. From the responses it is clear that the parents of the present elderly were taking care and responsibility of their parents and the same attitude is passed on to the present elderly. 88.5 percent of the respondents started taking responsibility of the family when they started earning.

C. Financial position:

In normal course youth starts earning between the age of 25-30 after completion of his education mainly to start his family life and also to share the burden of his parents if necessary. But for various reasons like poverty and death of earning member in the family one has to start earning much earlier. From the responses it is seen that 9 per cent started earning when they were less than 16 years of age. 48 per cent started earning during the age range of 20 to 25 years.

While earning one should ensure proper financial planning not only to meet the present needs in the family like family running expenses, education and marriage of the children etc., but also to save for old age. 81 percent of the respondents had planned to save for the old age. 7.5 percent of the respondents could not plan for the old age because of meagre income.

Due to increase in the longevity proper financial planning for old age is a must. Savings should start from the pay of the first month itself.

D. Emotional attachment:

Emotional attachment among the family members is a quality which brings and keeps together both in the favourable and adverse circumstances. 84.5 percent of the respondents have said that they have emotional attachments with the family members. This is a good sign. In the fast changing family structure it is all the more necessary to have emotional attachment with family members which is a great psychological strength to share good and bad days. It also gives strength to spare time for social work and also develop one's hobby like writing, painting etc. From the responses it is seen that 59 percent had developed hobbies before retirement.

Family life and involvement:

The questions mainly pertain to the years of life after retirement, by which time the children also would have grown up, started earning, got married and started their family life. Living arrangements after retirement is very important factor in making the retired life happy. Also occupation to keep oneself busy, social contacts, attitudinal adjustments are necessary to make the old age graceful.

From the responses received it can be said that by and large the respondents were well prepared for the old age. As regards living arrangements majority stayed with sons and daughters, indicating their preference for joint family system. Of course their role in the family affairs had necessarily to be changed. Nearly 56.5 percent have said that their role in the family was changed while 34 percent have said that they continue to play the same role as while in service, business etc. Nearly 75 percent continue to remain active after retirements. With adequate financial security they could pursue their hobbies also. 64.5 percent of the elderly said that their children were ready t finance the parents whenever they need it.

On the question whether government is taking enough care of the elderly only 15 percent said Yes and 6-7.5 percent said No. The state should understand the feelings of the elderly and take more concrete steps to keep the elderly happy.

It may be stated at the end that the responses are mostly from the middle class elderly and from their views expressed frankly should enable the family members and policy makers to think about "how to make elderly of all categories poor, middle class and well to do feel that old age is worth living".

(*The questionnaire was designed, responses obtained and analysed by Dr. G. B. Kolhatkar, aged 78, a social scientist of Pune. Address: B-60, Woodland, Kothrud Tel: 25383630*)

C. ARTICLES BY EMINENT SENIOR CITIZENS

Old Age and Attendant Problems

~ *M.V. Kamath*

(*Madhav Vittal Kamath, aged 92, is a senior Indian journalist and author of over 40 books. He was the former chairman of Prasar Bharati. He was Washington correspondent of* Times of India *during 1969-78. He has also served as editor of the Illustrated Weekly of India. Currently, he is the Honorary Director of Manipal Institute of Communication. He was awarded Padma Bhushan in 2004.*)

I saw a report in *Harmony* magazine that said middle age starts at forty-eight years and "old age" at seventy-five. That seems to be not quite fair as matters go. One normally retires at the age of sixty and, if the employer is generous, this may be extended by two years. Old age, thus, begins in the early sixties and the possibilities are that one may live for another fifteen years, considering that life expectancy is now around seventy-two. Way back in 1947, when India became free, it was round a low twenty-seven years which would mean that only a very minute percentage lived beyond seventy-five. As matters stand now, Indian citizens live longer with, in many instances, grievous results.

It is now a well-known fact that the problems that the aged face are threefold: fak.kia n , financial and health related. One presumes that those who belong to the upper middle and upper classes are financially well-off and could well take care of themselves. My thoughts go to those who belong to upper lower to the middle middle classes: how do they handle old age? The joint family is now a thing of the past. There are no large households. Couples aged, say sixty-five years onwards, live practically alone, their children having either left them for making a living abroad or having decided to live separately from their elders for greater privacy. This seems to be a growing feature. Who takes care of the elders then? Here, I must make a broad division between people who live on a pension and people who are dependent either on their savings or on the goodwill and grace of their grown up children. And there is the rub. I don't have statistics on people who, as government servants, draw a pension. They are a class apart. Percentage wise, I don't expect them to be more than 10 to 12 of the plus-60 retirees. Whatever their pension is, of one thing they can be sure: at the end of the month, they know that some cash awaits them on which they can live if not well, at least comfortably. But what about those, employed in private firms and who, aged sixty, are left to fend for themselves? Who takes care of them, especially in regard to health and medical expenses? To the best of my knowledge nobody has made a study of this situation which cries for detailed study.

I have heard painful accounts of parents neglected and left unattended only to die slowly and in deep distress. One of the new developments is the growth of old age homes, but we do not yet know who their resident customers are and their financial status. Such homes do not come cheap and an average individual or a couple may have to shell out anything between ₹10 to ₹20 lakhs as deposit, apart from having to pay a monthly sum of anything between ₹5,000 to ₹10,000. How many among the middle class can afford to pay such large sums of money? Would close relations like, say, brothers/sisters/sons/daughters come forward with financial help? How many of the old age homes again, are caste-based? Is there any way that insurance companies can help?

The saddest part of today's family sets-up is that many are increasingly becoming "nuclear"—one child based, with both parents employed leading to attention to the child's growth outsourced to nursing homes with inevitable consequences. Feeling neglected, the child looks for emotional support beyond the confines of the home. Parents begin to realise it only in their later years. At the poorer level, old people have some reason to feel more at ease. According to the media, to widen the scope of social security scheme for poor senior citizens, the government is set to revise the rules of old age pension.

The Ministry of Rural Development has apparently proposed to revise the rules for old age pension. It has, it is claimed, proposed to lower the age of those who can avail of the pension from sixty-five to sixty years while, at the same time, increasing the monthly allowance from ₹200 to ₹500 p.m. to handle the increasingly rising high cost of living as a result of inflation. That would amount roughly to about ₹16 a day which is nothing much to speak about, but would at least guarantee one meal a day for the poor pensioner. As is not so well-known, the Central Government has the Indira Gandhi National Old Age Pension Scheme to provide some money to senior citizens below the poverty line that would be in addition to the subsidised food grains the poor are entitled to every month under the government's public distribution system. According to the media, the ministry's current proposal would mean that one crore more poor would come under the Direct Subsidy Scheme. Persons who earn less than ₹589 p.m. in the urban areas and below ₹450 in the rural areas will be the beneficiaries.

But is this concern for the poor, commendable as it is, applicable to one and all—including those from the middle classes? Take, for example, a teacher who retires at age sixty and can find no employment, or a clerk in similar circumstances but whose children are reasonably well-to-do, and yet are separated from their offspring? Who is to decide on the eligibility of applicants for government support? There are many such issues that need to be addressed. But in the end there is no question but that the care of old people is the primary responsibility of their children and of none else. To assign such responsibility to government is demeaning and does not say much about people's adherence to dharma. But here a word about caste responsibility may not be entirely out of place. Whatever one may say about caste, the bare truth is that it exists and if it cares to, it can play a role in taking care of the elderly. Funds can be raised, suitable old age homes can be set up and run for the old and the infirm at manageable costs.

But, as the saying goes, who is to bell the cat? The situation being what it is, one suspects that for a long time to come the old and the infirm have no other option hut to suffer uncomplainingly. Or go on a Kashi Yatra and die en route unattended and unsung. Taking sanyas is no option unless it involves fasting unto death, if that is its hidden meaning.

Towards the Glorious Sunset

~ Usha Thakkar

(*Ms Usha Thakkar is Hon. Director, Institute of Research on Gandhian Thought & Rural Development, and Hon. Secretary, Mani Bhavan Gandhi Sangrahalaya*)

As I try to collect my thoughts on old age and strategies of coping with it, I wonder what old age is. Is it gradual loss of physical strength, weaning of faculties, increasing aches and pains and dimness of memory, all ultimately convolving into a long wait for death. Or is just the final stage of life, when one can sit and reflect on the years that have passed by, the rich time to savour experiences of the years that have gone by. Perhaps both the perspectives contain some elements of truth. The important question is how to cope with the advancing years of life.

As one lives longer one has to be a helpless witness to declining physical energy as well as the passing away of dear ones. It is not easy to cope with a situation that seems to be overwhelming with a sense of loss—loss of vitality as well as loss of near and dear ones. The golden dreams of life seem to fade into shades of gray, and slow pace of life descends softly. In the words of Mathew Arnold,

It is to spend long days
And not once feel that we were ever young.
It is to add, immured
In the hot prison of the present, month
To month

On the other hand, it is also the stage when one finds time to pay attention to some unfinished tasks and neglected interests. Advance in medical science and awareness about health and hygiene have increased the lifespan of an individual with a promise of good life in later years. Opportunities for the elderly in contemporary times are unprecedented. It is not uncommon for the elderly to seek new areas and avenues for their talents and interests. It is not unusual to see an elderly person developing hobbies of singing or writing or gardening or art. It is certainly not a stage of senility and infirmity. Tagore took up painting in his later years. Morarjibhai Desai occupied the chair of prime minister late in life. Churchill bloomed as a politician in his later years. John Kenneth Galbraith wrote regularly in the later years of his life. Recent times have witnessed "old" leaders like Silvio Berlusconi of Italy, Manmohan Singh of India, Mwai Kibaki of Kenya and Queen Elizabeth of U.K.

Some develop a life-long liking for power and find it difficult to vacate the positions of power even at an advanced age. However it is prudent to leave such positions at a certain age and stage in life. Every stage in life from childhood to death has its own joys, responsibilities and obstacles; one has to welcome all stages of life with equanimity. A person has to retire after putting in certain years of hard work making space for another to occupy her/his chair and moving to some different activity or even take life easy, provided the person has worked hard in young days and has really earned restful living. A person earns the right to be free from the work of repetitive drudgery she/he has done for years. Relinquishing a post after certain age is a welcome step. Ratan Tata gave up a position of power voluntarily after a certain age. Recently the news that caught our attention was that Pope Benedict XVI became the first Pope since the middle ages to step down. Even in families it is nice to see the transition of power and responsibilities from older to the younger generation. The patriarch of the family and the ruling queen of the household in their old age have to learn to give up the power positions and to adapt themselves to the roles of nurturing wise persons.

Retirement does not mean living in seclusion or giving up social interaction. It is the time to stop being in a formal position and to experience the joy of living. One can continue to do some useful work and if the circumstances demand earn a little. It is the zest for life that determines the outcome. Voluntary social work can fill up the void of the declining years. Such work may vary from working for an organisation or reading to the blind or helping the deprived. There comes a time when one thinks of doing something different, something pleasant, and also to return to the society whatever she/he can. Persons like Bill Gates and Warren Buffet return their due to the society. One does not have to return in financial terms only; such return can be in terms of talents, time, skills and experience.

Our ancient texts associate the advanced age with wisdom that is acquired by experience and learning over years. In the famous *Yaksha* questions narrated in the *Mahabharata, Yaksha* asks *Yudhisthir* what makes a person intelligent, and the latter's answer is the association/company of the aged (*Vriddha).* The word *Vriddha* comes from the root that means growing, so the old or the aged is one who has grown, not only physically but also intellectually. One is also reminded of a quote in *Vidurniti* that states clearly that an assembly is not an assembly, where there are no aged (*Vriddha)* persons, and those aged (*Vriddha)* persons are not aged if they do not tell the *Dharma.* Thus the link between the advanced age is established with wisdom, experience and knowledge.

An advancing age in our times demands medical care and

financial security. Women in our society need extra care. For most part of their life they look after the family and children. In old age they need respite and affectionate care. Looking after grandchildren is a joy, but cannot be a full time work. Household work after a certain age can be a burden. Senior persons, men and women, must maintain their dignity and independence. Sensitive response of the family, society and state can be of enormous help in providing this. Some countries, starting from Germany under Bismarck before more than a century, have made special provisions for the elder citizens.

The contemporary times have witnessed an increase in the number of the elderly. The phase of life after sixties requires good health, congenial family as well as social relations and balanced wealth management. It will also be comfortable if one has completed social responsibilities and is willing to learn new skills and to take up new challenges. It is heartening to see the elders getting computer savvy and having wonderful rapport with younger generation. This stage of life offers freedom to make choices in the manner of life one wants to live. One has to discover one's own potential and interests that never got opportunities. One has to learn to give up negative traits and to make way for the next generation, and yet to be around if any help is required.

With advance in age, decline in health and memory are inevitable. One must learn to live with that. A tender approach from the people around at this juncture can be comfortable.

If youth has its beauty and vitality, old age has is own charm, if one cares to find it. A toothless smile of Gandhiji could put a stranger at complete ease. As sunrise is beautiful, so is the sunset. After experiencing the richness of life, going through the hustle bustle of life, one reaches the stage of sunset, not the dreary end of the journey but a resplendent time full of richness of experience. One, however, has to prepare for this journey to the glorious sunset and enjoy the richness of the remaining years of life.

The Evening of One's Life

~ *Satish Sahney*

(*Shri Satish Sahney is a former IPS Officer. After his retirement in December 1996, he joined Nehru Centre, Mumbai, as its Chief Executive, from January 1997 and has been working as such ever since.*)

Getting on in years is a natural process and there comes a time when one retires from the daily grind of ten to twelve hours of work. It is certainly not the onset of old age. It is entering into a new phase of life which can be fruitful and extremely satisfying because it provides the freedom to do what one wishes to do. To make it so there are four essential requirements: a place to live, financial independence, sound health and an occupation to keep the mind constantly engaged in meaningful pursuit.

Theoretically the formula sounds very well but how many in reality are able to meet all the requirements? May be those who have been professionals or in a service of some type which provides the benefit of provident fund, gratuity and life-long pension are able to do so. Even amongst them it may not be all that easy. For example, health cannot be taken for granted. One has to be lucky to inherit strong and healthy genes coupled with self-discipline in matters of health and avoidance of excessive self-indulgence. Everyone is not so blessed.

In the context of India's huge population the percentage of such people would be very small. Millions have to struggle throughout their life to survive. When age catches up with them and their physical strength ebbs away, they face deprivation, illness and humiliation and slip into a life of indignity. Only a welfare state will be able to address this enormous human problem; a state which provides security of an income to the unemployed, old age pension and old age homes and free national health service.

While moving towards the evening of one's life one must try to become gracious, humble and patient. It requires a great deal of the practice of mind control, particularly for those who have been in positions of pomp and power. The quality of patience prevents one from getting angry, annoyed and irritated. It also helps one become a good listener who does not interrupt others while they are speaking. Humility pushes false pride out of the system and one gives up the practice of constantly proving one's worth by bragging about one's achievements and accomplishments. In return, one develops an inner confidence in oneself that does not require any praise from anyone for its sustenance.

Cultivating a spirit of detachment is yet another very great quality. It may well be asked that the idea of detachment is contrary to the suggestion that an occupation is necessary to keep one purposefully occupied. Rajaji in his marvellous book on Bhagvad Gita explains the spirit of detachment as "not wanting in expertness or efficiency in work, but vigilantly guarding against the development of selfish attachments". This spirit of detachment, if developed, though not easy to nurture, will keep the body and mind healthy and free from worry all through life and especially when one is not young any more.

On Growing Old

~ *Vispi Balaporia*

(Prof. Vispi Balaporia is a member of the Senate at the University of Mumbai. She retired as the Vice Principal and Head of the Department of English in Jaihind College in 2011. At present she is Advisory Member on the Jai Hind College Managing Board.)

Fear has many definitions and descriptions, but the constant is that it is embedded in every human being—almost from birth. In that sense it is a primeval emotion. As children, we fear the dark, and the dark can be linked to the unknown. Children also tend to have overactive imaginations, which feed ravenously on fear, heightening the terror of the unknown. As we grow into adults and learn to rationalise our fears, we may succeed in taming them. But they continue to haunt our subconscious.

The average adult gets caught up in the hurly burly of everyday life, leaving no room for vague anxieties, except perhaps at fleeting moments. The ever increasing demands of daily life provide their full load of worries and problems, and all one's energy is diverted to coping with these. Old age, death, and the unknown get pushed into the background.

It is only when this hectic pace slows down that the individual begins to introspect on these realities of life. In our birth is our death is a universal law; but how many of us give much thought to this. Moreover, to think of death every moment we live would perhaps be too morbid. But there comes a time in every human's life when one needs to start looking at this eventuality. And that is when one needs to work out a coping strategy, without panicking.

There is no readymade recipe for such a coping strategy. It is dependent on innumerable factors, such as the individual's nature, personality, mental preparedness, ability to rationalise, as well as one's social, financial, and emotional situation. So let me briefly give my personal approach to this universal situation.

Having now moved into the seventies, I have accepted the fact that the major part of my life is done. How much remains is an open question to which I am not looking for answers. I take each day as it comes, fulfilling the tasks lined up for that day. But that does not mean that I do not plan for the future, though a future more near than far. Consequently, I am happy and agreeable to accept suggestions made by either family or friends, and look forward to accomplishing these. And that, too, makes all the difference: having tasks and commitments that require time, effort, and energy to fulfil; having a number of affectionate family members that want to include you in their plans and their concerns; having friends who want to do things together with you. All this keeps me going, despite the loneliness and the void created by the very sudden and unexpected death of my husband a couple of years ago. There are private moments of sorrow, and fried, and remembrance. But these, too, I accept as the inevitable part of being the survivor in a happy marriage of forty-seven years.

It is, then, with this philosophy that I face old age, hoping that my health, both physical and mental, will not desert me, as I wait for that final curtain to come down.

Second Innings

~ *Indu Saraiya*

(*Indu Saraiya is a freelance writer and journalist whose book reviews feathers and interviews have appeared in leading newspapers and magazines. She was founder editor of BEAM, the literary biannual of the Bombay English Association and has authored a book* Dateline Independence.)

"Grow old along with me!
The best is yet to be,
The last of life for which the first was made;
Our times are in His hand
Who Saith 'A whole I planned,
Youth shows but half; trust God: see all,
Nor be afraid!'"

("Rabbi Ben Ezra" by Robert Browning)

Browning wrote this and similar poems three years after the death of his beloved but ailing poetess-wife, Elizabeth Browning. Theirs was an intensely happy marriage of fifteen years. Overcoming grief, Browning then began to explore through his poems the larger concept of human love vis-a-vis divine love. Accepting the inexorable passage from youth to age, life to death, he imagined advancing age as a second birth, a chance to reinvent oneself, obtain the interest from the capital invested in one's youth. Browning followed his own mantra, and went on to lead a rich social and literary life in England.

Would this mantra work in today's very different, chaotic, globalised, space-age world? Certainly, provided one is not killed prematurely in an earthquake, or by a terrorist, or by penury, or by a disabling disease, or by any of the scores of accidents not of one's own making. Though the mortal coil decays, the mind and spirit are independent of the body; they can be cultivated to become a source of renewed energy, strength, and joy of life.

However, the equations between the young and the elderly of today have broadened from the purely personal and philosophical like Browning's, to the familial and the sociological. Dependable parental care can no longer be guaranteed. This is the age of "Dinks" (double-income couples). Married working couples can hardly find the time or the energy to cultivate among their already over-burdened children, hobbies like sports, music, stitching, dancing, reading, writing, carpentry, hiking and so on. Again, with joint families breaking up into nuclear families, the grandmothers are no longer around. This is one lamentable loss for children growing up today. Another threat is the easy access to drinks and drugs. Indeed, binging up children in today's day and age is an onerous task for parents.

With nuclear families comes another cruel problem—no room for ageing parents in two and three bedrooms flats. I once read a news report of an elderly grandmother in Chennai being dumped as garbage next to the bin! However, this is more the exception than the rule, as I found out when I was working for "Bombay Magazine" in the 1980s. One of my assignments was to write a feature on Old Peoples Homes in Bombay. It was published in the issue of 7-21 May 1983.

The assignment took me far and wide—from Mother Teresa's Asha Daan at Byculla, to the Shepherd Widows' Home nearby, built for the care of 65 year olds and above (interestingly, every inmate had to submit a copy of her will to the managing committee), to the Little Sisters of the Poor Home for the Aged on Mahakali Road, Andheri, to the Cheshire Home, also in

Andheri, appropriately named Bethlehem.

Let me give you just four illustrations. As I entered Asha Daan, my hand was grabbed by a distraught, bejewelled, spectacled lady. "Are you Sindhi like me?" she asked; and without waiting for an answer, burst into tears and said, "My children threw me out but I get more love here than I ever did at home."

"It is like home here," asserts 74 year old Maude Callaghan who has lived in this small, cosy Shepherd Widows' Home for 9 years. Her two daughters live in Canada, and she would have gone there to live, except that the weather defeated her.

In contrast, the Little Sisters of the Poor Home for the Aged is a spacious haven of peace for almost 300 needy men and women of over 60 years. The place is like a beehive, with inmates gardening or mending or typing or painting the furniture and so on. To feel useful is in itself an antidote to age, and the humiliation of total physical and emotional dependence is taken care of by the Sisters' reassuring care. "When death approaches," says Sister Patricia, "as it often does here, people gather round, praying or attending to the person's needs, and never allowing the person to feel alone and unwanted in death."

At Bethlehem, I saw John Mercel who had lost both arms and both legs many years ago in a factory accident, bring out an artificial arm and write out in clear, regular lettering "Cheshire Home" on the blackboard for the village pupils.

But now, with the Great Indian Diaspora, a new dimension between parents and their expatriate offspring, has sprouted. Today, NRI sons and daughters can send funds several times more to their relatives in India than either side could ever have imagined. Such parents need no longer be a burden on their children. And in the United States, domestic help is either too expensive or not easily available, and home-tending fathers and mothers can earn a few dollars side-wise through baby-sitting, or catering, or even driving! The world is full of surprises.

It is dangerous to generalise, but by and large, the tradition in Indian culture has always been for the young to respect the old. Although this tradition largely continues in this day and age, it is under stress. Our forefathers had realised centuries ago the burden ageing parents would put on their growing families' resources, and had wisely advocated *vanaprastha*—that is, voluntary retirement to the forest. But in fast-urbanising India, where are the forests? Perhaps the practical answer to *vanaprastha* today lies in old people's homes.

There is nothing more satisfying than spending one's autumn years pursuing one's childhood hobbies like reading, piano-playing, stitching, socialising—even if it only on one's evening walks with others, or playing Bridge, or Badminton, Gold and so on. The spiritually-minded, like my late widowed mother, can read scriptures, attend *kirtans* or go on pilgrimages. What most ageing people need is love and human companionship; it is important not get isolated, but to remain involved with people. A kind of peace comes with a feeling, hopefully right, that one has tried one's best to live a useful life, that one has fulfilled one's duties to one's children and elders, and with that peace comes an urge to love everybody, and be loved by everybody.

After all, age is just a number.

How I View and Use my Old Age Years

~ *Dr. P. M. Kamath*

(Formerly Professor of Politics, University of Bombay, currently, Adjunct Professor, Department of Geopolitics and International Studies, Manipal University, Manipal and Hon Director, VPM's Centre for International Studies (Regd), Mulund, Mumbai.)

When I retired from the University of Bombay in 1997, I thought it is time to plan for one's own death. Then just to warn me that I am not going to live forever, within two years after my retirement, in August 1999, I had a mild stroke and I spent seventeen days in ICCU. Another thought also convinced me that I am not immortal: all great men have died; that also consoled me. Death often comes all of a sudden; and one does not plan or propose for one's own death.

In my case my stroke was caused by my own inadequacies in managing people in an educational trust with which I was associated with since 1962 in various purely honorary capacities. I have used the term "purely" because in this trust we do not take even any honorarium. Since my association with this trust has been for a long period, I tend to care for its growth and development. But incapable, incompetent, insecure and insensitive people, who come and go would like to think that I might be enjoying some hidden advantages!

But I learnt many new ideas and lessons in the retired life by working in this educational trust as well as in academic field. One thing is: As the age advances, people who are doing some useful social work will have their ego inflated as age goes by. Longer they live, higher the position they hold, bigger is their ego. Hence though they may guide and extol others on the virtue of working without ego, they never realise that they too are the victims of their inflated ego. You may wish to know, how I have tried to overcome the impact of this phenomenon. I have simply refused to occupy the highest position!

Second, senior citizens ought to know the rule that they cannot change the past. Hence, do not harp on the past. I encounter practically on every day during my walking sessions in the garden, seniors telling me: That he could have done this or that and brooding over it and repenting for his not doing it, then! One illustration is necessary. I have known an auditor by profession, who is a good yoga teacher. He would demonstrate that even after sixty he can still perform shirshasana! But wherever he went seeking an assignment after his retirement as a yoga instructor, he was turned away for not being able to produce certificate/s proving his having undergone yoga training.

Senior citizens have to realise that past cannot come back; future is unknown, hence, not subject to change as on *today*. What is important therefore is: Today, the day you live is important and you can use it as you wish. You can change its impact on you. You can mould it the way you wish. You being able to do it can bring you rich dividends; it helps to keep you happy; thereby you unknowingly help yourself to live longer and purposefully. Hence senior citizens in their old age must always cultivate a positive attitude. If I can have confidence that I can shape the day I live, I will achieve so much, which one cannot simply foretell.

If you follow the second principle of life, you will be a young man always in hurry to make best use of the day in hand. This has helped me in the academic field as well as in my social work. Whenever, some issue has bothered me, I have taken pen in hand to express myself to reach out to a larger audience. I am not a social reformer, I am not a civic activist; yet I have influenced many decisions of the government at all levels: federal, state and local. In many cases impact has been seen and experienced; and in cases, it has been slow to be seen.

If I narrate all instances here, my article might turn into a book. But let me narrate one instance, at the federal level and one at the local level: Soon after the Indian nuclear tests, I wrote an article on "Post-Pokhran Permutations" in the *Tribune* (Chandigarh) on 17 June 1998 justifying Indian nuclear tests and suggesting further steps to be taken to augment Indian power. The article drew the attention of the then defence minister, George Fernandes. He wanted more information and supporting documents. I was then in Shimla. He traced me there by evening six on the same day as it was published. I had immense satisfaction that I could contribute a little bit in the government's policymaking. Second, I wrote an article in *Mid-Day* on evil effects of spitting. I met the then commissioner of Mumbai. He was so pessimistic. But I kept on harping on the issue. Now you see some impact of it in your city of Mumbai.

I have nothing but full satisfaction of having done so much

during the post-retirement period. I have published two books of my own, and one manuscript is ready to go to press; I have also edited three books and three edited books are in pipe line for publication. In addition to it, I have authored numerous articles in peer-reviewed journals and countless—running into thousands, articles in popular magazines and newspapers in India and abroad.

In the field of social work, again using the precious time available in hand today, I could expand the institutions under the banner of VPM in Mulund. No doubt many others have contributed their mite into it, but nobody can ever say that these were conceived by someone else. My intellectual inputs, planning of implementation and administering to show them sunlight, will speak volumes for ever by themselves. In pursuing these goals, if any one says to me that we will do it tomorrow, I have tried to convince him. But if one does not listen to any of my proposals, wherever I am convinced, I have succeeded to sideline such naysayers. Additionally my time and money have gone into enriching them. Many of my friends who know me, do not hesitate even for a second to acknowledge my contributions. I am sure my detractors, at least, even if grudgingly, will admit my contributions in the growth of these institutions. My contribution to society at large is so significant that I have donated my body for medical students to study rather than burn in the crematorium.

The message is clear: if I were to go after money earning as most of my retired friends have done, I could have been a millionaire by running a coaching class, in which I never believed. But what I would have left in such a case is a pot full of money to my successors—may be, to fight among them. But what I leave today for future generations is: my lifelong work in academic and social field for them to build on and keep the idea that senior citizens can do social and academic work with lasting impact.

D) RESOURCES FOR SENIOR CITIZENS

I) CONCESSIONS AND FACILITIES FOR SENIOR CITIZENS

Concessions and Facilities given to Senior Citizens by Different Ministries/Departments of the Govt

1) Ministry of Social Justice & Empowerment

Ministry of Social Justice & Empowerment is the nodal Ministry responsible for welfare of the Senior Citizens. It has announced the National Policy on Older Persons covering all concerns pertaining to the welfare of older persons. The National Policy on Older Persons recognizes a person aged 60 years and above as a senior citizen.

The Ministry is also implementing following schemes for the benefit of Senior Citizens:

- An Integrated Programme for Older Persons (Plan Scheme) - This Scheme has been formulated by revising the earlier scheme of "Assistance to Voluntary Organisations for Programmes relating to the Welfare of the Aged". Under this Scheme, financial assistance up to 90% of the project cost is provided to NGOs for establishing and maintaining Old Age Homes, Day Care Centres, Mobile Medicare Units and to provide non-institutional services to older persons.
- The Scheme of Assistance to Panchayati Raj Institutions / Voluntary Organizations / Self Help Groups for Construction of Old Age Homes / Multi-Service Centres for older persons (Non Plan Scheme) - Under this Scheme, one time construction grant for Old Age Homes/Multi-Service Centre is provided to non-governmental organizations on the recommendation of the State Governments / UT Administrations.

2) Ministry of Finance

- Income tax rebate upto an income of Rs. 1.85 lakh p.a.
- Higher rates of interest on saving schemes of senior citizens.
- A Senior Citizens Savings Scheme offering an interest rate is 9% per annum on the deposits made by the senior citizens in

post offices has been introduced by the Government through Post Offices in India doing savings bank work.

3) Ministry of Road Transport and Highways

- Reservation of two seats for senior citizens in front row of the buses of the State Road Transport Undertakings.
- Some State Governments are giving fare concession to senior citizens in the State Road Transport Undertaking buses and are introducing Bus Models, which are convenient to the elderly.

4) Ministry of Health & Family Welfare

- Separate queues for older persons in hospitals for registration and clinical examination.

5) Department of Telecommunications

- Faults/complaints of senior citizens are given priority by registering them under senior citizens category with VIP flag, which is a priority category.
- Senior citizens are allowed to register telephone connection under N-OYT Special Category, which is a priority category.

6) Ministry of Railways

- Indian Railways provide 30% fare concession in all Mail / Express including Rajdhani / Shatabadi / Jan Shatabadi trains for senior citizens aged 60 years and above.
- Indian Railways also have the facility of separate counters for Senior Citizens for purchase / booking / cancellation of tickets.
- Wheel Chairs for use of older persons are available at all junctions, District Headquarters and other important stations for the convenience of needy persons including the older persons.
- Ramps for wheel chairs movement are available at the entry to important stations.
- Specially designed coaches with provisions of space for wheel chairs, hand rail and specially designed toilet for

handicapped persons have been introduced.

7) Ministry of Civil Aviation

• Indian Airlines is providing 50 per cent Senior Citizen Discount on Normal Economy Class fare for all domestic flights to Indian senior citizens who have completed the age of 65 years in the case of male senior citizens and 63 years in the case of female senior citizens subject to certain conditions.

• Air India is offering discount to senior citizens of 60 plus on flights to USA , UK and Europe. Further, Air India has now decided to reduce the age of 60 plus for discount on their domestic routes as well with immediate effect.

• Sahara Airlines is offering 50% discount on basic fare for travel on its domestic flights only to senior citizens who have attained the age of 62 years. Discount is applicable in economy class only.

8) Ministry of Consumer Affairs, Food and Public Distribution

• Under the Antyodaya Scheme, the Below Poverty Line (BPL) families which also include older persons are provided food grains at the rate of 35 kgs. per family per month. The food grains are issued @ Rs.3/- per kg. for rice and Rs.2/- per kg. for wheat. The persons aged 60 years above from the BPL category were given priority for identification.

• Under the Annapoorna Scheme being implemented by the States/UT Administration, 10 kgs. of food grains per beneficiary per month are provided free of cost to those senior citizens who remain uncovered under the old age pension scheme.

• Instructions to State Governments for giving priority to the Ration Card holders who are over 60 years of age in Fair Price Shops for issue of rations.

9) MCD, Delhi

• MCD, Delhi, has opened a separate counter to facilitate the senior citizens for submission of property tax bills.

• A rebate of 30% of the property tax due on the covered

space of a building up to one hundred sq. mtrs. of the covered space has been allowed by the corporation in the case of any self-occupied residential building singly owned by a man who is 65 years or more in age.

10) Miscellaneous

• Courts in the country accord priority to cases involving older persons and ensures their expeditious disposal.

• Under the Old Age Pension Scheme, monthly pension is given at variable rates to the destitute old by various State Governments/UT Administrations.

II) TRAVEL CONCESSIONS FOR SENIOR CITIZENS

(Note: The information provided is valid as of October 2013. This is subject to change in the future.)

Air India

50% discount of basic fare of normal economy class fare for senior citizen of Indian Nationality, permanently residing in India and should have attained the age of 63 years on the date of commencement of journey. Documents valid are photo ID with date of birth e.g., Voter's ID card, Passport, Driving license, senior citizens ID card issued by Air India etc . Theis is applicable to any sector within India. The validity of these tickets are 1 year from date of issue. Ticket can be purchased any time. For refunds/cancellations, permitted –fee applies. Source: www.airindia.com

Jetkonnect

Senior Citizens (65 years and above) are entitled for concession on basic adult fare in Economy class, on all domestic sectors operated by JetKonnect. To avail of this concession, you have to fill the "Concession Form" and submit it along with a photograph and proof of age. This discounted fare can either be issued through any of the JetKonnect ticketing offices or any of it authorized Travel Agents. All taxes are paid as applicable to an Adult guest. Senior Citizen's concession forms are available with your local Travel Agent, any JetKonnect offices. This concession is available subject to applicable terms and conditions. Note: Foreign nationals need not fill up a Concession Form or apply for an Identity Card, but can avail of the Senior Citizen concession simply on production of proof of birth (e.g. Government issued Photo ID, Passport). Source: www.jetconnect.in

Jet Airways

Jet airways senior citizen concession for domestic travel: Applicable on tickets sold and ticketed only in India. Guest must be over 65 years of age at the time of commencement of journey, irrespective of the gender status. Fare only applies if purchased before departure. If a guest wishes to avail this fare, ensure that tickets are reissued before departure. After departure post facto refund is not permitted. Senior citizen concession fares can be applied on one way or return journeys. The period of application if unless and otherwise specified, there is no restriction. Tickets are issued only on Jet Airways documents or any neutral document validated on Jet Airways. Ticketing on other airline document is not permitted. The applicable booking class can be Premiere - I Class and for Economy - S Class. Unless and otherwise specified, the ticket is valid one year from the date of issue. Stopovers are not permitted for intermediate ticketed points. This concession is valid on Jet Airways only. The ticket can be refunded as per applicable charges. Tickets issued in conjunction are considered as one document. This charge is not applicable on request or open dated tickets which were not holding confirmed status at any point of time. Senior citizen tickets are issued either for round trip or for circle trip journeys. After commencement of journey if guest wishes to collect refund for unused sectors, same can be done after deducting the normal sector fare for used sectors. Senior Citizen Discount will be offered on submission of either of the following documents to conform

guest's age / date of birth, School Leaving Certificate, Passport, Certificate from Employer from public sector undertaking or Govt. organizations where the senior citizen was employed, Ration Card, Election Commission Card, Jet Airways Senior Citizen card, A document confirming the Resident Status of the Senior Citizen.
Source: www.jetairways.com

Indian Railways

Travel by Indian Railways is 40% cheaper for all male Senior Citizens who are 60 years in age or above, while women aged 58 years or above are entitled to 50% concession in fare. Indian Railways provides this fare concession to elderlies in all its trains including Shatabdi, Rajdhani and Jan Shatabdi trains. Kindly note that while travelling all Senior Citizens need to carry proof of their Date of Birth / Age with a Photo ID Card. (b) There are separate Counters / Queues for Senior Citizens at all Railway Stations for purchase, booking or cancellation of tickets.
(concessions on demand)
Should carry documentary proof of age during travel, otherwise the difference of fare will be collected.
Source: www.indianrail.gov.in

Senior Citizen Card

The Indian Government provides several benefits to senior citizens through its schemes in various sectors of development. Apart from various tax benefits, travel and health care facilities provisioned for them, the Indian Government has given reasons for Senior Citizens to feel happy by providing them an identity card called the senior citizen ID Card. Even though this card plays an important role for all senior citizens, it plays a particularly crucial role in easing the burden of poor/ underprivileged senior citizens.

Benefits available for the Senior Citizens under this senior citizen ID card:

Railway concession - 30% (60 Years)

Maharashtra State Transport - 50% (65 Years)
Air travel concession - 50% on only basic fare (65 Years)
Some private hospitals give discount - 30% (60 Years)
Govt. hospitals give treatment free of cost - (60 years)
Banks give extra interest - ½ % (60 Years)
High court will give priority hearing (65 Years)
Maharashtra professional tax - 100% (65 years)
M. T. N. L. - 25% discount on monthly rentals (65 years)
Railways have separate queue for senior citizens
Income tax relief
Old age home- admission free or at nominal cost.

Documents required for the senior citizen ID Card:

Proof of age- Birth certificate or school / college leaving certificate or election card or passport (not expired) or PAN Card or pension card. Any one is sufficient. If none available, obtain doctor's certificate from ONLY Govt. Hospitals or Municipal Dispensary regarding age.

Proof of name: The name you give on the form should be the same as indicated in the supporting document. If the name has changed, proof of Govt. Gazette publication should be submitted or marriage certificate produced.

Proof of residence: In order of preference: ration card or valid passport or election card.

Doctor's certificate: required for: blood group, illness/ diseases, medication in use, medication allergies. The certificate has to be on the doctor's letter head with his / her signature, stamp & registration no., a practitioner of Indian medicine WITH register number can also certify.

Photographs: 3 stamp size photos, stick 2 photos on white form and stick 1 photo on the pink form.

III) SELECT LIST OF OLD AGE HOMES IN INDIA

Chandigarh

All India Pingalwara Society
Chandigar Branch
Palsora
Chandigarh
0172-2697625

Chandigarh Child & Women Development Corporation Ltd
Town Hall Building
3rd Floor, Sector 17-C
Chandigarh
0172-2623365

Home for Old & Destitute People
Social Welfare Department
U.T. Administration,
Sector 15 -B
Chandigarh 160015
0172-704676, 708690

Lions Home for Old & Destitute
Sector 15-D,
Chandigarh 160015
0172-2784610

Sri Sathya Sai Trust
Haryana & Chandigarh
2093, Sector 15-C
Chandigarh 160015
0172-2781307, 2641747

Satya Sai Baba Trust
Sector - 15-C
Chandigarh 160015

Shanti Dan
Sisters of Charity
Sector-23
Chandigarh 160023

Chhattisgarh

Catholic Diocese of Jagdalpur
Lalbagh, Jagdalpur
Bastar
Chhattisgarh 494001
07782-264726, 264632

Chhattisgarh Bal Avam Vridh Kalyan Parishad
Near Police Station
Mana-Camp
Raipur
Chhattisgarh 492015
0771-2226307

Delhi

"Aashirwad" Senior Citizens Council
X-22, Karkardooma

Institutional Area
Opp. Central School
Vikas Marg Extn.
New Delhi, Delhi 110092
011-64684018

Elder Home Society
Dr. Katju Marg, Plot No.
Psps-4
Adjacent To Mcd Office
Sector-17, Rohini
New Delhi, Delhi 110085
011-26153004, 27570684

Home for the Aged &
Infirm
Khadi Gramodyog
Bhawan Building
Narela
Delhi 110 040
011-27786078

Johns Day Care and
Boarding for Senior
Citizens Association
Plot 106-107, G-Block,
Phase-6, Aya Nagar
New Delhi, Delhi 110047
011-26501513

Old Age Home (Delhi Govt.)
Dept. Of Social Welfare
Tilak Vihar Near Crpf
Camp, Tilak Nagar
Delhi 110018
011-28332323

St. Mary's Home for the
Aged Women
6, Rajpur Road
Delhi 110 054
011-23928868

Haryana

Bhagat Labha Mal Kartar
Kaur Charitable Trust
Nirmal Dham
Model Town
Karnal, Haryana 132001
0184-2266904

Hope Senior Citizens
Home Society (Regd.)
U-215, New Palam Vihar,
Phase-II
Baba Prakashpuri Marg
Opp. Village Jhajgarh
Gurgaon, Haryana 122017
0124-2468383, 4071721

Protective Home
(Home For The Aged &
Infirm)
Near Neelam Chowk
Sector - 5, Faridabad
Haryana
0129-212554

S.S Rao Madho Singh
Memorial Trust
Village & P.O. Maandi
Tehsil- Narnaul

Mahendergarh
Haryana
01282-52146, 51502

Himachal Pradesh

H.P. State Social Welfare Board
Shimla
Himachal Pradesh 171001
0177-2624007

H.P. State Welfare Board, Shimla
Old Age Home
Basant Pur, Shimla
Himachal Pradesh 171001
0177-2784432

Home for the Aged
Garli, Kangra
Himachal Pradesh 177108
0177-220985

Madhya Pradesh

Asha Niketan Hospital & Rehabilitation Centre
E/6, Arera Colony
Bhopal
Madhya Pradesh

Ashagram Trust
Barwani
Madhya Pradesh 451551
07290-222186, 224201, 202513

Jeev Sewa Santhan
2nd Floor, Jaslok Bhawan
(Vidyasagar Public School)
Sant Hirdaram Nagar
Bhopal
Madhya Pradesh 462 030
0755-2522714, 2523081

Social Welfare Centre
Road No. 12, Nandanagar
Indore
Madhya Pradesh 452003
0731-2551547

Punjab

All India Pingalwara Charitable Society
"Apna Ghar"
Sangrur Branch
Dhuri Road
Sangrur, Punjab 148001
0183-2584586, 2584713

Home for the Aged
Salvation Army Compound
Jail Road, Gurdaspur
Punjab 143 521

Red Cross Senior Citizen's Home
G.T. Road, Near New Sabzi Mandi, Jalandhar
Punjab 144005
0181-2255724

Senior Citizens
Association
Vridh Ashram
Opp. Police Post,
Haibowal Kalan
Ludhiana, Punjab 141 007
0161-477119

Shri Vivekanand Swarg
Ashram Trust
Jawaddi Road
Model Town Extn. - B
Ludhiana, Punjab 141002
0161-2455758, 2459991

Rajasthan

Sewa Samiti
Old Unn Mill
B/H Railway Quarters
Pali Marwar
Rajasthan 306401
02932-280784

Indian Council of Social
Welfare
Sect. 6, Heera Path
Mansarover, Jaipur
Rajasthan 302020
0171-2392895

Swami Brahmanand
Vridhashram
Brahmanandji Ki Bagichi
Udaipur Road, Beawar
Rajasthan 305901

Apana Ghar (Vridh Ashram)
Mahavir International
Charitable Trust
Suratgarh Road Chak 5 E
Chhoti Sriganganagar
Rajasthan 335001
0154-2423932, 2421261

Shri Manav Verdh Ashram
197-202, Manavpuram
Baral Ii, Bijainagar
Ajmer, Rajasthan 305624
01462-231510, 231151,
230147

Uttar Pradesh

Jan Kalyan Trust
Anand Niketan Vridh
Sewa Ashram
C-5, Sector-55, Noida
Uttar Pradesh 201 302
095120-2581475, 2582480

Methodist Home for the
Aged
Community Development
Centre, Vrindaban
Mathura
Uttar Pradesh 282 121
0565-442696, 442167

Manvayatan Society
Plot No. 2, Block A.L.T.
Sector-37, Behind
Community Centre

Adjacent To Hanuman Murti,
Noida, Uttar Pradesh 201303
095120-2432195, 2432383

Old Age Home
Indian Red Cross Society
53, Bahadur Ganj, Allahabad
Uttar Pradesh 211003

Senior Citizen Home
All India Women's Conference
Tarash Mandir, Vrindaban
Mathura 281121
Uttar Pradesh
09758960851

Uttarakhand

Indian Institute of Community Development (Iicd)
Hope Old Age Home
Vill. & Po. Gumaniwala
Via. Rishikesh, Dehradun
Uttarakhand 249 204
0135-452590, 452330

Little Flower Home for the Aged
Kathgodam P.O. Nainital
Uttarakhand 263 126
05942-22132

Tibetan Homes Foundation
Happy Valley
Mussorie
Uttarakhand 248179
0135-2632608, 2631491

Vriddha Seva Ashram
Bharat Sadan, Po Sadhubela
Sapt Sarovar Road
Haridwar
Uttarakhand 249410
01334-260111

Andhra Pradesh

Anaada Vrudha Vishrama Asramamu
Amancharla Village (Canal)
Nellore Rural Mandal
Nellore
Andhra Pradesh 524345
0861-2378054

Aram Ghar
Indian Council of Social Welfare -Ap
Shivrampally, Hyderabad
Andhra Pradesh 500 252
08413-23391620, 23329587

Asara Home for the Aged
12-1-334/1712 Lalapet
Behind Vidya Mandir
School Secunderabad
Andhra Pradesh 500017
08715-7015612, 7000620

Association for the
Care of the Aged
(Ashram Sravana) 2-515,
Opp. Bank Of Baroda
Street Ramanayyapeta
Kakinada
Andhra Pradesh 533005
0884-2378324

Old age Welfare Centre
No. 28, Huda Colony
Via Chandanagar,
Miapur Hyderabad
Andhra Pradesh 500050
08413-23045261

Govt. Home for the Aged & Disabled
Victoria Memorial Hall
Saroornagar, Hyderabad
Andhra Pradesh 500035

Sri Ramakrishna
Vanaprastha Ashrama
Saradanagar
Ramalingampalli Po
Nalgonda
Andhra Pradesh 508126
08418-265321

Karnataka

Home for the Senior
Citizens
Shri Vadiraja Trust(R),
#43, 5th Temple
Street, Siddanthi Block,
Malleswaram, Bengaluru
Karnataka 560 003
08152-24793, 080-3316557

Jeevan Sandhya Trust
C/O Vasavi Vidya Niketan
Trust
3, Vani Vikas Road,
Visveswarapuram
Bengaluru
Karnataka 560 004
080-642 448

Old and Infirm Peoples
Home
P O Tibetan Colony
N Kanara
Karnataka 581 411

Our Lady of Light (Sneha
Jyothi)
Anchaipalaya
Kumbalgud Po
Bengaluru
Karnataka 560074
080-28437239, 28437383

The Bangalore Friend In
Need Society
Home For The Aged
No. 3, Colonel Hill Road
Bengaluru
Karnataka 560051
080-22865519

Sarvamangala Charitable Trust (R)
"Premsadan",Flat No-212
Santosh Apartments,
Nal Road, Bengaluru
Karnataka 560017

Kerala

Elders' Village Owners' Society
Eruvely
P.O. Chottanikkara
Kerala 682312
0484-2714155

Govt. Old Age Home
Near Govt. Fisheries School, Thevara Ferry,
Kochi, Ernakulam
Kerala 682001
0484-2663641

Home for the Aged & Infirm
Chunangamvely
Erumathala Po Aluva
Kerala 683105
0484-2837229, 2837255

J.J. & S. Charitable Trust
Sneha Nivas
Ambayathode,
Thamarassery,
Kozhikode, Kerala 673573

Manavaseva Charitable Trust
Po Maniyancode
Near Iti, Via Kalpetta
North Wayanad
Kerala 673122
04936-205199, 202092

Puducherry

Cluny Home for the Aged
Hospice Convent
2, Laporte Street
Puducherry U T 605 001

Imm Heart of Mary's
Home for the Aged
Canuvapet, Villianur
Puducherry U T 605 110

St. Joseph's Convent
Hospice
Jawaharlal Nehru Street, Karaikal
Puducherry U T 609 602

Tamil Nadu

"Sai Charan" A Senior Citizen Home
3/1 3rd Street
Santhiniketan Colony
Madambakkam Jhambaram
Chennai
Tamil Nadu 600073

Amaithi Old Age Home
Unit-I, No. 91-A, Ist Main
Road, Shanthi Niketan
Colony, Madambakkam
Chennai,
Tamil Nadu 600073

Dharmapuri Madhar
Sangam Old Age Home
No. 1 Venkata Sarrma
Road, Dharmapuri
Tamil Nadu 636 701

G.S. Senior Citizens Home
New No. 34, (Old No. 18a)
Mylai Ranganathan
Street
(Near Dr. Natesan Park),
T. Nagar, Chennai
Tamil Nadu 600017

Helpage India
Tamaraikulam Elders
Village
Periyakanganamkuppam
Uppalavadi Post
Cuddalore
Tamil Nadu 607002
04142-212352

Senior Citizens Centre
I/180 East Coast Road
Muttukadu Post
Via-Kovalam, Kanchi
Tamil Nadu 603112

Assam

Assam Chah Mazdoor
Multipurpose Social
Education Association
Rangajan T. E.-Titabar
Jorhat, Assam 785 630

Bahumkhi Krishi Avam
Samaj Kalyan Samitte
Nurnagar,
P.O.Hiranpanthi
Haibangaon, Nowgaon
Assam 782002

Bahumukhi Krishi Aru
Samaj Kalyan Samity
Noor Nagar, Po Herapati
Via-Haibargaon
Nagaon, Assam 782002

Dr. Ambedkar Mission
Day Care
Center,Dhopatari
P.O.Changsari
Kamrup, Guwahati
Assam 781101

Geetashram Janaseva
Kendra
Geetanagar
P O Bhoukumari Pathsala
Barpeta
Assam 781 325

Bihar

St. Mary's Orphanage
Fakirana, Banuchaper
Bettiah Po
West Champaran
Bihar 845438
06254-232750

Jharkhand

Vihar Samaj Kalyan
Sansthan (Viskasan)
Vill. Kalendey Kulgu, Via
Piska Nagri
Block Ratu, Ranchi
Jharkhand 835222
0651-2502087, 2252013

Manipur

Integrated Rural Dev.
And Educational
Organisation Wangbal
P.O. & P.S. Thoubal
Thoubal
Manipur 795 138

Rural Service Agency
(Rusa)
Laiching, Nongpok
Kakching
Imphal East, Manipur

South Eastern Rural Dev.
Organisation (Serdo)
Sangaiyumpham Part-Ii
Wangjing
Manipur 795148

Meghalaya

Society of Sisters of
Charity
Mercy Home-Home For
The Aged
Dem-Thring, Shillong
Meghalaya 793021

Orissa

Association for Social
Reconstructive
Activities (Asra)
Satyabadi Press,
Premises
Pithapu, Cuttack
Orissa 753 001

Adarsh Sewa Sangathan
Mundkul,
P.O-Mangalpur,
Dhenkanal
Orissa 759017

Kalinga Shelter
B/22, Indradhanu Market
Complex Nayapalli,
Khurda, Bhubaneswar
Orissa 751 015
Shree Ramakrishna
Ashrama

At/ Po M. Rampur
Kalahandi
Orissa 766102

Tripura

Abalamban
Airport Road, Barjala
(Near Trtc Workshop)
Agartala
Tripura 799001

Apna Ghar
C/O Abalambam
Airport Road
Po Barjala (Via Kunjaban)
Tripura 799006

Tripura Govt. Old Age Home/
Infirmary
Vill. Narsingarh
Po Binangarh
Tripura 799015

West Bengal

Adorations Sisters of the
Immaculate Heart of Mary
Bridha Ashram (Home For
The Aged)
Krishnagar, Nadia
West Bengal 741 101

Barrackpore Swami
Mahadebananda Giri
Briddhashram
48, Middle Road
Barrackpore
North 24-Parganas
West Bengal 743 101
033-5607328

Home for Old & Infirm
Political Sufferers
Po. South Garia
South 24-Parganas
West Bengal 743 613

Mahadevi Birla Niketan
Bagirhat (Near Amtala)
South 24-Parganas
West Bengal 743503
0470-9287

Nava Nir Home for the
Aged
30, Ashok Avenue
Kolkata
West Bengal 700 040
033-2758172

Santi Nivash (Home For
The Aged)
Oxford Mission
Barisha, Kolkata
West Bengal 700008
033-24466307, 24471179

Goa

Bom Jesu Home for the
Aged

Portavaddo
Siolim, Bardez
Goa 403 517
0832-272246

Ishaprema-Niketan
Bhonvta Vaddo,
Assaganv, Bardez
Goa 403 507
0832-262913

St Joseph's Home for the Aged
Portovaddo, Siolim
Bardez
Goa 403517
0832-2272246

Missionaries of Charity
Asilo-Near Don Bosco
Mahatma Gandhi Road
Panjim, Goa 403 001

Gujarat

Anand-Dham
Opp. Hanumanji Temple
Lambhvel, Anand
Gujarat 388310
02692-51384, 51998

Bharti Bapu Ashram Seva Trust
Opp. Railway Station
Sarkhej, Ahmedabad
Gujarat 382 210
6620116, 6610575

Kutch Vikas Trust
Shanti Niketan Old Age Home, Raidhanpar,
Nagor Po, Bhuj, Kutch
Gujarat 370001
02832-274230, 274283

Ramnik Kunwarba Vruddhashram
Akhil Mahila Parishad
Gondal Road, Rajkot
Gujarat 360 001
0281-2445572

Sandhya Vishram, Home For The Aged
C/O Sisters of Charity Of St. Anne P.B. 15 Irana Road,
Kadi, Mahesana
Gujarat 382715
02762-277864

Maharashtra

A S R A - Apar Nath Senior Citizen's Home
Shiva Farm, P.O.
Konregaon Mull
Urlikanchan, Punesholapur Rd. Pune
Maharashtra 412 202
0212-816921, 816087

Anandadham
At Jambhulpada
Taluka Sudhagad,
Raigad
Maharashtra 410205

Durgawati Old Age Home
Swami Vivekanand
Charitable Trust
J-13, Laxmi Nagar, Nagpur
Maharashtra 440 022

Home for the Aged
Little Sisters of the Poor,
Mahakali Cave Road,
Andheri East, Mumbai
Maharashtra 400 093

Madhuban Vrudhashram
Kondheshwar Road
Badnera, Amrawati
Maharashtra 444701

IV) HELPLINES FOR SENIOR CITIZENS

AHMEDABAD
Agewell Foundation: 079 2662 0606
HelpAge India: (079) 26860758, 1800-180-1253

BENGALURU
Banglore City Police & Nightingale's Trust Helpline: 1090
HelpAge India: 22124594
Dignity Helpline: 080 - 41511307
Nimhans' helpline for elders: 080-26685948 and 09480829670

BHOPAL
HelpAge India: 1800-233-1253
BHUBANESWAR
HelpAge India: 1800-345-1253

CHANDIGARH
Chandigarh Police Senior Citizens Helpline: 1090
HelpAge India: 1800-180-1253

CHENNAI
HelpAge India: 25322149/ 1800-180-1253
Dignity Helpline: 044 – 42133002
Chennai Police Senior Citizens Helpline: 1253

DEHRADUN
HelpAge India: 1800-180-1253

DELHI
Delhi Police Senior Citizens Helpline: 1291
Senior Citizens' Security Cell: 23490010, 23494336, 23490233
HelpAge India: 42030400
Agewell Foundation: 29836486, 29840484

GURGAON
Gurgaon Police Senior Citizens Helpline: 0124-2221559

GUWAHATI
HelpAge India: 1800-345-1253

HYDERABAD
HelpAge India: 27428472, 27427066
Heritage Trust Helpline: 23390000

INDORE
Senior Citizen Helpline: 0731 251 0308/252 2111

JAIPUR
HelpAge India: 1800-180-1253
KOCHI
HelpAge India: 1800-180-1253

KOLKATA
Senior Citizens' Helpline: 9830088884

MANGALORE
Nightingale Helpline: 1090

MUMBAI
Mumbai Police Senior Citizens Helpline: 1090, 103
Dignity Helpline: 022 - 61381100
HelpAge India: 26370740, 26370754
Senior Citizens' Helpline: 23898078, 23898079

NAGPUR
Nagpur Police Senior Citizens Helpline: 0712-2564333

PUNE
Shweta Association for Vitiligo: 09923709210
Pune Police's Senior Citizens Helpline: 1091/26111103
Dignity Helpline: 020 – 30439100
Aadhar: 022 2421 0683

V. WEBSITES OF SOME NGOS WORKING FOR THE ELDERLY

AISCCON: All India Senior Citizens' Confederation
http://www.aisccon.org/

FESCOM: The Federation of Senior Citizens Organisations of Maharashtra
http://www.fescom-for-sr-citizens.org.in/index.htm

HelpAge India
http://www.helpageindia.org/

Dignity Foundation
http://www.dignityfoundation.com/

Harmony
http://www.harmonyindia.org/

The Family Welfare Agency
http://www.familywelfareagency.org/

ARDSI (Alzheimer's Related Society of India)
www.alzheimer.org.in

Shree Manav Seva Sangh
http://shreemanavsevasangh.org/index.html

Silver Inning Foundation
www.silverinnings.com

GLOSSARY

Abuse of Elderly	Physical, psychological and emotional, also financial, by spouse, partner, relative, friend or neighbour, volunteer, practioner, solicitor or other individuals
Atharva Veda	Last and latest of 4 vedas - ऋक, यजु, साम & अथर्व - was composed circa 1000 B.C.
Acid Peptic Condition	Pungent, hot and spicy and sour food causes burning sensation in stomach; leading to ulcers. This is called acidity in common terminology
Alternative Medicine and alternative therapy	System of treatment other than allopathic. Commonly called Ayurveda.
Cybercrime	New form of crime using computer communication and operation
Chakras or energy centres in bodies	These are nothing but subtle energy centres placed along Sushumna Nadi (nerve), a subtle body channel in spinal column each of which is represented as a lotus with specific number petal. Mooladhar Chakra situated in Coccyx and is a seat of 'Kundalini' the great dynamic energy.

Chinese wisdom	Acupuncture and Acupressure
Freud	Called grandfather of regression work
Gerontology	Science dealing with phenomena and problems of aging and old age
Globalisation	Social and commercial communication amongst countries of entire world. Absence of commercial barriers.
Healing thru music therapy	Music has the power to sooth, inspire, energise and uplift and heal chronic pains and depression.
Insomnia	Sleeplessness or disturbed sleep pattern
Karma yogi	Those who perform prescribed religious and social duties with complete detachment, just as a duty.
Lifestyle disease	Usually hypertension (blood pressure) diabetes and heart attack. Too much stress at work irregular eating habits, giving into smoking, alcohol and drugs may be direct causes.
Live-in relationships	Living of an adult man and woman out of wedlock by legal arrangement or otherwise
Manu & Manusmriti	A sage of Rishi, who wrote "Laws of Living" for Hindus. Likely to have been composed in 5th century B.C.
Nuclear Family	Family consisting of husband, wife and their children.
Old Old Age	Age above 80 years
Plato	Greek philosopher who wrote about youths of his time (2300 years ago)

Purushartha	4 aims of man's life धर्म, अर्थ (wealth), काम (Desire) & मोक्ष (Final deliverance)
Pranayam or breathing technique	Controlled breathing clears up body, mind and spirit and hence produces good health.
Psychological (Mind control) techniques	Methods and practice of Reiki, meditation, hypnotism, past life regression therapy (PLRT)
Ragaragini Chikitsa Kendra	Established by Shri Ganpathy Sacchidanand Swamiji who has identified Ragas for treatment of diseases.

SELECT BIBLIOGRAPHY

Babu,Talari Anantha, *God and the Householder,* Caxton Printers, Hyderabad.

Bhatia, Ravi,*On Ageing Within and Without,* New Quest – Quarterly Journal.

Census of India 2011 – Provisional Population Totals – Registrar General and Census Commissioner India – New Delhi.

Chakraborti, Rajagopal Dhar, *The Greying of India: Population Ageing in the context of Asia,* Sage Publications India Pvt.Ltd., New Delhi.

Chaudhary, Aabha, ed. *Active Ageing in the New Millennium,* Anugraha, New Delhi.

Chetana Foundation for Social Awareness, Research and Development – The British Council Division – Mumbai, "Causes and Remedies of Abuse of Older Persons in a Domestic Setting".

Chopra, Deepak, *Ageless Body, Timeless Mind,* Harmony Books – Crown Publisher, New York.

Desai ,Sonalde B., Amaresh Dubey, Brij Lal Joshi, Mitali Sen, Abusaleh Shariff, and Reeve Vanneman, *Human Development in India: Challenge for a society in Transition,* Oxford University Press, New Delhi, 2010.

Ghosh, Rajarshi, ed., *Ageing Society: Social and Economic Issues,* The ICFAI – University Press, Hyderabad.

Gokhale, Dr. S. D., Dr. Aarti Kaulavkar Nagarkar, and Dr. Bhooshan Patwardhan, *Longevity 21st Century Revolution.*

Kanitkar, Tara, Sharvani Shukla, "Demographic Profile of Elderly in India", International Longevity Centre, Pune, India.

Ojha, Ruby, *Challenges for Development in 21st Century,* B.R. Publishing Corporation, Delhi.

Rajan, S. Irudaya, G. S. Mishra, and P. Sankara Sarma, *India's Elderly: Burden or Challenge,* Sage Publications, New Delhi.

Raju, S. Siva, ed. *Voice of Elderly in India,* B.R. Publishing Corporation, Delhi.

Raju, S. Siva, ed. *Networking of Organizations Working for Care of Older Persons in Mumbai*, B.R. Publishing Corporation, New Delhi.

Seminar – April 2000 – Ageing: a Symposium on Greying of our society – Malvika Singh, New Delhi.

Swami Chinmayananda, *The Holy Geeta*

Trehan, B.K., and Indu Trehan, *Retired But Not Tired* - The Lotus Collection, Roli Books Pvt.Ltd., New Delhi.

Vivekananda Kendra Patrika, Indian Youth Achievements and Challenges, Madras.

News papers and Periodicals:

Times of India

2006: November 11

2007: October 13

2008: March 13

2011: September 8 / 20

October 18

December 20

2012: June 14

November 24

Maharashtra Times

2012: March 16

November 29

Free Press Journal

2011: November 21

2012: July 4

DNA
2007: July 15
2011: September 29
2012: May 30

Afternoon
2011: January 17
September 7 / 28

Hindustan Times
2006: May 15
2011: June 15
2012: May 3

Mumbai Mirror
2011: May 23

Indian Express
2011: January 15

Economic Times
2013: February 26

The Age
2011: June 15

Pune Mirror
2012: August 9

ABOUT INDUS SOURCE

We are a niche, independent publishing house passionately committed to publishing good and relevant literature. Although our primary focus is publishing books on spirituality and philosophy, we also publish general non-fiction in diverse genres. We seek to provide positive, spiritual insights for harmony and better living. Through our publications we would like to share the received wisdom, lighting the way for fellow-travellers. We are committed to our goal of promoting understanding of the Self, between faiths and cultures, and of the world in which we live.

Visit our website www.indussource.com for more details.

Indus Source Books
PO Box 6194
Malabar Hill PO
Mumbai 400006
India
www.indussource.com
info@indussource.com